Technology-as-a-Service Playbook

How to Grow a Profitable Subscription Business

Thomas Lah
J.B. Wood

Contents

1 | Disruption Happens

How can you spot a tipping point? Malcolm Gladwell, whose book, *The Tipping Point*,[1] helped popularize the term, says it's that magic moment when an idea, trend, or social behavior crosses a threshold, tips, and spreads like wildfire. Well, we think one has come to dozens of business-to-business (B2B) and business-to-consumer (B2C) technology industries.

Ten years ago, we first stood in front of thousands of tech executives and worried aloud that the cloud era was going to disrupt the tech industry more profoundly than any other transformation in its vaunted 50-year history. Our worry was not rooted in disruptive technology but in disruptive business models. Big companies like IBM, HP, and Oracle have all weathered generational changes to computing models and architectures many times. Handling new waves of technology is old hat; they have plenty of plays for that. But we worried that this perfect storm of new technology *and* new business models could re-cast the very foundations of market leadership in the industry.

A lot has happened since that decade. Unless you have stubbornly avoided all business media over the past few years, it is impossible to have missed the interest in subscription business models, not just in IT but it nearly every technology-related industry. Today's energy surrounding subscription business models is the follow-on to the buzz a few years ago about the "sharing economy"—something that *Time* magazine said was one of the top 10 ideas that would change the world back in 2011. The attraction of the sharing economy was and is the ability to simply access rather than own physical and human assets. For the provider, it produces recurring revenue streams that keep customers spending for years—even decades.

Although subscription business models and the sharing economy can manifest themselves in many industries, this book is concerned only with tech and near-tech industries. Even more specifically, we are focused on highly cloud-enabled, technology-as-a-service offers. The categories of these offers take many popular names. There are software-as-a-service (SaaS) offers, platform-as-a-service (PaaS) offers, infrastructure-as-a-service (IaaS) offers, managed services, and so forth. To keep it simple for the rest of the book, we are going to refer to them collectively as XaaS. You can make the "X" whatever you want. It simply means that you are offering sophisticated computer software, hardware, industrial equipment or devices, and/or services in an "as-a-service" consumption model to your customers. We would expect some or all of the offer to be delivered through the cloud. If you are selling subscriptions to razor blades or fine wine over the Internet, this book probably isn't for you. On the other hand, if you are involved in the strategy, development, finance, marketing, services, or sales of complex, cloud-based technology solutions in IT, industrial equipment, health care, or consumer markets, and terms like SaaS and managed services resonate with you and your team . . . then keep reading. We have some interesting observations to pass along. Very importantly, if you are involved in traditional (asset-based, on-premise) technology and you are wondering what XaaS technology will mean to your job and your company . . . then *definitely* keep reading. That's because your company is about to be caught up in the business model tipping point. To remain competitive, you will not only need new offers, but you will also need a new way to operate. Being connected to your customers is the catalyst.

Before you begin, you might be asking yourself: Just where are these observations coming from? OK, fair question.

Our answer begins with this statement: We don't know all the answers, and anyone who tells you they do should be shown the door. It's still early days in assessing how the cloud era of tech will fully disrupt the technology industry; predicting the future is dicey. It's like predicting the future of the clean energy industry. It's hard enough to figure out which technical approaches will ultimately win the market, much less what the best business practices of the new leaders will be. So, who are we and why this book? The answer is that we run the Technology Services Industry Association (TSIA). As one of tech's largest industry associations, our company gets to uniquely study and talk with hundreds of the world's most successful technology and industrial companies each and every day. We are an incredibly research-intensive bunch. We have experienced industry executives, PhD researchers, and data analysts looking at all the data we collect from public sources and from the companies themselves. We field thousands of formal inquiries annually from management at both traditional and XaaS companies wanting to know about the trends and best practices in running a successful business in this time of radical change. They want to know what lessons we are learning from our research on top-performing companies because we have access to data that is simply not available in the public domain. It's from all this research and interaction that we draw our observations. So, though we can't predict the future, we think we may be in one of the best positions to dissect and debate it. Most importantly, we think some winning patterns are emerging. That is what we want to share in this book. You might not agree with all of our observations, and not every one might play out. But, we think they are important for every executive and manager in the tech world to be aware of and consider. It's a tricky time. Are we at a tipping point? If so, what will it mean to the traditional business models we know and love? How do we prepare? What will successful XaaS organizations of the near future look like?

In a nutshell, here is what we have learned after studying the topic from multiple angles for 8 years: XaaS is not just technology that is priced by the month and hosted in the cloud. If it were that simple, you wouldn't need this book. We believe that, as the enigmatic smoke clears around the cloud, what's emerging is an image of success in XaaS business models that is fundamentally different from traditional tech. It's something that goes way beyond the technology and the pricing model . . . something that cuts deeply into the underlying business model the tech industry has grown comfortable with. It's just a new way of running a tech company. And it's powered by your real-time connections to the customer. What's most interesting—why we wrote this book—is that NOBODY truly knows what that new way is! It's a fact that there is no B2B subscription business that is as rapidly growing *and* as profitable as the traditional tech bellwethers were in their heyday. Only the XaaS CEO who can make that claim can write the definitive book. And really, they should accomplish it more than once to prove that they have perfected the formula. Until that day, we are all in this together—all trying to break the enigmatic code for the profitable XaaS business. We are debating whether the tipping point has arrived and what life after that will look like. Let's face it: The cost of building software is dropping fast. We think it's the business execution around the code—not just the ability to write code—that will determine the success or failure of future icons.

Just how different might the winning B2B/B4B XaaS company look? Here are 10 assertions that are a sample of things we will cover:

- The ability to "prove deliverable business outcomes'" will supplant "win the feature bake-off" as the central focus of senior leadership at tech companies. This will cause a dramatic re-thinking of investments and top talent allocation. Offers will "go vertical" in order to better deliver full value to the customer. Services will move from the back of the bus to the front of the bus. But at the same time . . .

- Software will eat services. The ability of technology companies to reduce technical complexity and build best customer practices into their software will be a defining characteristic of successful XaaS providers. Value-added services will survive and prosper as a concept. However, labor-delivered services (except highly consultative expertise) will still be viewed by management as a boat anchor. Eventually, development will accept that their charter includes the "full product" and not just a collection of features. They will build all the capabilities into the product that are needed not only to win the feature bake-off but also to enable the differentiated services that will drive adoption, encourage expansion, reduce sales costs, and have a plethora of other objectives. These are the capabilities needed to create downstream profits and sustained competitive advantage.

- Suppliers and customers will increasingly compete as every company becomes a tech company. Low-cost software development will turn industrial buyers of technology into technology producers themselves. Technology resellers will find their original equipment manufacturer (OEM) suppliers competing with them through cloud-enabled, direct models. Large XaaS providers will manufacture their own hardware and build their own software, no longer being a buyer of technology but actually overseeing the manufacture of the products they use. (By the way, all of this is already happening at scale.)

- The act of selling will undergo radical change. Customers can now self-serve a huge amount of the information they need to make a technology purchase decision. They will be able to self-serve on simple purchasing decisions like low-cost XaaS trials or renewals. Even on more complex decisions they will have less and less interest or patience for "company overviews" or "demos" from their sales rep. They will know all that. They will want to discuss the "last mile." They will want to know specifically how your key features will lead to improved business outcomes for companies in their specific industry. Selling will become a process, not a heroic act!

- Delivering and measuring customer success will become a defining characteristic of market leaders. If you don't have a systematic way to make more than 90% of all your XaaS successful, you will not be profitable. We are not just talking about success in your terms; we are talking about success in the customer's terms.

- Organizational structures will be significantly reinvented with highly integrated development, marketing, sales, finance, and service teams swarming around specific customer segments. Regional autonomy over international markets will decline, and centralized processes and systems will ascend. Even traditional departmental profit and loss statements (P&Ls)—the archaic command and control systems we dearly loved—will collapse under the weight of the new operational and organizational models, where expense dollars in one department yield revenue growth or cost savings in a totally different department.

- Channel partner models will get re-thought and reconstructed. Many resellers will perish in the transition. New kinds of partners will be added. How the OEM and their partners work together for a particular customer will be radically redefined as the old notion of direct or indirect customers is replaced by a model where both parties serve every customer.

- The employee skill sets that companies covet will expand from the traditional obsession with hiring technical and sales skills (that built the last generation of tech companies) to including deep vertical industry and business process expertise. Suppliers will start hiring experts from their customers. Any human being that combines both deep vertical market expertise *and* either great technical skills or great sales skills will write their own ticket.

- The market advantage pendulum between innovation and scale—the one that has swung so far toward innovative new companies that are taking share against much larger, traditional tech companies—will begin to swing the other way. Large tech companies will begin to enable their global footprint of customers, partners, and employees to create competitive XaaS advantages that many small but disruptive companies struggle to match. Right now, the traditional companies just want to study the disruptors. As the disruptors grow, their interest in how to scale globally will grow. Suddenly, they will become curious as to how the traditional tech companies operate at such huge scale.

- The traditional cost structures that high-tech and near-tech industries have supported with high unit prices for their products will be destroyed. Unit prices for nearly everything will continue to come down. The labor-intensive operating models for marketing, sales, services, and general and administrative expense (G&A) will be torn apart and reinvented. Heroic acts will be replaced by processes. Those processes will become automated. They will interact with data and best-practice models. That unified model will "own" the customer—who they are, what outcomes they are trying to achieve, where they are in the process, what interactions are needed next, and how they can expand to higher levels of value. We will still need a human face to the larger customers, but they will be talking about what the model tells them to talk about.

The Magnitude of the Transformation

As part of our research, we have been tracking the performance of 50 of the largest providers of technology solutions every quarter over the past 10 years. In 2015, the companies in the TSIA Technology & Service 50 (T&S 50) index were generating average operating incomes, on average, north of 11%. Figure 1.1 demonstrates the high operating incomes of these enterprise tech companies compared to other well-known profitable companies.

As we discussed in our last book, *B4B*,[2] the B2B technology industry created some of the most profitable business models in the history of business models. As Figure 1.1 indicates, the *average* profitability of the 50 companies in this index is higher than that of blue-chip companies like General Electric (GE) and Walmart. But now these beautiful business models are under duress. Since 2008, the combined top-line revenues of companies in the T&S 50 index have been shrinking dramatically. By the fourth quarter of 2015, product revenues were shrinking at an average rate of −8% per year for companies in the index. Remember, these are

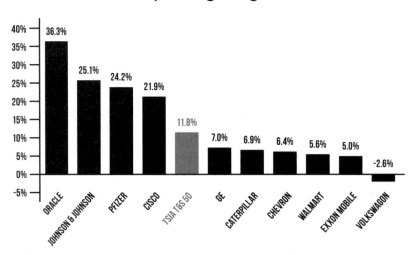

Operating Margin

FIGURE 1.1 Operating Income of Legacy Technology Providers

companies that were always considered high-growth and high-margin product businesses! Figure 1.2 documents the dismal decline of combined product revenues and the rise of service revenues for these companies since 2008.

Legacy technology companies have become desperate for top-line growth. The natural place to pursue that growth is the fast-growing world of XaaS and subscription revenues. However, the profitable business models for XaaS have yet to be proven. For the past 3 years, we have been tracking another index called the Cloud 20 that consists of the largest publicly traded XaaS companies. Although revenue growth for these companies has been phenomenal, profitability has been elusive. Figure 1.3 provides a comparison of key performance metrics of revenue growth and net operating income between XaaS companies and traditional technology companies we track.[3]

In theory, these new XaaS business models have incredible potential. Tien Tzuo is founder and CEO of Zuora, a SaaS company that provides software for subscription billing, and former chief marketing officer at Salesforce. He has become an outspoken advocate for the subscription business model. In many of his

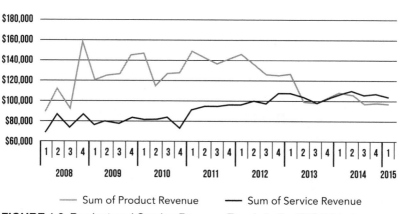

FIGURE 1.2 Product and Service Revenue Trends in the T&S 50 Index

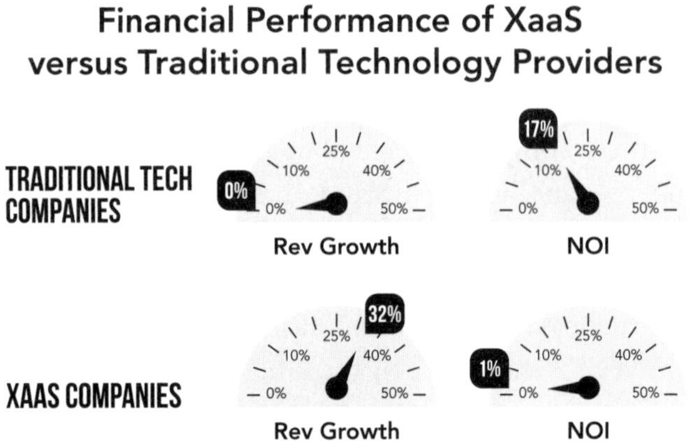

Financial Performance of XaaS versus Traditional Technology Providers

FIGURE 1.3 Financial Performance of XaaS versus Traditional Technology Providers

articles, interviews, and speeches, he points to the following benefits of the subscription business model:[4]

- Customers in all marketplaces want flexibility in how they consume.
- Customers only want to pay for what they use, and subscription models are designed to support that desire.
- Subscription relationships provide greater insight into what customers are consuming and what they value.
- Subscription business models create predictable, renewable revenue streams.
- Subscription business models create the opportunity to produce highly profitable revenue streams as more and more customers are served from a common platform.

Mr. Tzuo has many valid points—especially when subscription business models are built on cloud-based platforms. A centralized delivery model enables several advantages over traditional on-premise delivery models where the customer installed and managed the technology on their own. Hosted offers allow providers to quickly release new capabilities to all customers. With customers interacting on a hosted platform, providers can gain visibility into which customers are adopting and which are not. Also, providers can use analytics to build best practices that all customers can leverage. XaaS companies should absolutely benefit from economies of scale. More users on the same platform should result in higher profits. These are just a few of the unique advantages of the XaaS model.

Unfortunately, at this point in time, the majority of XaaS companies that we track are not exhibiting proof that scale automatically equates to higher profitability. Figure 1.4 compares the financial performance of SaaS providers with annual revenues of more than $500 million against traditional license software companies of the same size.

Clearly, there are challenges facing technology companies executing subscription business models. In a subscription model, you obviously need to acquire customers. More importantly, you

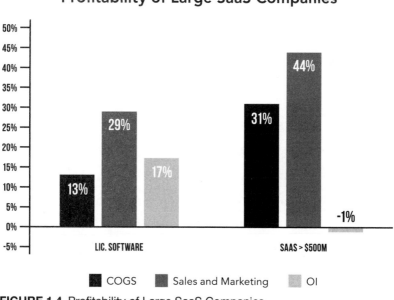

FIGURE 1.4 Profitability of Large SaaS Companies

need to keep those customers on the platform. Most importantly, you need to convince those customers to spend more money with you over time. High sales costs, customer churn, and offer commoditization create downward drag on the profitability of the subscription business model. The sharing economy is not yet proving a panacea of profitability in tech.

For now, investors seem to be OK with this reality for high-growth, pure-play XaaS companies like Salesforce and Workday. However, investors have high profit expectations for legacy technology companies such as Autodesk, Cisco, Microsoft, Oracle, and SAP. As these legacy companies attempt to pivot to XaaS offers to secure growth, Wall Street becomes apprehensive. All these head-lines—and many more—have starting appearing since late 2014:

- "Wedbush Downgrades Autodesk, Worried about Business Model Transition"[5]
- "Will Oracle's Transition to Cloud Impact Its Margins?"[6]
- "When Will Microsoft Have to Stop Milking Its Windows Cow?"[7]
- "SAP Profit Down 23% after Cloud Move[8]

As these companies attempt to navigate the expectations of investors, they are dealing with the reality that new XaaS offers require a significant investment in multiple areas such as:

- New technology platforms
- New pricing and financial processes
- Revised sales and marketing motions
- New service offerings and capabilities
- Reengineered partner models

So at the same time that revenues decline from our highly profit-able legacy offers and we begin to replace them with new sub-scription offers, additional investments must be made. In *B4B*, we referred to this phenomenon as "the fish" (Figure 1.5).

The Fish Model

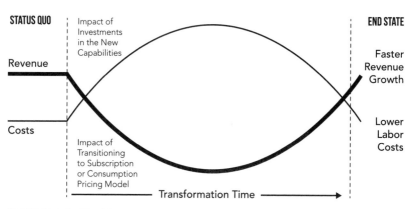

FIGURE 1.5 The Fish Model

Before this industry transition is completed, *every* legacy technology company will need to swallow this financial fish as they migrate from old to new business models. You can already see the consequences of this transition as companies begin navigating the rough waters. Some legacy companies signal tepid growth and lower profit expectations in the short term as they navigate the transition:

- "Adobe's (ADBE) Strategic Shift Will Lead to Growth in the Long Term"[9]
- "SAP Sees High Cloud Profit Potential in Long Term"[10]

    Other companies simply take themselves out of the public eye:

- "Dell Officially Goes Private: Inside the Nastiest Tech Buyout Ever"[11]
- "JDA Software to Go Private in $1.9 Billion Deal"[12]
- "BMC to Go Private in $6.9 Billion Deal Led by Bain, Golden Gate"[13]
- "Dell Buying EMC: Is This the End Times, or the Road to Salvation? (In any case, the enemy is now Amazon)"[14]
- "Informatica, Now Private, Announces New Leadership Team"[15]

And other companies are breaking into smaller companies:

- "HP's Big Split: The Good, Bad, and Potentially Ugly"[16]
- "Why Symantec Split Up into Two Companies"[17]

Regardless of the tactic, the fish is still sitting there—waiting to be swallowed. The pivot from traditional technology business models to new XaaS is inevitable. Almost every legacy technology company will need to establish some form of a XaaS offer. At the same time, new, pure XaaS providers will eventually need to pivot from unprofitable, high-growth business models to business models that generate more money than they spend. This book is designed to assist in both scenarios.

The Purpose of This Book

It does not matter if you are a 50-person, well-funded XaaS start-up or a $1 billion license software company: You will need to answer these three questions in the next few years:

1. How will we make our XaaS offer successful and how will we evolve our portfolio?
2. How are we going to cost-effectively land, deliver, expand, and renew customers of our XaaS offer?
3. What is our sustainable financial model for XaaS?

We have been collaborating with the industry for the past 8 years to find realistic answers to those three questions. This book provides a series of frameworks, observations, and recommendations that can help any size company navigate the gauntlet of decisions that must be made as you enter the brave world of the subscription economy. The content of this book will be highly relevant if you find yourself in any of these three scenarios:

- *I am responsible for helping my company stand up and optimize a XaaS offer.* If you find yourself in the middle of a XaaS offer, then this book is for you. It doesn't matter if you are the product manager for this new offer, the services executive responsible for supporting the new offer, or the CFO who is scratching your head over how to make money with this offer. There is detailed information on the plays your company will need to run to build a profitable XaaS offer.

- *I need to educate others in my company on how they need to change in order to empower our new XaaS offer.* If you are convinced that XaaS disrupts many company functions but you are struggling to convince others of this reality, this book is for them. Use this book to help carry key messages to these organizational functions. Sales, marketing, services, finance, and product engineering can all benefit from the content in these pages.

- *My company is not even talking about XaaS offers, but I want to understand how XaaS may impact my company.* Our point of view is that this industry transition to XaaS models will eventually impact every company in some way, shape, or form. The shiny new capabilities that are part of XaaS offers are making traditional offers look, well, traditional. Dated. Limited. This book can serve as a wonderful primer for ramping yourself up on the nuances of XaaS business models.

One warning concerning the content in this book: We cover a lot of ground. Not every chapter will be for every reader. For that reason, we recommend you leverage Figure 1.6 to prioritize which sections of the book you should tackle in your first read-through.

Using the XaaS Playbook

Unlike previous books we have written, the *Technology-as-a-Service Playbook* glides up and down between overarching strategic frameworks and "rubber meets the road" tactics. For that reason, we have created a cheat sheet to help prioritize the content that will be most relevant to various readers based on the specific questions the reader is attempting to answer. Figure 1.6 lists some of

AREA	QUESTION	CH 2: XAAS 3X3	CH 3: ECONOMIC MOATS
Strategy	Can we make money with a XaaS offer?	X	X
	How do we communicate with investors about our XaaS strategy?	X	
	Why are so many XaaS providers unprofitable?		X
	How long will it take our company to make this transition to XaaS?		
Finance	What financial models make sense for XaaS offers?	X	
	What metrics make sense to monitor for XaaS offers?	X	
	How do I communicate our XaaS transformation to investors?	X	
	How does our company P&L structure change?		
Product Mgmt & Engineering	What do we put in our XaaS offer?	X	X
	How do we price our XaaS offer?	X	
	How do we differentiate our XaaS offer?		X
	What is different about engineering XaaS offers?		X
Sales	What is different about selling XaaS?	X	X
	Why can't we bundle everything into one simple price?	X	X
	Why should we be selling managed services?		
Services	What is different about providing services around a XaaS offer?	X	X
	What new skills and processes will be required to service XaaS offers?		
	How should we price our services in XaaS offers?	X	
	What new services will we need to offer?		X
Partners	How will XaaS change our partner model?	X	X
	What do I tell our partners about our new XaaS offer?		
	What needs to change in our XaaS product to better support our partners?		X

CH 4: ORG. STRUCTURE	CH 5: SWALLOWING THE FISH	CH 6: PORTFOLIO AND PRICING	CH 7: CUSTOMER ENGAGEMENT MODEL	CH 8: FINANCIAL KEYS	CH 9: MANAGED SERVICES	CH 10: CHANNEL
				X		
	X				X	
		X		X		
	X			X		
		X		X		
			X	X		
	X			X		
X			X			
		X			X	
		X				
		X				
X		X	X			X
			X			X
		X		X		
					X	
X			X		X	
X			X		X	X
		X				
		X	X		X	X
			X		X	X
			X		X	X
		X	X			

FIGURE 1.6 Technology-as-a-Service Playbook Reader Cheat Sheet

the most common questions related to XaaS offers and highlights the recommended content.

The tipping point is nigh. Traditional product sales are declining. XaaS revenues are growing at double and triple digits. Sitting on the sidelines is no longer an option for traditional companies. At the same time, running a cash-burning XaaS financial model is becoming a riskier proposition every day. Something has to change. We hope you find this playbook useful, and we hope you enjoy the journey.

2 | The 3x3 of XaaS

So Many Choices

This is a book about the plays a company can run as they work to establish and optimize a technology-as-a-service offer. Obviously, the offer has to have value to the user, or as it's frequently called, product-market fit. We can't help you with that. It's up to you and your team of experts to target the opportunity and establish a uniquely valuable proposition. Fortunately, the cloud and the Internet of Things (IoT) will open up thousands of chances to do just that. But believe it or not, that's just the beginning. Once you have the opportunity in sight and the core product working, an entire new set of issues begin to play out. That's where this book comes in. We want to promote discussions among your team that can accelerate your thinking and increase the chances that your great idea is a commercial success.

But where to begin? What can we learn from the cacophony of XaaS offers and activities already in the marketplace? Some of these offers lead with free trials, such as McAfee's suite of security-as-a-service offers. Customers can try the service and then determine if they want to continue paying.[1] Some XaaS offers provide all the customer requires in one simple subscription price.

Apptio property management software provides a great example of this approach. On its web page, it leads with the tag line: *"No surprises. No complicated list of features that cost extra. Everything you need to run a more successful business."*[2] Still other XaaS offers list multiple components a customer can choose to purchase based on business requirements. Veeva Systems, which secures over 25% of its revenue from add-on services surrounding the core technology subscription, offers professional services, managed services, administrator training, environment management, and transformation consulting.[3]

Looking across XaaS providers, it may seem challenging to discern common patterns related to things such as offer types and pricing models. One industry article defines 12 distinct ways to price a SaaS offer.[4] What pricing model makes sense for your XaaS offer? What should be included in the offer? One way to bring some clarity to the chaos is to use the filter of time.

Profit Horizon

As we have studied the XaaS marketplace, we believe there is one defining factor in determining XaaS offer strategy: the profit horizon, as illustrated in Figure 2.1.

> *Profit Horizon: The length of time targeted to achieve significant GAAP profits.*

By GAAP profits, we simply mean a company is considered profitable when applying traditional, generally accepted accounting principles. This is an important distinction, because many XaaS providers are currently applying non-GAAP metrics to communicate the financial health of their businesses. The argument for non-GAAP is that non-cash items, such as employee stock option expenses or the amortization of intangible assets obtained through acquisition, should be excluded to provide a more meaningful

Profit Horizon

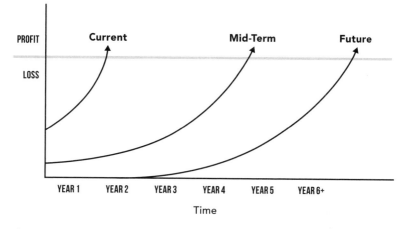

FIGURE 2.1 The Profit Horizon

view. We don't want to get into the debate about GAAP or non-GAAP, so we choose to set GAAP profits as the bar since no one will argue with you once you have achieved them!

A plethora of companies are building XaaS offers that they believe may take many years to capture significant market share, aggregate customers, and create the economies of scale needed to make GAAP profits. They may not even fully understand how those revenues will be monetized or how profits will be created. These companies have a "future" profit horizon. There are different profit horizons for companies that feel they need less time. Perhaps a company established a XaaS offer several years ago. It expects to achieve a critical mass of customers and revenue in the next few years or so. Its profit horizon is "mid term," but not current. Finally, if you have a XaaS offer that you believe can get to a critical revenue mass and be profitable within the next year or two, then your profit horizon can be defined as "current." You are expecting or needing the offer to generate profits for your company relatively quickly.

The 3x3 of XaaS: The First Dimension

Applying this concept of a profit horizon to XaaS offers in the marketplace, we can easily recognize three common, distinct profiles of XaaS solution providers, as seen in Figures 2.2, 2.3, and 2.4 and described below.

1. **Future Value Aggregator (FVA).** These are XaaS providers that believe the real financial value of the offer will be realized at some date in the distant future. The method of achieving profitability may be vague or unproven, but there is an initial mass of believers (investors, customers, analysts) that has provided adequate support to get the company to believe in its direction. The critical success metric for these offers is the unit of future value. This is the item that the provider believes will be monetizable at scale. That item could be users buying subscriptions, but it could also be page views in an advertising model or transactions in a web services model. For one XaaS offer we analyzed, the unit

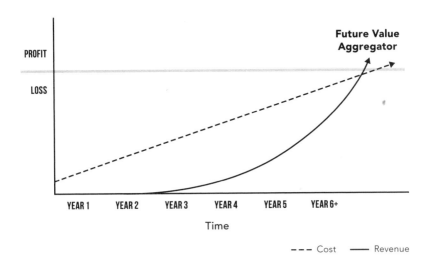

FIGURE 2.2 Profit Horizon: Future Value Aggregator

of future value was the number of project plans under management on their platform. In the early days, FVAs are likely to be experimenting with revenue models; customer spending may be erratic or even nonexistent as the company endeavors to find the levers to add visitors and translate them into reliable revenue. FVA doesn't necessarily mean that companies are not monetizing customers at all, it's that they are in an immature—and likely unprofitable—state of monetization. The per-customer unit economics are likely to be negative or sub-optimal.

2. **Mid-Term Wedge (MTW).** These are XaaS providers that expect to achieve profitability in the not-too-distant future (3 to 5 years, or so) selling their core subscription. This is the most commonly advocated SaaS business model. These companies have, or believe they will amass, enough customers on the platform in this time frame to achieve the economies of scale required to be profitable. We refer to this as the mid-term wedge profile, because these are companies that are exiting the

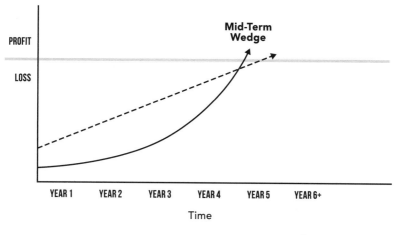

FIGURE 2.3 Profit Horizon: Mid-Term Wedge

left-hand side of the classic XaaS financial curve, where the provider is investing in the platform, and entering the right-hand side of the model, where each additional customer drives more and more revenue that brings the company one step closer to profitability. Importantly, the wedge model assumes that, at some point, costs are no longer increasing in a linear relationship to revenue. MTW is where companies start to hone in on their "balanced state." Losses shrink and the economies of scale that are driven by positive per-customer unit economics begin to really become visible. The balanced state of growth + profits becomes clear and accurately projectable. It is the proof moment for the business model.

3. **Current Profit Maximizer (CPM).** These are XaaS providers that are focused on maximizing the revenue and margin opportunity surrounding their XaaS offers as soon as possible. Instead of capturing market share at the expense of profitability, the companies are very focused on maximizing profitability

Profit Horizon

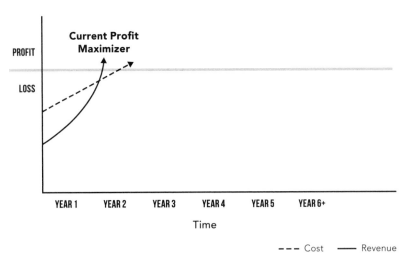

FIGURE 2.4 Profit Horizon: Current Profit Maximizer

per customer in the short term, this year or the next. Often these are large public companies with shareholders who are demanding profits now, or XaaS companies who are fairly mature and are ready to make the switch from revenue valuation multiples to profit growth valuation multiples. Most importantly, what both companies have in common is that they believe they can get their revenues to critical mass soon. Potentially this could be a new company with meteoric growth, but that usually requires a longer horizon than 1 to 3 years.

So this leads us to the three profiles of XaaS, as summarized in Figure 2.5. These profiles are the first dimension of the 3x3 of XaaS.

Shareholder Appreciation Drivers for Each Profile

What profile is applicable to your XaaS offer? There are a few key attributes you can test for:

- **Drivers for the Future Value Aggregator.** This profile is applicable when there is a significant market—that may or

The Three Profiles of XaaS

	FUTURE VALUE AGGREGATOR	MID-TERM WEDGE	CURRENT PROFIT MAXIMIZER
Unit of Consumption by Customers (users, pageviews, clicks, etc.)	Rapid growth (usually triple-digit)	Growth (high double-digit+)	Growth, could be slowing
Confident in Pricing/ Revenue Model	Not yet	Yes	Yes, usually multiple
Revenues Growing Faster Than Expenses	No	Yes, maybe barely	Yes
Profitability Horizon	5+ years	3 to 5 years	Current to 3 years
Examples	Twitter Transitioning: ➞ Docusign Box	Workday Transitioning: ➞ Salesforce.com AWS	Google, Adobe

FIGURE 2.5 The Three Profiles of XaaS

may not be well understood by the marketplace itself—to create and/or dominate. The premise is that the XaaS offer with a dominant share of this large market will be best positioned to maximize future profits. However, to assume this profile, a company needs a critical mass of investors that drink the Kool-Aid and believe in the future payoff. If investors are not excited about the potential future state, then it is hard to raise capital to support the investments required to acquire customers. Over the past few years many venture investors have been placing high valuations on unprofitable XaaS providers with the hope that over a long horizon profits will flow.

- **Drivers for the Mid-Term Wedge.** This profile is applicable when the company believes it has a 3- to 5-year line of sight to making the current offer profitable. The company believes it can manage the three attributes that kill the profitability of XaaS offers: churn, costs, and commoditization. The company can keep the majority of customers on the platform for multiple years. Economies of scale are kicking in so it costs less to serve each customer. The company will be able to fend off commoditized pricing due to hyper-competition. It knows how many customers are required to cross the line to profitability.

- **Drivers for the Current Profit Maximizer.** This profile is applicable when a company needs or expects to generate high profits in the near term to meet shareholder approval. As just mentioned, the two common classic examples would be a highly profitable, publicly traded software company that is now in the process of starting up a new XaaS offering that competes with the legacy license offering, or a mature XaaS company that is ready to show off its ability to throw off profits and cash. Occasionally there may even be a highly disruptive and high-priced entrant that is confident it can get to profitability early in its XaaS childhood. In the first case, investors are accustomed to substantial profits from the company and may not have much appetite for significant losses related to a new XaaS offer. In the second example, investors are salivating at finally reaping the rewards of the multiyear investment to get the subscription business model to become a money-making machine.

Common Behaviors

When companies assume one of these profiles, recognizable behaviors emerge:

- **Common Behaviors of the Future Vaule Aggregator.** Companies in this profile care more about attracting new potential customers than anything else and are willing to do whatever it takes to make that happen—almost no matter what that costs. They will offer "all in," simplified pricing models, up to and including free and freemium. They will throw in services required to enable the customer at no cost, not focus on monetizing value-added services. Sales and marketing expenses will range from 50% to over 500% of total company revenues as the company aggressively invests to acquire new customers, add units of future value, and increase market share.

- **Common Behaviors of the Mid-Term Wedge.** Companies in this profile have clear signals that their revenue model and product-market fit are valid. Subscription or transaction revenues are consistently trending up each quarter. Cost of goods sold (COGSs) as a percentage of revenue might be beginning to shrink as economies of scale kick in. Sales and marketing expenses might also be shrinking as a percentage of revenue. B2B companies in this profile are often in the early stages of monetizing premium account services around the core subscription. These services typically represent 2% to 10% of total company revenues at this stage. The company has realistic models that indicate positive cash flow, and even GAAP profits, as it passes through the wedge inflection point in the next 3 to 5 years.

- **Common Behaviors of the Current Profit Maximizer.** Companies in this profile either have, or quickly will have, a critical mass of revenue enabling them to pass the wedge inflection point within 1 to 2 years. They are typically exhibiting slower top-line growth than the other two profiles, but are forecasting positive operating income in this fiscal year or the next. From that point forward, their models indicate strong and predictable cash flow and profit increases. If you look at their websites, you will typically see a diverse listing of multiple product and service offerings customers can purchase for additional fees. These companies may offer multiple consumption models. They may also offer to run the technology operations as a managed service.

3x3 of XaaS: The Second Dimension

Once you identify which XaaS profile you would like to pursue, you will need to answer the following three questions:

1. What is the offer portfolio and pricing model?
2. What is the customer engagement model that we will use to sell and deliver this offer?
3. What are the financial keys that will allow us to make money with this offer?

We refer to this as the iron triangle of offer definition, as seen in Figure 2.6.

A key premise of this book can now be stated: *The profit horizon of the XaaS offer should drive how a provider engineers the financial model, designs the portfolio, sets the pricing, and matures the customer engagement model for the offer.* While we will cover all three elements in later chapters, here is a bit more elaboration to help clarify the focus of our 3x3 matrix.

Portfolio and Pricing

Obviously, a company must determine exactly what it intends to take to market. The company needs to clearly define the XaaS

Iron Triangle of Offer Definition

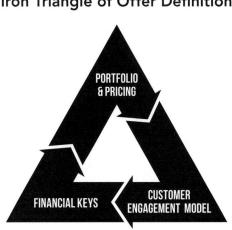

FIGURE 2.6 The Iron Triangle of Offer Definition

offer and how it should be priced. Double-clicking into this area, the company must make decisions in the following areas:

- **Technology Offer Definition.** What form will the core offer take? How will you package the high-value capabilities? What is the differentiation of these offers from competitive alternatives? Will you have a single offer or multiple, complimentary offers inside a portfolio?

- **Value-Added Services Offer Definition.** Are there any additional services the customer may need in order to be successful with the technology? Services could include traditional customer or technical services as well as information/ analytic-based services.

- **Offer Pricing Model.** How will the offer be priced? Will the price be based on consumption of specific features, number of users, business outcomes, or other factors? Will required services be bundled or sold separately? How will these services be priced?

As discussed in the opening chapter, the answer to these portfolio and pricing questions are wide and varied in the marketplace today. Understanding what answers maximize success within each XaaS profile becomes key.

Customer Engagement Model

Next, a company must work through the appropriate customer engagement model for the XaaS offer. We break the customer engagement model into four distinct phases we call LAER (pronounced *layer*):

- **Land.** All the sales and marketing activities required to land the first sale of a solution to a new customer, and the initial implementation of that solution.

- **Adopt.** All the activities involved in making sure the customer is successfully adopting and expanding their use of the solution.

- **Expand.** All the activities required to cost-effectively help current customers expand their spending as usage increases, including both cross-selling and upselling.

- **Renew.** All the activities required to ensure the customer renews their contract(s).

Customer engagement models for XaaS offers are highly diverse in the industry today. There is often particular confusion and conflict around the involvement of the channel. Many traditionally channel-focused tech companies find themselves in the awkward position of bringing out new XaaS offers that allow customers to engage directly. This channel conflict is particularly hard to avoid in many cloud XaaS models because customers often can completely self-serve from the company's website. Partners, particularly those who sell to small and medium business (SMB) customers, find that some customers do not need to engage with them directly.

So far, many of the engagement models companies have deployed are poorly aligned with the profit horizon of the offer, often resulting in offer failure or financial failure due to intolerable levels of sales and marketing expense. One objective of this book is to help companies reduce the probability for these misalignments.

Financial Keys

When working through the financial keys, a provider is creating the parameters for how success will be measured for this XaaS offer. And as indicated in the 3x3 model, success is not always defined by profitability. But in any model, the main areas a company must discuss when setting the financial keys for their XaaS offer include:

- **Revenue Mix.** What percentage of total company revenue will come from the core technology subscription(s), and what percentage of revenue will come from other value-added services you intend to monetize with the customer? We often refer to this as setting the "economic engine" of the offer.

- **Margin and Profit Targets.** What are the gross margin expectations for each revenue stream we have identified? What is the profitability we expect from the overall economic engine associated with this XaaS offer?

- **Sales and Marketing Costs.** What will the cost of our LAER model be as a percentage of revenue? How do we project that these costs ratios will change over time as our profit horizon shrinks?

- **Key Performance Metrics.** What are the specific metrics we will monitor to determine if we are on track to meet our financial objectives? Some of these metrics may not be financially oriented but can predict our ability to achieve our financial objectives in the appropriate time horizon as selected in the 3x3 model.

Once again, how a company answers these questions will be very different based on the XaaS profile it is pursuing. Figure 2.7 summarizes a view of the 3x3 of XaaS that provides an outline of the critical conversations a management team must have when defining a XaaS offer.

The Basic 3x3 of XaaS

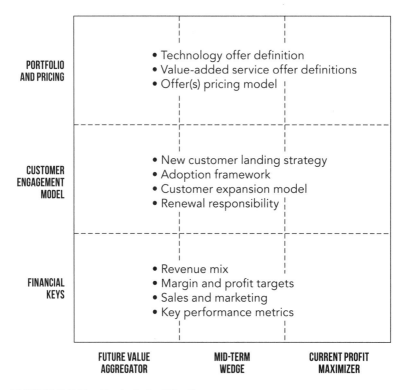

FIGURE 2.7 The Basic 3x3 of XaaS

Friction Curves

We have one final but critical thought before we continue the journey through the technology-as-a-service playbook. As you work through all the decisions associated with your XaaS offer, you will be optimizing between one of two extremes (Figure 2.8). At one extreme, you are doing everything possible to make it easy for the marketplace to acquire and adopt your core XaaS offer. On the other extreme, you are—at some point—doing everything possible to maximize the profits you extract from the offer.

On the left side of the diagram, you want to minimize any possible friction that prevents your units of future value from

Extremes

FIGURE 2.8 XaaS Offer Extremes

being acquired. That might mean free use of the product for a period, free services, and so forth. On the right side, you may be presenting concepts in your offers that add friction to the buying decisions but have the potential to increase per-customer revenue and profits. Maybe you are charging a premium price. Maybe you have a big professional services price tag to get the offer implemented correctly and you want to make money at that service. Maybe you have broken the offer into several separately priced modules that have the potential to increase total customer spend if the customer selects two or more. In any case, friction is a critical concept in the XaaS playbook. Most importantly, your friction strategy can and should change over time as your priorities, and your offer, mature. So let us introduce you to a model that TSIA calls the friction curve:

> **Friction Curve**: *The amount of offer complexity that balances the ease of customer purchase decisions with optimal per-customer economics.*

Every parameter you set regarding your XaaS offer will move the offer up or down the friction curve, as seen in Figure 2.9.

There are friction curves related to offer definition, pricing, and so on. We will refer to the concept of friction throughout the book. Understanding your profit horizon objective helps you understand how much friction to insert into your portfolio.

The Friction Curve

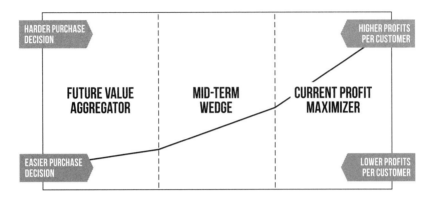

FIGURE 2.9 The Friction Curve

Now we know that there are a lot of people in the XaaS industry who might fundamentally disagree with this premise. They argue that the best way to profitability is to make it quick, easy, and fun for new customers to enjoy the offer. The idea is to get as many as you can as fast as you can. Eventually you will have enough to make money. In a perfect world you could find a highly profitable, frictionless offer model. If you can, good for you! They do exist and that could be your goal. But we think that is also the path to commoditization. Our observation is that most of the more profitable technology offers also force customers through some amount of complexity and trade-off as they choose from among multiple, sometimes premium-priced offers within a provider's portfolio of products and services. You may be faced with this reality as you make your playbook decisions. Again, we think friction is best thought of according to your profit horizon. You may start off with a low friction model when you are an FVA but intentionally place more and more expensive choices in front of your customers as you evolve into a MTW and CPM player.

So now let's put together all the elements of the 3x3 of XaaS, shown in Figure 2.10.

The 3x3 of XaaS

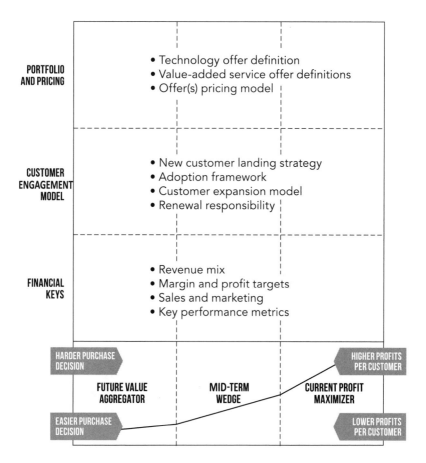

PORTFOLIO AND PRICING
- Technology offer definition
- Value-added service offer definitions
- Offer(s) pricing model

CUSTOMER ENGAGEMENT MODEL
- New customer landing strategy
- Adoption framework
- Customer expansion model
- Renewal responsibility

FINANCIAL KEYS
- Revenue mix
- Margin and profit targets
- Sales and marketing
- Key performance metrics

HARDER PURCHASE DECISION   →
HIGHER PROFITS PER CUSTOMER

FUTURE VALUE AGGREGATOR   MID-TERM WEDGE   CURRENT PROFIT MAXIMIZER

EASIER PURCHASE DECISION   →
LOWER PROFITS PER CUSTOMER

FIGURE 2.10 The 3x3 of XaaS

Upcoming Chapters

In Chapter 3, we will discuss how to create a XaaS offer that has the potential to create the highest and most sustainable profits possible by combatting the three "killer Cs" of XaaS success: customer *churn*, high *costs*, and offer *commoditization*. This is an important concept because many XaaS offers are creating a race to the bottom in terms of pricing and profitability. Chapter 4 tries to sort out how profitable XaaS businesses might eventually

organize and operate differently than traditional tech companies. Chapter 5 is targeted at all those large, legacy technology
companies that are struggling to pivot from traditional technology offers to new XaaS offers. In Chapters 6 through 8 we will
explore the three elements of the iron triangle of offer definition
in more detail. Chapter 6 will explore the power of portfolio
in XaaS. We will provide frameworks for defining your XaaS
offer and setting the pricing strategy. Chapter 7 will cover the
LAER customer engagement model and why the concept and
science of customer adoption is the best strategy for battling the
three killer Cs. Chapter 8 explores the specifics of setting target
financial models and metrics for a XaaS offer. Chapter 9 looks at
the special case of managed services as entrée into XaaS. Chapter 10 will explore the changing channel models—how the role
and success factors of go-to-market partners can alter in XaaS
marketplaces.

Playbook Summary

This book is designed to provide a set of plays you can run to
move your XaaS business forward. At the end of each chapter, we
will provide a summary of the plays that have been defined in the
chapter. As of now, you need only make one simple decision and
you will have run the first play in your XaaS playbook.

Play: Setting the Profit Horizon

Objective: Align your entire management team on what
profit horizon the company is pursuing for this XaaS offer.

Benefits:
- Provides context for the wide variance in behaviors of XaaS
  providers in the marketplace.
- Identifies the right XaaS offers to compare yourself against
  and model yourself after.

- Identifies the key parameters the management team will need to set for the XaaS offer.

- Minimizes behavior schizophrenia when setting the parameters for the XaaS offer.

Players (who runs this play?): The executive management team runs this play and should include senior leadership from the areas of product development, marketing, sales, services, and finance.

3 | Digging an Economic Moat for Your XaaS Business

As we just discussed, all kinds of companies are creating XaaS offers these days. Regardless of the profit horizon for your XaaS offer, at some point in time the offer will need to become profitable. It will need to generate more revenue than it costs to sell and deliver. Unless you are a market anomaly like Amazon,[1] that is just a basic business reality. But what level of profitability would you consider a success? If your XaaS offer generated an operating income percentage of 10%, would you declare financial victory? Would less than 10% be acceptable? Boards and chief financial officers (CFOs) love to set firm, and often aggressive, profitability objectives. But just because the board of directors *wants* a XaaS offer to generate a certain level of profit, it does not mean the offer (or the company) will ever achieve that level of profit. Why not? The answer can be found in the concept of economic moats. But before we introduce that framework, let's review the historical profitability levels of technology companies.

The Tech Cash Cow
In Chapter 1, we introduced the data in Figure 3.1 that demonstrates how profitable even the average large technology companies

Operating Margin

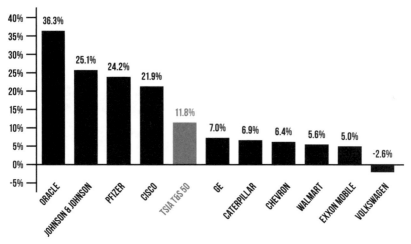

FIGURE 3.1 Operating Profit Comparisons

have been. The average profitability of the TSIA Technology & Services 50 (T&S 50) index of companies is superior to large-cap icons like General Electric (GE) or Exxon Mobile.

To provide additional context, Figure 3.2 tracks the net operating incomes of leading technology companies through the Great Recession of 2007–2009 compared to some other well-known companies. Although General Motors (GM), General Electric (GE), and Exxon all experienced significant dips in their operating incomes in 2009, Cisco, EMC, and Oracle exhibited little pressure on their profitability.

Figure 3.2 also highlights a strike zone where we are picking operating incomes: a range from above 5% to 15%. This is a healthy range of profitability by most standards. Accenture, GE, and Exxon are operating comfortably within this range, year after year. EMC runs at the high end of the range. A few exceptional performers like Cisco and Oracle (and some other technology companies) have been operating beyond the range.

Operating Income Profiles

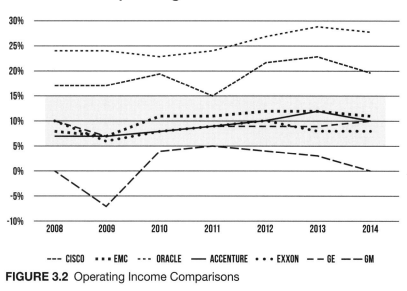

FIGURE 3.2 Operating Income Comparisons

But we are choosing 5% to 15% as a reasonable initial profit target for a XaaS offer. A big basket of hardware and software companies have been operating in this reasonable profitability range—undisturbed—for quite a long time, so we know it's a number that the financial markets will accept. Although some companies may be able to do even better, let's set some modest sights and start there. Let's get our XaaS offer to a 5% to 15% GAAP profit by working together; then, you can feel free to take it to new heights from there.

So how do we do that? Well, first we set our profit horizon as was done in Chapter 2. Now we need to figure out what strategies we can build into our offers that will be the foundation of our eventual 5% to 15% GAAP profit. Let's approach that task by looking at the lessons of the tech industry so far. Why were large technology companies like Oracle, EMC, and Cisco so incredibly profitable, even through the difficult 2008–2009 recession? Our answers can be found by applying a framework leveraged by several sophisticated investors.

Economic Moats

The investment firm Morningstar coined the term "economic moat" to describe how some companies are able to consistently generate above-average profits. Here is how Morningstar describes the concept:

> *"The idea of an economic moat refers to how likely a company is to keep competitors at bay for an extended period."*[2]

However, Morningstar is not the only investing entity that embraces this concept:

> *"In business, I look for economic castles protected by unbreachable 'moats.'"*[3] —*Warren Buffett*

Buffett and others are searching for companies that have a unique ability to generate highly profitable revenue. But how can you tell if a company has developed an economic moat that other competitors will find difficult to breach in the short term? Combining the insights of multiple publications on the topic of economic moats, we would like to proffer six attributes that will help determine if a XaaS offer can generate strong and consistent profitability. These attributes will be introduced from our view of least important to most important.

#6 Attribute: Virality and Other Paths to a Low-Cost Sales Model

Virality is the concept that a company has a product or service that almost sells itself. There is organic demand for the product. Word of mouth and reputation drive sales as opposed to heavy spending on sales and marketing. Think of the old Vidal Sassoon commercial: "And they told two friends, and so on and so on."[4] Low sales costs mean the company has an offering customers are excited about, and it usually means that more money drops to the bottom line. Virality is just one path to a low-cost sales model. We will discuss other paths later in the book.

A XaaS example of virality and a low-cost sales model is mobile ride-hail company, Uber.

#5 Attribute: Diverse Revenue Streams

Most consistently profitable companies have been able to diversify their revenue through multiple offers. The existence of several revenue streams in a portfolio allows them to better weather a difficult period or intense margin pressure faced by any one offer. As an example, during the 2008–2009 recession, large tech companies faced huge pressure on new product sales revenue as customer uncertainty brought IT purchases to a virtual standstill. Fortunately, these same companies had also built strong revenue streams for both their maintenance/support and professional services businesses. Because customers were not adding new products, they relied more heavily on maintaining and increasing the productivity of the products they already owned. For many profitable tech companies, maintenance renewal rates actually increased during this period. In addition, many customers contracted for professional services to help them better leverage existing systems to the new business realities they faced. The fact that these tech suppliers had a diverse portfolio of products and services enabled them to cushion the blow to the top line and achieve continued profitability on the bottom line. Perhaps even more important, diverse product or service revenue streams give you more ways to make money. Hewlett-Packard (HP) never made much money on printers, but they did pretty darn well on ink. Diverse revenue streams are usually a win-win. They are not only good for the provider, but they also usually mean that the customer has an array of products and services that provides a more complete solution. They don't need to shop multiple providers, and they have one throat to choke.

A good example of a XaaS company with diverse revenue streams is Veeva Systems. The company currently has over 20%

of total company revenues coming from value-added services wrapped around the core product subscription. The company, unlike many similarly sized SaaS companies, is generating an operating income of almost 10%.

#4 Attribute: Network Effect

Another economic moat similar to virality is the concept of a network effect. This is the phenomenon whereby a good or service becomes more valuable when more people use it. Telephone service is a great historical example. The more people who got phones in the late 19th and early 20th century, the more valuable it was to have a phone. If a company has an offering that is valuable because many people are using the same product, then the marketplace is incented to stay with that offer. This is not the same as market share. One company may dominate the market in mittens, but that does not benefit consumers in any special way when they buy a pair of mittens. However, if a person uses the TripAdvisor website to research travel decisions, that person benefits if more and more people are using the site and posting helpful reviews. The network effect can also be achieved by becoming a technology standard, building your brand into a standard, or by having uniquely broad compatibility with a surrounding ecosystem of products from other providers. If there is a vast network of complimentary products that easily interact with it to form a more complete and robust solution for the customer, your XaaS offer can achieve this effect.

Good XaaS examples of the network effect include LinkedIn and Salesforce's Force.com and AppExchange platforms.

#3 Attribute: Economies of Scale

A powerful economic moat for your XaaS offer can be dug when economies of scale play a significant role. This gives a company the power to have either higher profitability than a competitor or choose to use lower prices as a competitive advantage. If a company has an offer where increasing volumes equate to higher unit margins (often called "subtractive manufacturing"), then companies with critical mass and market share are in the pole position to extract high margins. Think of Intel in the computer processer marketplace. Because cloud-based XaaS offers are almost always based on multi-tenant architectures, where each incremental tenant reduces the providers' average hosting cost per tenant, you get subtractive manufacturing economics.

In infrastructure-as-a-service (IaaS) markets today, we see Amazon Web Services (AWS) and Microsoft Azure beginning to leverage their massive scale to apply price pressure to smaller rivals like Rackspace.

#2 Attribute: Unique Capabilities

Of course, something powerful must be said for having a truly unique capability. If a company can do something few others can do, then that company is in a position to create higher-than-average profits. Unique capabilities can be created through patents, specialized expertise, or even geographic presence. Also, brand equity built up over time can be viewed as a unique capability. Why is this only number two on our list of economic moats? It's because this moat seems to be getting narrower and shallower in the cloud. The cost and time to build or replicate features is rapidly shrinking. One XaaS offer's unique functionality is soon commoditized as all of its competitors quickly catch up—sometimes with an even better version than the original. In addition, recent trends in patent law are making it even more difficult to secure and defend software patents. All these add up to a markedly different outlook for the decades-old tech strategy of betting the whole company on the sole strategy of having perennially differentiated features.

A great XaaS example of unique capability is Google, whose search algorithms and ad placement software are both highly proprietary and highly effective.

#1 Attribute: High Switching Costs

The traditional trump card in creating highly profitable tech revenue has been high switching costs for customers. If it is expensive or painful for customers to switch to a competitive offer or substitute, then a company is in the perfect position to extract maximum profitability from the customer. When we present this model to MBA students, they are often incredulous that this is our number one attribute. They can't believe customers would fall for this in the long term—especially sophisticated buyers in business-to-business (B2B) markets! Yet, there are many ways to create high switching costs for customers that include:

- Requiring a large capital up-front investment that creates a sunk investment the customer will not readily abandon.
- Technically, making it difficult for customers to migrate all their data off of your offer.
- Contractually, making it financially painful to switch.
- Requiring a large training investment that makes it painful to retrain employees on substitutes and cause a protracted negative impact on productivity.
- Embedding your capabilities within the customer's business processes so your offer becomes critical to the customer's success.

Many SaaS application companies still benefit from high switching costs in much the way their on-premise predecessors did.

Companies like Salesforce and Workday are good examples of XaaS offers with high switching costs.

In summary, a company can generate highly profitable revenue when some or all of these attributes are present in their offers:

- Costs of selling the offer are low.
- The company has a diverse stream of revenues that surround the core offer, which helps balance out revenue or margin pressure in any one stream.
- The more customers that buy the offer, the more valuable the offer becomes to all customers.
- The more of the offer the company delivers, the lower the cost per customer becomes.
- The offer delivers a unique capability or experience to the customer that they cannot get elsewhere.
- It is very painful for customers to switch from the offer once they have decided to purchase it.

Next, let's review how the traditional technology industry has done on building deep economic moats around its offers. This is an important exercise because, as we will later see, not only the traditionally profitable tech companies but also the XaaS companies that are highly profitable today are both leveraging multiple economic moats. Quite simply, the more economic moats you can dig, the more successful and profitable your XaaS offer is likely to be!

Economic Moats in Traditional Technology Product Markets

#6 Attribute: Virality and Other Paths to a Low-Cost Sales Model

Companies in the T&S 50 index spend an average of 22% of revenues on sales and marketing—not exactly a small number. Software companies spend an average of 29%. Accenture, with all of its advertising and direct sales costs, spends 11% to 12% of revenues on sales and marketing. Ford Motor Company spends

10% to 11% on selling expenses. So in comparison, low cost of sales has not necessarily been a strength of the traditional high-tech business model.

Score: LOW

#5 Attribute: Diverse Revenue Streams

In addition to the diverse revenues emanating from their famously enormous and complex product portfolios, most large tech companies also have large and diverse service portfolios. On a combined basis, the companies in the T&S 50 index now have more than 50% of their total combined company revenues coming from services. Over the past five years, their collective product revenues—even with their diverse product port-folios—have declined 35%, and most hardware products have also suffered substantial margin erosion. But by diversifying into services that are growing at between 2% and 35% compound annual growth rate (CAGR)—many of which often have margins far superior to the products they are sold with—traditional tech companies have been able to better withstand the myriad pressures on their core offers and continue to deliver earnings per share (EPS) growth over time. So the traditional technology industry has done an excellent job of having diversity across both products and services.

Score: HIGH

#4 Attribute: Network Effect

Performance here has been a mixed bag among traditional tech companies. A few, like Microsoft Windows, have taken advantage of their vast network of users to build their products into true technology standards. A handful of others have built their company brand into a "safe choice," like IBM or Cisco, or a social fad, like Apple. Some have even used the network effect by achieving a broad base of IT workers who were familiar with the products. This was good news for any customer who wanted to operate their technology. Some traditional high-tech companies benefited enormously from the network effect. But rarely were they able to leverage the most powerful of the network effects where each new customer they sold added to the value being received by the base of existing customers. Many of them did, however, take advantage of the vast community of third-party resellers who could make money by reselling products and delivering attached services. The greater the demand the original equipment manufacturer (OEM) could create, the more partners flocked to resell the product. The more partners that did that, the more successful the brands became, and the more other partners felt the need to follow suit. In this instance of the network effect, the traditional tech industry was successful.

Score: MEDIUM

#3 Attribute: Economies of Scale

Clearly, economies of scale apply to technology products. We already mentioned Intel, which has made massive investments in plants to build processors. That has allowed the company to maintain roughly 80% of the processer marketplace decade after decade. But those economies have not created widespread competitive advantage for most hardware companies. Only a few have been able to use price to sustained benefit or enjoy product margins substantially better than their competitors.

In perhaps the industry's best example of how to make use of economies of scale, companies like IBM and Oracle have built vast piles of customer support and maintenance customers who pay to access a single technology service infrastructure. Once that structure was built, the incremental cost of supporting one more customer on the platform was negligible. Over time, as customer after customer was added and renewed, these maintenance empires became huge and incredibly profitable. Figure 3.3 reports on the product and support margins we track in our industry benchmarks and demonstrates how powerfully

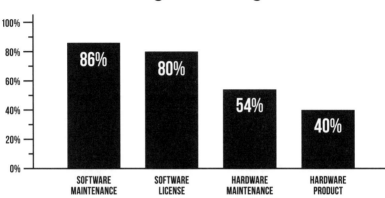

FIGURE 3.3 Margin Profiles for Technology as a Product

the economies of scale in the software support and mainte-nance business have led to gross margin that can exceed soft-ware itself!

Score: MEDIUM

#2 Attribute: Unique Capabilities

Technology companies have spent the last 40 years positioning around the unique technical capabilities of their products. These feature wars have resulted in a mind-boggling number of features per product. Microsoft Word alone has more than 1,200 features a user can access. Competing on differentiated technical capabilities has been the hallmark of high-tech strategy. Technology sales reps are trained to compete on "speeds and feeds" or software features. This has worked consistently and pervasively.

Score: HIGH

#1 Attribute: High Switching Costs

But as we have mentioned, the trump card of the technology-as-a-product business model, especially for software companies, was high switching costs. Technology companies pulled nearly every lever to make sure customers could not easily switch off a technology product. That meant that all downstream purchases by that customer would not be truly competitive situations. Solid revenues at solid margins could be counted on. Revenue from the existing customer base became the economic engine that propelled the company and its stock. It has been a beautiful thing.

Score: HIGH

Putting these observations together, we can rate how well traditional product revenue streams align with the attributes of high profit revenue, and seen in Figure 3.4.

As shown, these economic moats were medium or strong in every attribute but low cost of sales. There are many reasons why technology companies have been generating so much profit. Both their product and product-attached service revenue streams contain attributes that create deep economic moats.

So how are these attributes carrying forward to the world of technology as a service? How well are current XaaS offers faring in their ability to create deep economic moats that unlock the same type of highly profitable revenue? Let's take a look.

Economic Moat
TRADITIONAL TECH ALIGNMENT

ECONOMIC MOAT	TRADITIONAL TECH
Virality/Low Cost of Sales	Low
Diverse Revenue Streams	High
Network Effect	Medium
Unique Capabilities	High
Economies of Scale	Medium
High Switching Costs	High

FIGURE 3.4 Economic Moat – Traditional Tech Alignment

Shallow Moats of XaaS 1.0

The 20 publicly traded XaaS companies we track in our Cloud 20 index have been growing top-line revenues at double-digit rates. Revenue is clearly flowing nicely into these offers. GAAP profitability, on the other hand, has been extremely elusive for most, as shown in Figure 3.5. The average net operating GAAP income

Operating Incomes of XaaS Companies

COMPANY	RANK BY Q4 2015 TOTAL SERVICE REVENUE	Q4 2014 NET OI %	Q4 2015 NET OI %	TREND NET OI
Google	1	22.5%	25.2%	2.7%
Salesforce	2	-1.6%	2.5%	4.1%
Rackspace	3	8.8%	11.1%	2.3%
Workday	4	-33.1%	-23.9%	9.1%
ServiceNow	5	-19.3%	-10.7%	8.6%
Athena Health	6	-.7%	1.4%	2%
NetSuite	7	-17.9%	-17.3%	.6%
Ultimate Software	8	10.7%	7.5%	-3.2%
LifeLock	9	7.7%	-57.5%	-65.2%
RealPage	10	-4.5%	-11%	-6.5%
Veeva Systems	11	23.8%	18.8%	-5%
Medidata	12	4.2%	10.8%	6.6%
Constant Contact	13	9.7%	10.5%	.8%
Cornerstone OnDemand	14	-14.5%	-19.5%	-5%
IntraLinks	15	-6%	-6.8%	-.8%
LogMeIn	16	4.8%	11.3%	6.5%
LivePerson	17	-.8%	3.1%	3.9%
Demandware	18	-13.3%	-20.4%	-7.1%
Jive Software	19	-26%	-17.6%	8.4%
Qualys	20	10.2%	16.2%	6%

FIGURE 3.5 Operating Incomes of XaaS Companies

for these companies is −3.32%, and only 8 out of 20 made a net operating profit greater than 5%.

In addition, there is no consistent trend of improved margins and profitability year to year. Some companies are improving while others are not.

Now, perhaps a majority of XaaS companies in the public domain would still consider themselves to be future value aggregators or mid-term wedge companies. They may be building new markets or chasing market share and be less concerned with profitability. That could indeed be the case. However, the inability of so many XaaS companies to be profitable can be disconcerting, especially if you are a traditional tech company trying to decide whether you should take the plunge into subscription business models. This is of particular concern because many of these companies have annual revenues well in excess of $500 million—far past the point where most traditional tech companies turn profitable. Our point of view is that many of the first-generation XaaS companies are suffering from shallow economic moats.

So, let's now apply our economic moat framework to this current generation of XaaS offers (we'll call them "XaaS 1.0").

#6 Attribute: Virality and Other Paths to a Low-Cost Sales Model

As seen in Figure 3.6, SaaS companies in the TSIA Cloud 20 index spend an average of 40% of revenues on sales and marketing—much higher than their traditional license software peers (which is yet higher than many other industries).

What is driving this incredible spending? Acquiring new customers is clearly the main culprit. These XaaS companies need new customers to feed their models, and the sales cost to acquire a new customer almost always is more than the initial revenue received from them. Ironically, the more successful you are at adding new customers in a particular period, the worse your sales and marketing costs might be. It's almost like negative leverage. If it

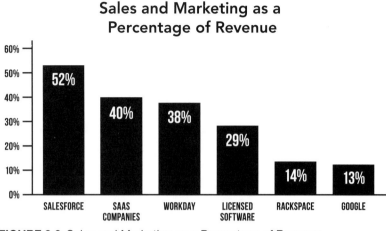

FIGURE 3.6 Sales and Marketing as a Percentage of Revenue

costs $10,000 to add a new customer but they are only going to spend $10,000 in the first quarter, you have just added revenue at a high cost of sales for that year. Do that hundreds of times and it's easy to see how sales and marketing costs in a XaaS world can skyrocket. But there is even more to the story here. In Chapter 7 we will introduce a framework on the XaaS revenue waterfall. That framework clearly demonstrates that if churn and down-selling are problems, it will take even more new customers to feed the beast of revenue growth because of the erosive effects of lost customer spending. Replacing lost revenue means that you need to land a certain number of new customers just to stay flat. If that void is too big and new customer sales costs to fill it are high, the XaaS company is destined to be unprofitable. And, the lack of cost-effective models to expand existing customer accounts can also cause sales expenses to soar. Having expensive field sales resources doing small upsell or renewal deals is simply not smart. It is our point of view that the selling models in these XaaS 1.0 business models have not yet been truly optimized. For most XaaS companies, cost-effective LAER coverage models have not yet been implemented at scale.

Score: LOW

#5 Attribute: Diverse Revenue Streams

This is an area of particular weakness for most XaaS companies or offers. Because these offers are often measured solely by the number of new users or some other unit-based metric, there is a massive temptation to eliminate any friction in the customer's selection process. That means throwing everything into the bundle at one low price—no separately monetized services or chunking of certain features into separate offers. Although we can understand that logic, we also think many companies will rue the day that the "eliminate all friction" mentality took root. Once an offer has established its value in the market, it is time to start building adjacent offers and diversifying the revenue streams associated with the core offer. Rainy days do come. New price-cutting competitors do emerge. Having a diversified revenue stream has proven again and again in the history of the tech industry to be a smart thing to do.

Score: LOW

#4 Attribute: Network Effect

Some XaaS companies have done an extraordinary job of leveraging the network effect. As we mentioned, companies like LinkedIn, TripAdvisor, Yelp, and Airbnb have built their entire business models on the network effect. But consumer XaaS companies are not alone. Salesforce's Force.com platform is a fantastic example of the network effect. The fact that a customer who chooses Salesforce knows there is a vast array of prequalified and highly compatible add-on applications is a mighty advantage for Salesforce. The more B2B XaaS providers that choose the Force.com platform, the stronger the advantage that Salesforce has over its customer relationship management (CRM) rivals. But not enough companies have built this moat into their strategy.

Score: MEDIUM

#3 Attribute: Economies of Scale

In theory, XaaS companies should absolutely benefit from economies of scale. Adding more users on the same platform should result in higher profits over time. Unfortunately, as we will discuss further in Chapter 7, the majority of XaaS companies that TSIA tracks are not exhibiting proof that scale automatically equates to higher profitability. Many of the SaaS companies TSIA tracks are becoming less profitable as they grow in revenue. Although these companies experience incredible top-line growth, their operating incomes remain in negative territory.

Now, we do believe economies of scale should be a positive attribute for XaaS revenue streams. Cost of goods sold (COGS) and general and administrative expense (G&A), in particular, should benefit. However, the economies are not yet consistently presenting themselves—even for multibillion-dollar SaaS companies. Without clear data to support this attribute of high-margin revenue, we cannot yet assume it is a given for XaaS offers.

Score: LOW

#2 Attribute: Unique Capabilities

As we will highlight in Chapter 4, XaaS providers are finding it harder to compete on features and are being forced to compete on price. For example, Microsoft, Amazon, and Google have been engaged in an aggressive price war related to hosted web services. The ability to differentiate their offers based on features has been challenging as the cost and time to develop new features become less and less. However, there continues to be evidence that features can determine market share, as SaaS start-ups quickly put competitive best-of-breed features on the table.

This moat works sometimes, but usually not for long. For example, have longtime competitive companies like Cisco WebEx, Citrix, and Skype been able to use unique product capabilities to win market dominance and avoid price commoditization? Not really. Many XaaS 1.0 offers have competitors that match one another on all the key features that define the category. So, unique capabilities are good when you can get them. But we see it as being a riskier and riskier strategy on which to base your entire business strategy.

Score: MEDIUM

#1 Attribute: High Switching Costs

How does the trump card of the technology-as-a-product business model relate to XaaS? In a recent study on customer success organizations, respondents from SaaS companies that were heavily focusing on customer adoption reported fighting average customer churn rates close to 20%. The TSIA benchmark tracking SaaS providers, in general, reports average customer churn rates of 8.4%.

The challenge for many XaaS providers is that an "easy on" XaaS offer can also be an "easy off" one. Many business customers of XaaS offerings are increasingly resistant to making massive up-front capital commitments or signing long-term agreements. If they dislike the offering after one year, they may indeed switch. In this regard, it is still true that the more complex your solution is to onboard, the stickier it is likely to be. Customers may resent a long and costly implementation, but from the supplier perspective it can be a powerful deterrent to attrition. So we still think high switching cost can be an important economic moat in XaaS, but like economies of scale, it seems to be present only in complex enterprise applications.

Score: MEDIUM

Putting these observations together, we can roughly rate how well XaaS revenue aligns with the economic moat attributes of high profit revenue.

Compared to traditional product revenue streams, we rate the current state of XaaS revenues the same or weaker on every attribute that drives highly profitable revenue—not for every company, certainly, but for the industry overall. We believe that just by looking at Figure 3.7, you get a better understanding of why many XaaS companies are unprofitable or barely profitable. And the argument that XaaS companies could be profitable if they chose to simply scale back on sales and marketing efforts is a shaky assumption—certainly an assumption that should make any CEO unsettled. If the core XaaS offer is surrounded by a shallow economic moat, then there is no reason to believe high margins and high profits will ever be realized. Keep in mind that there is not one real-world example of a XaaS company flipping negative GAAP operating income to positive operating income by simply slashing sales and marketing costs. No one has really tried because of the obvious and potentially huge negative impact on growth rates of such a move. If your stock price is largely supported by your growth rate, cutting sales and marketing costs is a risky call. It could work as a way to increase profitability, but to date no one has really played that card.

Overall, we think XaaS 1.0 is weaker in its economic moats, *but* this also brings us to a critical point: Not all XaaS businesses are losing money. A precious few are highly profitable on a GAAP basis. Why? We think it's largely because they have been able to

Economic Moat
XAAS 1.0

ECONOMIC MOAT	TRADITIONAL TECH	XAAS 1.0
Virality/Low Cost of Sales	Low	Low
Diverse Revenue Streams	High	Low
Network Effect	Medium	Medium
Unique Capabilities	High	Medium
Economies of Scale	Medium	Low
High Switching Costs	High	Medium

FIGURE 3.7 Economic Moat – XaaS 1.0

build and maintain multiple economic moats around their core XaaS offer.

As a reminder, looking at the Q4 2015 operating incomes for the Cloud 20 index on page 52, we see the following breakouts:

- 45% (9 of 20 companies) were unprofitable.
- 15% (3 of 20 companies) were marginally profitable (5% or less operating income).
- 35% (7 of 20 companies) were VERY profitable (over 10% operating income).

Let us look at four of those seven companies that were highly profitable. Why were they so profitable? The short answer is that they are all leveraging multiple economic moats (as listed below), and the more they employ, the more profitable the business.

Google: 25% operating income.
　　Economic Moats in Place:

1. Unique capabilities (product patents).
2. Low cost of sales.
3. Network effect.

Rackspace: 11% operating income.
　　Economic Moats in Place:

1. Unique capabilities (managed services, not product).
2. Low cost of sales.
3. Diversified revenue streams.

Veeva Systems: 18% operating income.
　　Economic Moats in Place:

1. Unique capabilities (products and services).
2. Diversified revenue streams.
3. High switching costs.

LogMeIn: 11.3% operating income.

Economic Moats in Place:

1. Unique capabilities.
2. Ability to offer outcome-based services.

So, it can be done. It is being done. These are levels of GAAP operating income that most CEOs would be thrilled to have for their XaaS offer. And it's being done by successfully surrounding the core offer with multiple economic moats.

Digging Deep Economic Moats for Your XaaS Offer

So in short, we believe XaaS business models can be profitable. We believe some XaaS business models will be *highly* profitable. However, to achieve profitability, XaaS providers must use economic moats and operating best practices to battle the three key enemies of XaaS profitability. We call them the killer Cs:

1. High selling *costs.*
2. High customer *churn.*
3. Rapid *commoditization* of the offer.

These killer Cs can and do weigh down XaaS profitability. How do we successfully combat them? XaaS companies must review each of the six attributes that create highly profitable revenue and determine how they can build as many economic moats as they can. Building these moats into your offer as early as your profit-planning horizon allows is the smartest thing you can do to increase your chances of having long-term GAAP profits for your XaaS offer. So let's look at ways you might be able to innovate around the six economic moats to combat the killer Cs.

#6 Attribute: Virality and Other Paths to a Low-Cost Sales Model

In our view, one of the primary challenges facing unprofitable XaaS companies, especially those in the enterprise space, is that they have pulled forward the expensive sales models of the traditional technology industry into their XaaS offers. These sales models rely heavily on a highly paid, field-based direct sales force to conduct nearly all the activities needed to build demand and land and grow new customers.

These conventional approaches are often proving to be too much cost to bear given the slow revenue recognition models associated with subscription and pay-per-use contracts. Successful XaaS companies will need to be open to different ways of creating demand that rely more on marketing and less on sales. They will need to debate alternative, less-costly sales models. And importantly, they must realize that in XaaS, profitable revenue is dependent not only on cost-effectively landing customers, but also cost-effectively renewing and expanding them. In traditional pay-up-front models, legacy tech companies really didn't even have to spend real sales and marketing dollars on these later-stage tasks. The only thing to renew was the maintenance contract, and any expansion was usually associated with the next big refresh a few years later. But XaaS offers face a different challenge in the form of the revenue waterfall model. They incur sales and marketing expense up and down the line throughout the entire customer life cycle!

At the same time that sales models are coming in for inspection and updates, the customer-buying landscape for purchasing technology is also changing, as shown in Figure 3.8.

Most traditional enterprise tech companies sold their wares to the IT buyer; it was a well-understood process both on the selling and buying sides. But XaaS has accelerated a shift that was bound to happen as the tech industry matured. Both TSIA and Gartner research indicates that conventional IT budgets are shrinking.[5] A growing number of enterprise technology decisions are now being made by business buyers. The complexity of implementing and adopting XaaS offers is often far less; the prices are often lower than many traditional on-premise solutions were and are available for monthly fees that fit neatly into the business buyer's

Shifting Sales Landscape

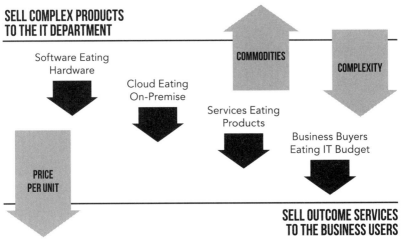

FIGURE 3.8 The Shifting Sales Landscape

own operating budget. That means HR picks its own tools; so does finance and marketing. XaaS offers give them the ability to choose best-of-breed cloud solutions and get them implemented with little or no involvement from the IT department. In many cases, individual employees are even making their own independent decisions to purchase personal technology tools.

These business buyers speak a different language. They are not interested in speeds and feeds. In fact, many don't care at all about the underlying technical attributes of the offer—they care about the business outcome the technology will lead to. This is causing massive reverberations in many traditional sales models. Sellers must now learn to speak the language of business, not the language of IT. They must know how their offers translate specifically into the business outcomes their buyers seek. They must be conversant in the business functions and in the industry each customer operates in.

The shifting buyer landscape and the killer Cs are all forcing successful tech companies to rethink and innovate their sales and marketing models for all the phases of the customer life cycle. How companies land new deals, drive broad adoption, facilitate systematic expansion, and efficiently achieve renewal is in the process of a major modernization.

Obviously, "going viral" is the land goal of every early stage XaaS offer. Achieving this, especially if you are a future value aggregator, is the central focus of both your R&D and marketing organizations. By combining an addictive and immersive technology, a compelling or fun experience, a cool brand, and a low-friction offer, early stage XaaS offers seek to achieve the holy grail of viral adoption. If you can do that, many of your sales cost problems go away. Together, these elements make up your brand experience. It's your secret sauce and, as we said, we don't purport to have simple or universal tactics for achieving the magic of a viral offer. And no amount of offer structure or go-to-market strategy is going to substitute for a serious weakness in these core areas. But offer structure and innovative sales tactics do accelerate the success of the core offering and increase their chance of long-term profitability. So, assuming your offer has at least some degree of success in the market and customers see value in it, now it's time to drive more customers onto the platform, but with an eagle eye on the sales and marketing cost structure you are building as you go.

Fortunately, there is new thinking and experimentation taking place out there. Here are some provocative approaches to selling up and down the LAER cycle that we see taking root in innovative XaaS companies:

- **Marketing-Led Selling.** You could argue this concept has been around forever. But as we look across the hundreds of TSIA member companies, we would assert that it has really not been a staple activity in tech. This is reflected in how sales and marketing dollars are allocated. In an informal survey with technology companies that we conducted in 2015, we found sales organizations were receiving five dollars to every one dollar spent on marketing activities. Most traditional tech companies simply have not trusted marketing to own the conversation with the customer once they have been identified. Leads from any source have typically been passed to field sales as soon as possible. It was up to the sales rep to qualify and cultivate the prospect, and sell the deal. This has resulted in expensive sales resources being allocated to very early stage—and often poorly qualified—opportunities. Marketing was often measured on lead *volume*, not lead *quality*. That is starting to change. Today's buyers are much better informed than at any other time in history. They can find information about your company, learn about the features of your product, and maybe even find pricing—all without talking to anyone. As a result, marketing's role is eating into the sales cycle. In addition, individual buyer behavior can now be tracked across marketing channels, and their engagement and propensity to buy can be "scored." Thus, marketing organizations at many XaaS companies are being charged with owning not only the identification of a lead but the cultivation of a lead, as well. That means when leads are finally turned over to sales, they are often highly qualified and deep into the sales cycle. This shortens deal windows, improves win/loss percentages, and increases sales productivity.

- **Bottom–Up Selling.** This is a marketing-led sales strategy where individual users or small teams within a large enterprise customer are approached to become customers individually. They use a credit card to make a personal decision to use the product. When that happens enough, the customer decides it needs an enterprise-wide license. Bottom-up selling reduces the enterprise license sales time and virtually locks out the competition.

- **Remote Selling Models.** This is another concept that has been around forever, but is now being beefed up and given far greater responsibility in XaaS. Historically, most inside sales teams either did lead generation for the field or sold only small, incremental add-on transactions to existing customers. But now some enterprise XaaS companies are successfully conducting the entire XaaS subscription sales process without ever going to the customer's site. These teams rely heavily on web meetings and phone calls as their key engagement tactics. In most cases, these sales teams are initially directed at small or mid-size customers, but as their effectiveness is proven, companies are experimenting with taking these teams "up market." By their nature, these teams can operate at higher efficiency and achieve greater volumes than their field-based counterparts. They don't have travel time, they don't wait in lobbies, and, when combined with the following tactic, they simply don't cost as much.

- **Process–Driven Selling.** Obviously, the number one expense line item in overall sales and marketing budgets is labor, specifically, sales labor. For decades, companies have been comfortable paying high annual compensation to recruit and maintain experienced enterprise sellers. But many XaaS companies are finding success with hiring less-experienced talent and then teaching and enforcing very tight adherence to a proven sales process. These multi-touchpoint sales processes control everything from who is contacted, what messages are delivered, what meetings are held, and what products are offered. This approach is often used in concert with remote selling and, thus, is usually piloted in smaller accounts. Most—but not all—companies are still relying on experienced enterprise sellers to manage their largest accounts. However, this is a trend we think has much potential for success.

- **Land-Only Sales Teams.** Due to the growing understanding and sophistication of the LAER model, some XaaS companies are bifurcating sales into two (or more) teams: The land team and the customer success team. In this model, sales lands. That's what they do. They don't own adopt, they don't own renew, and they even don't own most of expand. These later-stage tasks are relegated to specialized customer success teams who use "extreme adoption" as their leverage to ensure easy renewals and certain expansion. In some cases, the adopt and renew motions are driven by customer success managers (CSMs), but in others, the renewal and expand motions are done separately by purpose-built remote selling teams. No matter what the structure, the net result is that the land sales team makes their money from landing. Usually, that's landing a net-new logo customer, but it can also be cross-selling a second major offer platform to an existing customer. In fact, we see this practice becoming fairly standard: The adopt/expand/renew team(s) own growing a customer's spending on the offer platform already in use (adding more users, more transactions, more services), but they hand opportunities to land an additional (major) offer platform at that customer to the land team. Land-only sales is a fascinating and potentially huge win for the company because it guarantees a steady stream of net-new customers every month. For the sales team, it's a real challenge because they cannot rely on renewals of easy expansion to retire some of their quarterly quota. Often the quotas are lower for these land-only reps for this reason. However, the company balances their overall sales costs by blending a higher cost of land with a much lower cost of expand and renew.

- **Automated Sales.** Everyone has had the experience of buying something or signing up for a subscription on a website. The site is optimized to inform you and escort you through a self-service buying experience. Often this experience is integrated with other marketing tactics designed to attract and inform the buyer, eventually leading them to the automated sales experience. Obviously, this is a great low-cost sales model, one we are all familiar with and are probably considering or using in our current XaaS offer. However, a new and far less-used tactic is to imbed upsell and cross-sell offers that present themselves to the customer directly through the technology. Customers encounter the offer contextually as they are using the product, and they simply click a button to complete the transaction. Apple has a classic example of this capability related to their storage services. When a subscriber is getting close to exceeding their current capacity, Apple sends an email providing options on how to reduce storage needs or to purchase more storage. To purchase more storage, you simply click a button. This offer can be made separately via email or during the use of the product. This mentality of making it easier for the customer is migrating to enterprise XaaS. Unfortunately, we have seen resistance to this tactic. We had a TSIA member company that created an automated offer that was presented to their SMB customers through email. If the customer wanted to buy the offer, they simply clicked a button. When the sales organization learned about the offer, they vocalized concern: "We are losing an opportunity to talk to the customer and potentially upsell them." As a result, the automated offer was killed. Now, if a customer wants to make even a relatively small purchase, they are required to speak to a salesperson. In our opinion, this is a step in the wrong direction if your goal is trying to optimize sales costs.

- **Blended Sales and Service Models.** At TSIA, we predict there will be a massive blurring of the historical lines that separated sales from services. In the 2009 book *Complexity Avalanche,*[6] we asserted that "helping will sell, selling won't help." By that, we meant that service motions designed to improve the business value that a customer derives from a technology solution is bound to lead to expansion opportunities that benefit both the customer and the tech company. You can call identifying that moment "selling" if you want, but we actually like the term we first heard used by TSIA member company Blackbaud called "up-serve" (who got it from the book *To Sell Is Human* by Daniel Pink). You empower service and marketing teams to up-serve the customer by both providing services or information *and* recommending those new products and services that the employee truly believes would benefit the customer. Just look at Rackspace with their Fanatical Support team. They sell by helping, and they start that motion in the pre-sales stage. They act as both the sales rep and the service rep, but it's all done in the context of making customers fantastically successful. We are seeing examples all over the industry of innovative practices designed to leverage the vast array of services touchpoints with customers to create logical, deftly appropriate sales transactions or leads. It just makes sense to leverage the trusted advisor status many service organizations have achieved to make trusted expansion recommendations to customers. Our TSIA touchpoint calculus indicates that service interactions can occur 15 to 20 times more than sales interactions. Service staff can be trained to listen and identify new sales opportunities. We are seeing technology companies implement incentive programs for service employees to identify and log sales leads. For one company, we saw a new program implemented to incent service employees to log new sales opportunities for the sales force. In six months, the services organization had identified more than $100 million in new sales opportunities. Of course, all of those leads do not close—but over time, the services employees become more adept at identifying highly qualified leads.

- **Outcome-Based Selling.** Let's face it: Tech has always been a product industry at heart. We love our products, and rightly so. So, it was just natural that our sales conversation with the customer started right there—with the product. The demo, the side-by-side feature comparison, trotting out the performance benchmarks . . . this is how we loved to sell.

And our traditional IT buyers loved it, too! They were connoisseurs of technology. They simply orchestrated the feature "bake-off" and leaned it toward the sales team they liked best wherever possible. Selling to business buyers is fundamentally different. They don't want to start the conversation with the product; they want to start the conversation with their business outcomes. How can more revenue be generated, how can costs be cut, how can competitive advantage be gained, how can end-customer results be improved? Business—not technology—is the new language of sales. Many XaaS companies are reorganizing their sales messaging to start with the customer's business outcome and work backward to the differentiating features of their products and services rather than leading with them. They are also becoming much more vertically aligned in order to ensure that sales teams can speak the language of the customer.

Score Improvement Opportunity: From LOW for XaaS 1.0 to MEDIUM for XaaS 2.0

#5 Attribute: Diverse Revenue Streams

As we mentioned, this is an area of particular weakness for most XaaS 1.0 companies. The low friction mentality of the early days often takes root and proves hard to shake from the cultural mindset of the team. More and more and more features get added, and more and more services get given away, all inside the core offer. Although this may be the right strategy in the early days to keep friction low among early adopters, the winning XaaS 2.0 company will have specific plans and time frames to diversify their revenue streams.

The obvious starting point is diversifying the product portfolio by surrounding the core offer with complimentary adjacent modules. Both Salesforce and AWS have done excellent market-leading jobs of diversifying their product portfolio. They are not only growing and diversifying their revenues, but they are also eating their way into adjacent markets and taking share from the legacy competitors that once owned them. They lever the strength of their core by creating adjacent offers that integrate seamlessly and create customer synergies when they choose to select the same provider for more than one application. AWS customers can manage more of their IT infrastructure from a single place, at lower overall costs, on a single bill. Salesforce customers can better coordinate the activities of the sales, marketing, and customer service activities when they are using modules from Salesforce. The lesson here is to be courageous and aggressive on your unbundling. Look for opportunities to create separate offers through acquisition or organic R&D, not just have your core offer endlessly grow its own footprint.

The same is true for your services portfolio. Traditional, on-premise technology products came with a classic portfolio of product-attached services designed to help customers scale the mountain of complexity that often came with installing, integrating, and maintaining what they bought. These legacy tech companies intelligently leveraged that need for assistance into multimillion (or billion) dollar service franchises. As we mentioned, collectively the T&S 50 index of companies has over half of their revenue coming from services today. The good news is that for many XaaS 2.0 companies, customers still want and are willing to pay for many of these same services. As we mentioned earlier, companies like Veeva Systems and Ultimate Software have very strong service revenues coming from professional services around their XaaS offer. In its last fiscal year, Workday got more than 20% of its total revenue from professional services. So, the opportunity to monetize traditional professional, education, and premium support offers still exists for XaaS offers.

But what is more exciting to us is that XaaS 2.0 companies can choose to build a host of next-generation service offers around all the products in the portfolio. Figure 3.9 shows TSIA's latest technology services portfolio listing for cloud-based offers. In it, you will see exciting new offers that can be built in operational services, adoption services, and information services.

By designing and engineering these service capabilities deep into products, you can create adjacent offers that result in a better customer experience, act as competitive differentiators, diversify your revenue, *and* do all of the above at very attractive margins. For

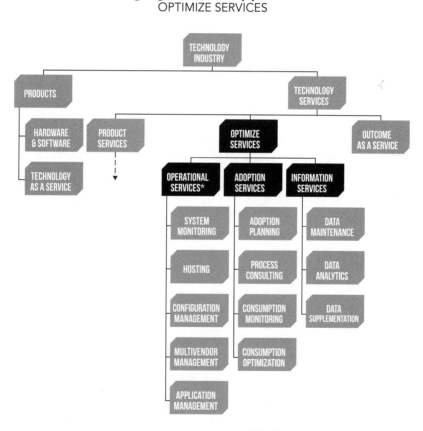

Also known as managed services.

FIGURE 3.9 Emerging Service Opportunities – Optimize Services

too long, traditional tech companies did not truly engineer new service capabilities into the products from the start. Services were largely an afterthought to the R&D teams, who often defined a set of end-user features or performance characteristics as "the product." Profitable XaaS companies will realize that the entire portfolio should be considered as in-scope for the R&D effort. By building service-enabling capabilities into the core products, services can be automated and delivered to the customer at margins equal to or better than the core offer itself.

There is no reason that XaaS 2.0 companies can't also one day count on having half or more of their revenues coming from cloud-enabled operational, adoption, or information services along with traditional professional, educational, or premium support services.

Score Improvement Opportunity: From LOW for XaaS 1.0 to HIGH for XaaS 2.0

#4 Attribute: Network Effect

The legacy technology companies took advantage of their product complexity to build network effects like partner reseller communities and vast technical talent pools that made their products easier to buy. XaaS providers have another network effect opportunity at their disposal by virtue of the vast data sets they are amassing. Every XaaS company is sitting on top of an incredible data set being generated by customers that use the offer. The opportunity here is to aggregate and analyze that data to create additional offers for customers. These are the adoption and information services mentioned earlier. Industry examples of these types of services include IT help desk benchmarking by Zendesk,[7] industry key performance indicator (KPI) benchmarking from SAP,[8] adoption scoring by Salesforce, cost optimization recommendations from Amazon,[9] and retail performance assessments from JDA Software.[10] Each of these offers creates unique, value-added insight to the customer, and each offer is driven by the network effect. The more customers on a specific XaaS platform, the more valuable and insightful these data-driven offerings become to customers.

In addition to benchmarking, technology suppliers can capture and promote many best practices as their network of customers gets larger and more diverse. Infor, an application software company offering both hosted and cloud offers, specializes in "micro-verticals." It has software for more than 400 highly targeted market niches. As an example, they don't just offer software for the food services industry; they have offers for beverage distributors and fast-food chains. Thus, they leverage their experience with a growing customer base to create ever-more-targeted offers that make competitors look broad and unfocused. So, the more customers you acquire, the more targeted and focused your offer can become. Although this may add to your R&D and marketing costs as the number of flavors of your offer increase, it might be more than offset by positive impacts on your market share and reductions in your selling costs.

Many cloud XaaS companies don't put enough emphasis on network effect, and this opens the door to new competitors. Take web meetings, for example. Cisco WebEx and Citrix each own a large share of the cloud-based meeting software. In a B2B environment, valuable meeting time is often lost when meeting organizers attempt to introduce new meeting tools that require participants to download and register—sometimes even leading to failed meetings when corporate firewalls prevent the new client app from being downloaded. Yet, why don't Cisco WebEx and Citrix leverage their "sure bet" meeting status against the numerous start-ups they face?

Another key strategy to leverage the network effect is to create compelling revenue generation opportunities for third-party partners. As we just mentioned, this is another of the network effects that traditional tech companies did quite well. However in a XaaS world, as we will discuss in Chapter 10, new models for incenting and rewarding channel partners may need to be devised, and new kinds of partners may need to be attracted. More on this later.

Score Improvement Opportunity: From MEDIUM for XaaS 1.0 to HIGH for XaaS 2.0

#3 Attribute: Economies of Scale

Cloud-based XaaS offers are naturals for this economic moat. That's because many of their incremental customer development and hosting costs are relatively low. The more customers they add to their platforms, the lower the average cost to serve. The incremental cost to serve a new customer can approach zero in some cases. No one is better at leveraging economies of cloud scale than Amazon. AWS has publicly committed to waging a volume-based price war with competitors Azure, Google, and Rackspace. They plan to use low prices to attract more customers, which allows them to reduce their average COGS per customer and thus to further lower prices.

The objective is to maximize spend per customer. As discussed in Chapter 5, a majority of XaaS companies are maximizing the addition of new customers but are under-focused on increasing the amount of money those customers spend. The XaaS 1.0 revenue mix is shown on the left side of Figure 3.10. This may be fine for the future value aggregator, but once a customer is on the platform, XaaS companies eventually need to maximize the revenue opportunity and create multiple economies of scale. Spinning up scalable new product lines or transaction offers or services is one method many enterprise tech companies employ. These tactics, as the right side of Figure 3.10 suggests, help both diversify the revenue streams and create the opportunity to generate several economies of scale within the offer or the company.

Score Improvement Opportunity: From LOW for XaaS 1.0 to MEDIUM for XaaS 2.0

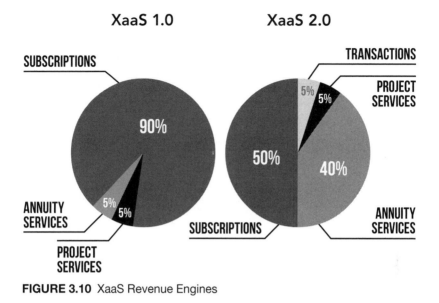

FIGURE 3.10 XaaS Revenue Engines

#2 Attribute: Unique Capabilities

As we pointed out, differentiating based on more user features or better technical capability is still a critically important tactic for XaaS companies. It's just getting harder to keep them as an advantage for very long these days. More and more XaaS companies are also successfully differentiating based on unique service capabilities enabled by technical capabilities. Industry examples of profitable XaaS offerings that leverage interesting service capabilities include the following:

- OpenText wraps both professional services and managed services around subscription revenues to generate an operating income of 16%.

- Granular is leveraging technology and analytics to create a managed service designed to help farmers maximize productivity and profits.[11]

- TravelClick combines a hosted cloud offering with value-added services to help hotels maximize revenue.[12]

Each of these offers is proof that service capabilities can marry with product capability to become a market maker for XaaS offerings.

Continuing to invest adequately in unique capabilities is always a prudent decision. What's changing is that companies are thinking much more broadly about what those capabilities are. It's not just about features; it's about any unique capability that expands the number, depth, or breadth of your economic moats. That might be building application programming interfaces (APIs) that broaden the interest of third-party channel providers, or allocating development resources to building a marketplace for supplemental offers by other XaaS companies. There are many great opportunities to leverage unique capabilities around your core offer in the cloud. It just takes imagination and a broad charter for your development and marketing teams.

Score Improvement Opportunity: From MEDIUM for XaaS 1.0 to HIGH for XaaS 2.0

#1 Attribute: High Switching Costs

As previously noted, technology companies have done an outstanding job of making it painful for customers to easily switch technology providers. Many first-generation XaaS companies have not done as well here. Yes, business process-intensive applications like CRM and ERP are always difficult to swap out, even if they are SaaS based. But even here, if the customer does not have a large sunk investment in licenses, they will be more tempted to make changes early if the cost savings are significant enough or if adoption of the current XaaS offer is low. However, there is a real opportunity for XaaS companies to make switching unattractive to customers. Once again, services can be of strategic help. XaaS providers that create sticky service offers that deliver business value that is hard to replicate are much harder to dislodge. The proof point is what TSIA sees regarding the renewal rates on managed service offerings from TSIA members. As shown in Figure 3.11, TSIA members with managed service offerings are

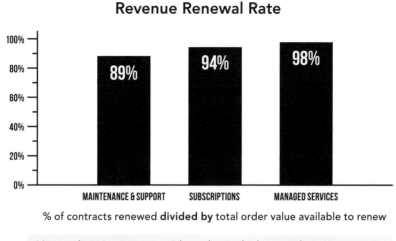

Revenue Renewal Rate

% of contracts renewed **divided by** total order value available to renew

*Managed services are very sticky and enjoy high renewal rates.
Subscription pacesetters are **growing** revenue, not just retaining revenue.*

FIGURE 3.11 Revenue Renewal Rates

experiencing higher revenue renewal rates than they achieve on traditional support. We know from our managed services benchmark data that renewal rates for managed service contracts hover in the high 90% range. If a customer is buying your managed service offering, they are also buying your technology.

It's the same logic for investing in a strong customer success capability. When XaaS companies drive high end-user adoption, they increase the barriers to switching. End-user training and business interruption due to the introduction of new software is a well-understood and feared cost to business customers. The more application software complexity in your XaaS offer, the greater the opportunity to drive business value lock-in through high end-user adoption.

In addition, stickiness can be achieved through very smart use of the data customers generate in your system. Every business trend report, every business outcome you can quantify, every usage report you can flash, every valuable analysis you can muster—all of these make the customer hesitant to turn your product off and turn a competitor's on. But like most everything else we have identified, this demands a broader line of thinking on how to design and build economic moats into your offers.

Score Improvement Opportunity: From MEDIUM for XaaS 1.0 to HIGH for XaaS 2.0

Putting It All Together

If a XaaS 2.0 company or organization pursued all of the tactics listed in this chapter, we believe their long-term profitability will be optimized (Figure 3.12). By developing intelligent product, service, and go-to-market strategies that wrap their offer in multiple economic moats, companies can accelerate growth, defend against commoditization, and optimize shareholder value.

No law states that technology companies should generate double-digit operating incomes. As Nick Mehta, CEO of Gainsight, likes to point out, "Not everything in business ends well. Look at the music industry. They are experiencing an all-time high for unit sales and plays. At the same time, their revenues are

Economic Moat
XAAS 2.0

ECONOMIC MOAT	TRADITIONAL TECH	XAAS 1.0	XAAS 2.0
Virality/Low Cost of Sales	Low	Low	Medium
Diverse Revenue Streams	High	Low	High
Network Effect	Medium	Medium	High
Unique Capabilities	High	Medium	High
Economies of Scale	Medium	Low	Medium
High Switching Costs	High	Medium	High

FIGURE 3.12 Economic Moat — XaaS 2.0

plummeting as disruptive new sharing models make buying music nearly a thing of the past."

Historically, the deep economic moats of traditional technology business models enabled wonderful GAAP profits. Most XaaS business models so far do not share that good fortune. XaaS companies will need to work harder and employ new tactics to create their own deep and wide economic moats. These tactics are designed to reduce the cost of sales, minimize customer churn, and prevent commoditization of the offer. Without these tactics, XaaS providers may want to begin comparing their financial models and profitability profiles to companies operating with shallow economic moats and in hyper-competitive marketplaces like the music industry. In the near term, many future value aggregators and mid-term wedge companies have stock prices that are being rewarded for catching the next wave of market disruption. However, in the long term, if they have shallow economic moats, they will face both razor-thin operating margins and anemic stock multipliers.

XaaS Playbook Play

The XaaS business models are currently proving much less profitable than the previous business models of the traditional technology industry. To determine how to add more margin and profit to a XaaS business, management should run the following play.

Play: Economic Moat Assessment

Objective: Determine what attributes you will leverage to create a more profitable business.

Benefits:

- Identifies attributes that have the potential to unlock higher profits.

- Aligns senior management team on what attributes they will invest in and optimize.

- If no attributes are found, forces leadership team to reset profitability expectations.

Players (who runs this play?): The entire executive management team runs this play: CEO, CFO, sales executive, services executive, and product executive.

4 | Stressing Traditional Organizational Structures

It's human nature to respond to any life disruption with one simple question: "What does it mean to me?" In Chapter 1, we emphasized our belief that the cloud and XaaS will fundamentally transform the business models of most tech companies. So, it's no surprise that human nature kicks in and business leaders want an answer to the question: "What does this mean to my/our organization? Who should own what?"

Fair questions. Organizational structure can reflect an organization's priorities as well as act as its command and control system. We totally understand why companies are keenly interested in having this conversation, but frankly we don't think it's the right starting point for your XaaS discussion. Our general recommendation is that technology companies delay the conversations on specific organizational structure until after they have designed the operating model they are building, how the customer experiences that model, and the capabilities needed to execute it well. They also should get some experience under their belt before they start stressing out the current organization. But, we know from our work with all these companies that they urgently desire to discuss and debate this topic. With this reality in mind, we wrote this chapter. In this chapter, we will cover some thoughts on XaaS organizational structure—but remember, it's still early, and the definitive, profitable XaaS model is not yet known. Areas we'll discuss include:

- Traditional technology supplier organizational structure.
- Drivers for change.
- Capabilities assessment.
- Wave 1 and Wave 2 moves.
- Timing.

We want to give you things to ponder concerning how profitable XaaS organizations might look and behave differently from traditional tech organizations. This is also relevant to many born-in-the-cloud XaaS businesses because most still look exactly like traditional tech companies. We think there may be more changes to come, even for those companies.

Traditional Tech Organizational Structure

We would assert that the common organizational structure in place at most enterprise tech companies today is built on three main intellectual pillars. They are:

- Emphasize the "make, sell, ship" organizations:
  o   R&D and sales, not marketing and service.
- Focus on maximum scalability:
  o   Horizontal go-to-market model, not vertical.
  o   Indirect channels for SMB.
- Establish clear command and control:
  o   Geography-based command and control of the field.
  o   Siloed P&Ls by organization.

We see these pillars at work not only in traditional companies but in most XaaS companies as well. That's because much of the senior leadership at large XaaS companies grew up in traditional tech companies. That's where they learned how a company organizes and operates. Often, they carry that forward into the XaaS businesses they now supervise. However, we're not sure that's going to ultimately deliver the profitable XaaS model we seek.

So, let's quickly review the legacy organizational structures at work in tech, and then discuss why your profitable XaaS offer may be better served with some slightly different approaches.

In *B4B*,[1] we explored the history of the high-tech business model. We traced the roots all the way back to the National Cash Register (NCR) company in the late 19th century, when CEO John Patterson established a formal R&D function as well as a large field sales organization to drive his company's products to market. His approach was mimicked by Thomas Watson when he left NCR to join the fledgling IBM Corporation. Many others then followed the IBM model. At the heart of this early B2B organizational model was a manufacturing mentality: "Make, Sell, Ship." The majority of technology product companies—including software companies—have kept Patterson's spirit alive by maintaining this manufacturing mentality. Product companies have optimized their organizational structures to develop differentiated product capabilities and then rapidly land those products in the marketplace at scale through sales. It worked well for most enterprise tech companies. Their deep economic moats didn't often force them to diversify their strategic investments into other organizations; they funded things like services and marketing almost like they were just COGS.

Not only did "Make, Sell, Ship" influence their organizational structures and strategic investments, but it also drove how strategic decisions got made. In *B4B*, we called it the B2B Decision Totem Pole:

> *In B2B suppliers today, the chief executive officer (CEO) is obviously the final decision maker. But what really happens is a*

strategic thought process conducted by a collective "brain" derived from many people on the executive team. However, those people, even if they are all at the same executive level, do not always have the same influence on the collective brain. The people often have a sort of status rank, almost like a totem pole.

In most large high-tech and near-tech B2B companies today, research and development (R&D) and sales own the two top "heads" of the totem pole. Which one is on top and which one is in second position on any given decision is not what is critical. What matters is that, as it was at NCR and at IBM, these same two influencers most often take the lead when B2B companies make critical decisions. At young B2B companies, R&D or engineering executives usually occupy the top spot. Once B2B companies become large, they come to have a huge investment in the sales force or reseller network that they rely on to provide a "return" in the form of revenue and growth. Together, the two influences work to keep sales channels fed with products to sell and optimized for coverage and quality. These become the driving considerations of the collective brain of most B2B companies. The two levers of growth are assumed to be adding products and adding salespeople.

By contrast, services and marketing are often seen as important but nonstrategic heads on the totem pole. Service quality is important because it maintains customer satisfaction and it can be a profitable adjunct to the core product business—important roles to be sure, but not strategic. Marketing in B2B companies often finds itself limited to making the sales effort easier, ideally by providing high-quality leads for the sales organization to pursue. Although B2B marketing may once have been the home of strategic planning, marketplace decision making, and business model selection, this is rarely the case today. In most B2B companies we see, those roles are ceded to the top two heads on the totem pole. Services and marketing usually occupy the spaces near the ground, not in the rarified, strategic air of sales and R&D. A key part of the sales organization's qualification for sitting in one of the top spots has to do with its esteemed position of speaking for the customer's wallet. If you walk into the headquarters of most medium-size or large B2B companies today and scream, "Who owns the customer?" the answer you are most likely to hear echoing through the halls is, "Sales!" That is one of the strongest legacies of men such as Patterson and Watson. They built pioneering, world-class bridges between their companies and their customers, and in most B2B companies, those bridges were—and still are— owned by the sales organization.

Because the critical success factors were what the product did and how big a sales effort you could mount, sales and R&D were the most heavily funded organizations. Currently, software companies in the T&S 50 invest an average of 28% of revenues on sales and marketing (S&M). The vast majority of those S&M dollars are spent on sales, not marketing expenses. These companies also spend an average of 18% of company revenues on R&D, making it the second best-funded organization (Figure 4.1).

But the complete thought for organizational structure and behavior doesn't stop at the top of the decision totem pole; we still have to deliver our offers successfully with the customer.

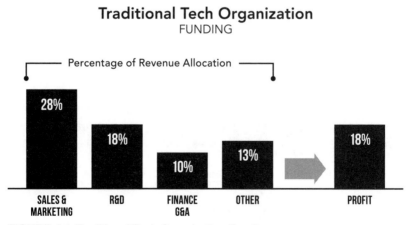

Traditional Tech Organization
FUNDING

FIGURE 4.1 Traditional Tech Organization Funding

That dramatically expands the complexity of global tech organizations. Many functions must be performed in many places around the world. This brings us to a critical point.

In traditional enterprise tech, the only one who had a chance to master the complexity of the technology was the supplier. After all, they built it. They support it every day, all over the world. They have seen thousands of deployments, and they employ far more experts on their products than any one of their customers does. For those and many more reasons, traditional tech companies became *full-service* suppliers, as illustrated in Figure 4.2. Throughout virtually every step in the customer life cycle up until the operate phase, they were in the lead. Today, managed services that help operate the technology are the fastest growing part of the traditional tech industry.

Think about the customer life cycle. For almost every major step in the journey, a separate organization inside the tech company leads it. Somehow, remarkably, the customer is handed from department to department as they make their way from being a new customer to a successful user. We call it the bucket brigade approach. And because many of these stages required activities at the customer's site, many or most of the employees in these organizations were in the field. To ensure local command and control, the field was thus logically organized by region.

Traditional Full-Service Business Model

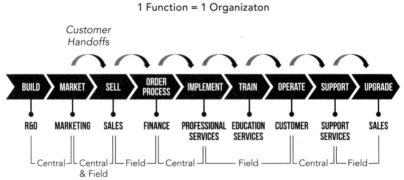

FIGURE 4.2 Traditional Full-Service Business Model

It's a familiar story. At their founding, most traditional tech companies designed a cool new product and defined some great use cases. They would then hire sales executives to land that cool product in specific global regions. How these regional sales leaders sold the product was largely up to them—just as long as they sold lots of it! As the region grew, the sales executive had significant latitude in how they ran the region. Service delivery and field marketing then followed suit, usually reporting to the head of sales in the region. The feeling was that each region had nuances that dictated management at the regional level.

This geocentric heritage means that resources within regions often report hard line up through the region—not hard line into a central or global function. This structure has always made it challenging to land global processes consistently. More importantly, it is challenging for regional executives who are primarily responsible for driving revenue growth to also be adept at driving delivery efficiencies or globally consistent customer experiences. It's just not job #1 for them, and they often lack scale. Over time, some functions have been globalized to create more consistency and efficiency. Global customer support is a classic example. Yet, the pull of geographic autonomy remains a strong influence on the organizational structure of tech companies of all sorts.

To make it easier and less costly to scale these organizations as they grew, they were instructed to take the same product and land it in as many vertical markets as possible with minimal customization in either the product or the surrounding services (Figure 4.3).

That horizontal go-to-market approach massively reduced complexity and cost for all the organizations in a tech company. It could successfully be argued that many infrastructure products, especially hardware, operated pretty much the same from industry to industry. Even most software products could claim they did the same. If the product needed to be customized to meet specific vertical market or customer needs, the customer or partners could

Horizontal Go-to-Market

FIGURE 4.3 Horizontal Go-to-Market Approach

go work on that. It was the right decision. Customers were en-amored of these products. They were willing to accept that the product wasn't a perfect fit, but its core value proposition was still compelling. They and their IT teams would make it work. So, if you were running that tech company and customers weren't demanding vertical solutions, why would you volunteer for the headaches of coming to market differently in each industry?

We would argue that these are the drivers of organizational structure in the world of traditional, full-service tech:

- Sales and development are highest influence organizations.
- Each function has its own organization.
- Field functions are organized geographically.
- Horizontal, not vertical, go-to-market.
- Each organization performs a task for the customer. Many handoffs.
- Budgets weighted heavily toward execution/delivery, less on planning/design.
- Goal: Optimize the function, control the organization's performance.

Each organization was focused heavily on two goals. The first was making their function the best it could be for the customer, usu-ally on a deal-by-deal basis—resulting in lots of heroic acts. Most of the budget for sales and service organizations went toward em-ployees who actually engaged customers, not ones who thought about, designed, and built an experience. The second was to control the human and financial performance of their vast organization. Most of their focus was intraorganizational. The most potent command and control device was the organizational P&L. They made decisions about how best to achieve their organizational goals; then, they memorialized that thinking in their budget. That budget got approved. They implemented it and held managers accountable for their revenue and costs. Importantly, because they were thinking primarily intraorganizationally, their P&L impact and return on investment (ROI) decisions were based on impacts inside their own organization. The majority of organizations inside traditional tech companies operate as siloed P&Ls. It's a great way to get everyone thinking about the bottom line, but it also leads to intraorganizational thinking and behavior. A dollar of cost in my P&L has to result in more than a dollar of revenue *in my* P&L. We'll come back to that thought later in this chapter. It also led to massive redundancies as these "businesses within the business" built capabilities that already existed somewhere else in the company. There is no doubt that this intraorganizational approach had pros and cons.

Before we go any further, we want to be clear on an important and undisputed fact. For traditional tech, this model works amazingly well. With these parameters in play, technology companies have established some of the most profitable business models in the history of business models. This heavy investment in sales and R&D combined with a geocentric bias, an intradepartmental approach, and a "one size fits all" go-to-market mentality has led to organizational structures that support highly profitable, multi-billion-dollar businesses. However, these structures do have four stress points that executive teams still debate to this day:

1. How seamless is the customer experience across all these organizational handoffs?
2. What processes and resources should be optimized regionally versus globally?

3. How do we optimize and account for resource investments that cut across the P&Ls of different departments?

4. As software and IoT eat the world, how do we align resources across sales, services, R&D, and marketing to develop and land vertical solutions?

Drivers for Change

Why rethink organizational structure now? After all, the current models have served the industry extremely well for decades.

The advent of XaaS is forcing almost every technology company to rethink and revise their product strategy. We also think it is going to lead to significantly different thinking about organizational behavior and operating models. Lex Sisney is a specialist and consultant on the topic of organizational structure and has written some great articles on the whens and whys of organizational change. He states that the number one mistake companies make is that they change their strategy but keep basically the same organizational structure:

> *"Every time the strategy changes—including when there's a shift to a new stage of the execution life cycle—you'll need to reevaluate and change the structure. The classic mistake made in restructuring is that the new form of the organization follows the old one to a large degree. That is, a new strategy is created but the old hierarchy remains embedded in the so-called 'new' structure. Instead, you need to make a clean break with the past and design the new structure with a fresh eye."[2]*

Now, we're not advocating for radical organizational restructuring. As you'll see, we don't think the big organizational boxes need to change, at least in the beginning. But the shift to XaaS offers is creating several drivers for organizational change within technology companies:

1. The organizational decision totem pole needs to broaden to capitalize on the opportunities for automation and direct

customer self-service throughout the customer engagement life cycle of XaaS.

2. New organizational capabilities are required to be successful with XaaS offers. They have to be identified and added.

3. You have to fix the old stress points:

   a. Create a totally seamless customer experience across the life cycle.

   b. Guarantee global consistency in the customer journey.

   c. Possess the flexibility to share resources and spread investments across functions and engineer out the redundancies in the operating model.

   d. Successfully develop and land vertical solutions (in many cases).

Let's start our discussion with a new picture of how we think XaaS, particularly SaaS, works or could work.

In Figure 4.4, the rectangles represent "objects" like the customer engagement technology platform. Another example would be the specific XaaS offers you can purchase and enjoy from the cloud. Together, customers might call it "the website" or "the product," but really it's much more. The ovals represent the organizations of the company. They are the people and functions that design, build, and augment the functions of the "objects." They are also the organizations that may interact with customers off the platform. The big arrows represent the customer engagement process.

In this model, marketing still has to go out into the world and locate prospects. They have to hand them off to sales. Sales has to land the deal that puts the customer onto the XaaS customer engagement technology platform. It is the existence of that platform, in our view, that is going to stress out traditional organizational behaviors. Although the friction points of traditional models might have been tolerable, they become much more dangerous if left unattended in XaaS. Lines are going to blur as ser-

XaaS Self-Service Business Model

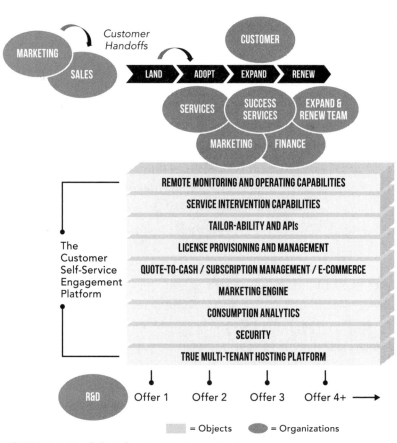

FIGURE 4.4 XaaS Self-Service Business Model

vices, customer success, sales, marketing, and finance become one big integrated motion, all delivered on the customer platform. Intraorganizational behavior and control are insufficient—even dangerous—thoughts here. We must truly increase the capacity of the organizations to think interdepartmentally. We need to think more about how one organization can improve the customer experience or create financial synergies that benefit other organizations. We have to learn to think and act with one brain, not several.

As consumers, we all experience this notion of the customer engagement platform every time we buy software or content on the web. When you go to the website, it's going to market to you, let you purchase, and aid in the delivery of whatever you bought. It will then help on-board and train you, even provide customer support. Once you are using the actual offer, it will market upgrades or other offers to you. When you purchase those expansion offers, it will lead you back through the adoption sequence.

In Chapter 2, we summarized the concept of the LAER operating model—the fact that XaaS offers require engagement activities that take a customer from the initial sale (land) through successful adoption, expansion, and renewal. In Chapter 7, we will double-click into the differences between traditional tech engagement models and XaaS engagement models. For the purpose of organizational structure, though, it is important to internalize that profitable XaaS offers will need a single, unified structure that cost-effectively drives customers across the entire LAER life cycle. To achieve this, we believe marketing and services, in particular, will need to be higher on the organizational totem pole. These two organizations will need to have a strong presence when designing the XaaS offer experience.

So, what are the key organizational thoughts around which a profitable XaaS will organize or operate? Below is a list of XaaS customer platform organizational constructs:

- Current organizations remain the same.
- Add customer success, success science, analytics, and infrastructure organizations.
- All organizations work closely together to build a single customer engagement platform that lowers sales and delivery costs.
- Customer self-serves through as much of the life cycle as possible.
- Budgets weighted more toward planning/design, less on actual customer delivery.
- Far fewer customer handoffs.
- Much more central, less geographic (field) orientation.
- Goal: great, easy customer experience.

As we will conclude later in this chapter, we don't think this needs to trigger a major rethink of organizational boxes on day one. The functions of business are the functions of business. Yes, we will need to add new capabilities and maybe even create a couple of new organizations, but we still have marketing, sales, services, and finance. What is different is how they think, interoperate, and very importantly, how they are measured.

Let's start with what we believe should be the two overarching goals of the combined organizations (beyond product-market fit, of course):

- Great customer life-cycle experience.
- Lowering cost of sales (COS) and overall delivery costs.

We don't need to explain why these are important. We have already pointed out how damaging a high sales cost can be to XaaS profitability. It is easy to imagine how great customer experience will make LAER operate more smoothly and achieve better results. But, let's spend a few minutes talking about how these need to play out as part of your profitable XaaS offer.

Earlier we pointed out the important idea that traditional tech companies offered a full-service experience. This was driven primarily by the complexity and risk associated with their offers. Customers paid us, or our channel partners, a lot of money to master that complexity. In XaaS, we have a completely new ball game. Complexity is your profit enemy, not your friend. You want to make it easy for prospects to learn and buy. Configuring and tailoring the product to their needs should be something that they can do for themselves. In the course of enjoying the offer, they should be able to get help or learn about new things they can do. They can choose to add new features or offers. They can pay their bills. In short, they can SELF-SERVE!

We think this "aha!" is significant as it relates to your organizational behavior. We think it puts some new realities on the table:

- You will have more direct customers—that is going to mightily impact your traditional channel strategies.

- You will have more central resources and fewer field resources—that is going to change budgets and command and control strategies.

- You will concentrate more on planning and design and less on actual delivery—the more you get the planning and design right, the fewer the customers who will require human engagement from you in the field during their delivery and realization of outcomes.

- The lines will blur—services will make sales, finance will design experiences, marketing will appear in the product. They will all be working together on one, interdepartmental customer experience. Ideally, the customer will not perceive any handoffs at all.

The impact of more direct customers is mostly an issue for your channels organization to ponder, and we are going to dedicate Chapter 10 to that. If channels are important to your business, please take a look.

Because your XaaS customer engagement platform can be accessed from anywhere, you may find that customers from around the globe can operate successfully without a lot of local resources. That has an impact on the balance of resources in traditional field-oriented organizations. They may have a greater percentage of their workforce in centralized locations versus in-region. A great example from the consumer world is how Netflix can open up a new country with only a small team of people. Yes, they have to source some local content and comply with local legal and tax regulations, but the countries largely rely on centralized technology and corporate resources as much as possible. To achieve that lean regional model, it takes real planning and investment in the operating platform. We don't see many XaaS companies doing this well. Either they struggle to grow internationally or they throw tons of people at the problem. Then, the geographies begin to grow, but they are wildly unprofitable. Just think of how much money you can save as you globalize your XaaS offer if you build a truly global customer engagement platform!

The point is that, in profitable XaaS, the emphasis shifts from the execution of a full-service model to the design of a self-service model as much as possible. The goal is to spend dollars and resources once on automating a task, not repeating it over and over again in the field. We think this is one reason why AWS is already profitable when some SaaS companies of equal or larger size aren't. Again, the key is to spend centralized cycles on the planning, design, development, and optimization of the function. That will change the capabilities and skills that organizations need. It will probably mean fewer hires that are deeply involved in the bits and bytes of technology and more that are steeped in how the customer uses the technology. The ideal staff member is someone who combines a product marketing mentality with some years in the field. After you find them, you focus them on working centrally and thinking interdepartmentally.

We predict that organizations will become more centralized, integrated, and focused on how the platform operates, and these XaaS teams will unite around a set of cross-company goals. Many departments and resources will work across organizational lines to create a single, killer platform. Often their activities may benefit other organizations more than their own. Maybe spending more R&D labor lowers service costs. Maybe more service costs result in more product sales. Maybe marketing is spending money to promote the adoption of features that lower customer success costs.

As a result, we would like to put a challenge on the table for chief financial officers in the industry: How will you develop budgeting, accounting, and performance measures that allow—even promote—this kind of cross-organizational activity? Departmental P&Ls have been the mainstay of organizational command and control. Managers could do what they wanted as long as their bottom line was at or better than plan. Then, companies added up all the departments and got to the company's overall profit number. Adding costs against their P&L that added revenue to another P&L was usually not encouraged. In fact, many times it was a non-starter. Arguing that was a sign of weakness, and the benefiting department rarely acknowledged the effect. The fact that they did better than plan was because of something they did, not something the other department did. In XaaS, that kind of mentality can kill your profitability. So Ms. and Mr. CFO, how will you cure that behavior? We think it's going to prove to be one of the most important contributions to profitable XaaS that internal finance and HR organizations can make.

So, again, the punch line is this: We don't think the big organizational boxes will need to change right away. Ultimately, some may converge. At some point soon, you will need to add one new box for customer success and one for the platform infrastructure. Up front, though, we think you can stick with the big organizational blocks. We will discuss a few specific adaptations later in the book. However, what does have to change right away is how the organizations work interdepartmentally, the skills they acquire, and whether their focus is central/global or regional. Skills-wise, we think you should be looking into the regions for people with deep customer expertise and the skills to engage in planning and design activities.

New Capabilities Assessment

But what skills? Well, the second factor forcing organizational change is the capabilities gap. As this book will hopefully articulate, selling and delivering XaaS offers is not the same as selling and delivering technology as an asset. Once again, we define organizational capabilities as *"the ability to perform actions that achieve desired results."* We organize the capabilities required by all organizations into the nine categories shown in Figure 4.5.

In each of these categories, there are capabilities that organizations must master in order to scale and optimize a XaaS business. Through interactions with technology companies, we have inventoried more than 380 distinct organizational capabilities.

Organizational Capabilities Categories

CATEGORY	EXAMPLE CAPABILITIES
Strategy and Planning	Annual business planning, aligning product and service strategies, stakeholder engagement and alignment.
Markets	Segmentation model, customer model, market requirements, competitive analysis.
Offers	Specific offer definition, offer development life cycle, offer management, bundling, SLA definitions, licensing and entitlement methods, pricing strategy.
Financial Model	Defining target revenue mix, margin profiles, investment profiles, and profit profiles for offer types.
Go to Market (GTM)	Defining alternate direct/indirect go-to-market models by offer type, including application ecosystems.
Product	Development capabilities, technology capabilities, tools and applications required to deliver offers.
Operations	Automation platform, services delivery resource optimization, support channel optimization, workforce planning.
Sales and Marketing	Direct sales structure, automation platform, sales metrics, sales methodologies, marketing programs.
Partner Management	Partner selection, partner establishment, outsourcing management.

FIGURE 4.5 Organizational Capabilities Categories

Currently, we tag roughly 150 of these capabilities as being tied to the success of XaaS business models, and we're adding more at a brisk rate. Figure 4.6 provides a sampling of some of these emerging capabilities.

You should inventory the specific capabilities needed to be successful with your XaaS offer. You need to identify the ones you already possess somewhere in the company. You need to identify the ones you don't have currently. If you do have them, you need to locate the specific people and teams who do them well. Their capability and skills need to be centralized and amplified. They have to change jobs to emphasize planning and design rather than daily execution. For the ones you don't have, you need to develop a plan to go get them. Maybe you need new technical skills to

XaaS Emerging Capabilities

GO-TO-MARKET

Service Capability

Customer engagement models to drive revenue growth.

Description

We have optimized how we have defined and engaged our roles across the customer engagement model of land, adopt, expand, and renew to accelerate revenue growth cost efficiently.

Business Drivers

Flat top-line revenue growth.

Service Capability

Renewal process for subscriptions.

Description

We have a well-defined process to achieve best-in-class renewal rates.

Business Drivers

Greater percentage of revenue coming from subscription contracts.

OFFERS

Service Capability

Monetizing services around product subscription models.

Description

We have developed profitable pricing models for selling service offerings on top of our product subscription.

Business Drivers

Requirement to make subscription business models more profitable.

Service Capability

Developing outcome offers.

Description

We have the ability to define and develop service offers that are designed to deliver specific customer outcomes.

Business Drivers

Desire to bring both revenue and margin dollars back into the customer contract.

OPERATIONS

Service Capability

User adoption KPIs.

Description

We have identified the key KPIs for assessing if customers have successfully adopted a technology.

Business Drivers

Need to understand if customers are successfully adopting technology. Prerequisite to account growth in subscription business models.

PRODUCT

Service Capability

Data handshake to enable new offers.

Description

We have identified the key data streams required to enable new adoption and outcome-based offers.

Business Drivers

Service organizations must successfully engage product engineering to prioritize features that accelerate adoption and create new revenue opportunities.

SALES AND MARKETING

Service Capability

Customer lifetime value.

Description

We have the ability to calculate the lifetime value of customers to our company.

Business Drivers

Requirement to understand which customers have the greatest financial potential in subscription relationships. Avoid investing finite resources in low-return accounts.

STRATEGY AND PLANNING

Service Capability

Establishing and/or leveraging a customer success organization.

Description

We use a customer success organization to drive customer engagement, adoption, and/or subscription renewal.

Business Drivers

Requirement to successfully drive customers from low to high to efficient adoption of technology capabilities.

FIGURE 4.6 XaaS Emerging Capabilities

build the customer engagement platform. Maybe you need to hire some customers who can close any knowledge gaps you have about how customers translate your offer into business outcomes. You might need a leader for your customer success organization. It doesn't matter. What matters is that you do a capabilities assessment. Start prioritizing and filling your gaps. Don't worry so much about where they report to for now. Just make sure they have the freedom to work together—interdepartmentally—to make sure you improve your product-market fit and build your customer engagement platform.

Still Wanting Some Immediate Actions?

So, the forcing functions are starting to bang on your door. Your company wants to rethink the organization, and they want to have that conversation NOW! You really want specific answers to the two most common questions we hear today about how future XaaS organizational structures might be different:

- Are there any massive organizational changes we should do right away?
- Who owns the new pieces/functions?

Some caveat emptors before we attempt to answer: We are not organizational theorists. Historically, our insights have been driven by the benchmarking we conduct. We can usually test for proven best practices and relate those to the industry. However, it is still early days on the topic of best-practice organizational structures for XaaS companies. All we can do at this point in time is try to put together pieces of the puzzle from what we see at the companies we work with and marry that to our perspective on how the industry will ultimately transform. Even the largest and most successful XaaS companies are continuing to experiment. Seventeen-year-old Salesforce is constantly reorganizing even today. The point is: The winning organizational structure for XaaS is a moving target. Yet, we do believe there is a model that can provide an interesting baseline for the conversation.

In short, our best answers to these questions are as follows:

No, the big boxes of sales, marketing, services, and finance do not need to be changed immediately. If you look at the executive team pages of most leading enterprise SaaS companies, the titles of the executives look just like a traditional software company. As we said, we think that partially stems from the previous experience sets of senior leadership. They are comfortable with traditional models. We also think that the major functions are the major functions. So, if the big boxes in the traditional organizational structures simply didn't work in XaaS, we would all already know that. However, as we will soon cover, there are several changes below the big boxes that will need to be considered.

The answer to the question about who owns the new pieces is covered throughout the book. Ultimately, there may be two big boxes added at the top. Many companies are creating chief customer officer (CCO) or chief revenue officer (CRO) and senior vice president of infrastructure roles.

In Chapter 7, we talk about the new functions of customer success, success science, and consumption analytics. There is a lot of context-setting to our recommendations, so please read that chapter carefully. Many XaaS companies have some of these functions reporting to the new CCO role, reporting directly to the CEO. You will see that in our "org chart of the future" diagram.

Who will own the new customer engagement platform infrastructure? Ultimately, you will want a senior vice president of infrastructure who is a peer to the top execs of all the other functions. You will see him/her on our chart, too. In the interim, we have seen R&D owns it, IT owns it, the CTO owns it, and the COO owns it. There are just so many layers, and they are a combination of in-house and third-party applications. Some companies put many of the operating characteristics inside individual products initially. However, as the portfolio grows, it makes sense to invest in a single, integrated, and branded operating platform infrastructure. It is that platform that becomes most of the customer experience. It doesn't make sense for one company to offer different shopping or payment experiences, or to offer the same service in different ways for similar products. What matters is not who ends up initially owning the platform. What matters is that the owner truly understands how incredibly important that platform is—both to the customer experience and to the cost structure of the business. It's one of the most important tools you have to ease the burden of customer success and lower the cost of sales. Put it where it gets the most attention and investment in the beginning, and make sure it's somewhere that considers all the heads on the totem pole to be equally important.

Wave 1 Moves

Altering organizational structure is painful—especially when departments and P&Ls are owned by executives that historically have been very successful. But, the times they are a changin'. We thoroughly believe that XaaS offers will demand organizational behaviors that are different from the ones tech companies have been perfecting since Patterson paved the way. If we had to pick, we would recommend the following six organizational changes early in the journey.

1. **Consolidate portfolio management.** Right now we see product managers and service marketing managers spread throughout different P&Ls within tech companies. Each of these people is working to maximize the revenue for their specific offers. Many of these offers are beginning to overlap. Where does premium support end and a managed service offer begin? Where does a managed service offer end and a new SaaS offer begin? These are just some of the grey areas that are quickly emerging. Bring all of these offer management resources together into one team. Ideally, they are part

of your revitalized marketing organization, but this group can also live separately and report directly to the CEO initially as they take ownership of rationalizing all company offers.

2. **Identify the key members of your platform infrastructure team.** This is truly a cross-functional team that focuses on customer experience design and the technical execution of the platform. You will need active interfaces with marketing, finance, services, R&D, sales, and channels. You can actually bring representatives from each of those functions onto a centralized team or you can just point them out, leave them where they are, and simply assign them as the liaison to the platform infrastructure team. In any case, you need to start thinking about who those people will be and who will lead the technology development strategy for the platform. In Wave 2, this becomes a department of the company.

3. **Establish a customer analytics team.** As covered in Chapter 3, data and analytics are a critical enabler to digging a deeper economic moat around XaaS offers. The sooner you start investing in this capability, the better. Also, this should be a shared resource being leveraged by both product and service groups within the company. Once again, ideally this capability is part of marketing or customer success, but that is not critical in the beginning. What is critical is to start building the capability.

4. **Establish a customer success team.** Someone in the company must take responsibility for driving customer adoption. The most common move we see in technology companies that are migrating to XaaS is to establish a new "customer success" team. We have seen this work well, but we have also seen it not have much effect, mainly due to poor implementation and half-baked commitments. If you can't get that strong commitment, an alternative may be to establish a customer success initiative and clearly identify what existing organization will now have the charter for customer adoption.

5. **Begin planning to migrate renewals away from sales resources you want focused on "land."** This is the first step in restructuring the sales motion to be optimized for the entire LAER life cycle. Some sales resources need to be laser focused on acquiring new customers or selling new offer types. By relieving them of renewal responsibilities, you free up selling cycles. Also, the renewal responsibility can be migrated to more cost-effective resources that are running a process, not a sales event. Now, we know this move may appear very risky. We recommend you work your way from the bottom up. Start by migrating your smaller accounts to this new model first. When you have proven the process, migrate larger accounts to this model. In Chapter 7, we will provide some specific tips on how to do this.

6. **Collapse the service delivery P&Ls.** As a first move toward creating a global service delivery capability that can seamlessly apply any type of service expertise to any offer, we recommend all of the current service P&Ls be pulled together under one executive. The objective of that executive will be to maximize and integrate delivery efficiencies across all service resources— to globalize and automate as much of the process as possible. The portfolio management team sets the revenue targets across offers. The sales and customer success teams are given quota to sell those offers. The consolidated services delivery team is responsible for having the capacity to deliver those offers. That is how the combined services P&L is achieved.

7. **Add a chief customer officer (CCO) or chief revenue officer role (CRO).** The purpose of these two roles is to look at end-to-end processes. The CCO is looking at the customer experience, and the CRO is looking at revenue generation processes. Both are trying to optimize a life cycle, one from the customer perspective and the other from an internal perspective. Both are working across functions. They have high influence but small staffs.

Some of these first moves are easier to make than others. However, we are already seeing evidence of large technology companies making some of these required changes. In 2015, SAP made the following announcement at their annual Sapphire user's conference:

> *"The different units of the services organization (support, education, consulting, custom development and cloud delivery), which have so far operated relatively independently from each other are going to merge their forces under a new "One Services" organization."*[3]

EMC has made moves to bring portfolio management resources from across multiple service lines into one team that focuses on rationalizing the entire services portfolio. Another large software company we are working with is in the process of moving subscription renewal responsibilities from sales account executives to service account teams.

Still not enough? Here is a pick list of guiding principles and specific actions we would encourage you to consider as you think forward. Pick the ones that resonate with you for immediate action.

- **Redundant functions focused on efficiency should centralize and standardize whenever possible.** Our friend Geoffrey Moore recently published a great book titled *Zone to Win*.[4] In that book, he discusses the six levers companies can drive to wring out efficiencies. Centralizing functions and driving common standards across regions are two key levers that Geoff and we advocate. This is a particularly good thought for services and customer success.

- **Maximize the ability to share resources across organizational lines.** Instead of running into the departmental P&L wall, the organizational and P&L structures should facilitate the ability to assign diverse resource types in various scenarios. This could include delivering a new managed service, building more service enablement into the products, or working cross-functionally with a high-potential account that is lagging with adoption.

- **Separate long-term focus from short-term focus whenever possible.** This is another Sisney observation where we agree. This is why sales (short-term focus) and marketing (longer-term focus) should not be combined into one organization. The same exists with offer development and offer delivery.

- **Leverage proven best adoption practices across regions.** Driving customers through the entire LAER life cycle will be a process that will be highly leveraged by both data and proven customer success science. We predict that asking individual regions to solve this adoption Rubric's Cube in their own way will prove suboptimal. Leveraging proven best practices across regions will be a necessary approach to accelerating customer success. It also provides the benefits of creating a consistent customer experience for global customers.

- **Expand sell in a cost-effective manner.** Historically, the main sales organization has owned all selling activities, from the initial landing of the customer, to any expansion large or small, and for any renewal activities. Not only do we recommend a separation of land and renewal responsibilities, but we also believe the new organizational structure should be optimized to drive the lowest costs possible related to renewing and expanding existing customers. We cover this in detail in Chapter 7.

- **Educate prospects and customers through marketing in a cost-effective manner.** As we mentioned earlier, the majority of sales and marketing dollars are spent on sales expenses. Marketing needs to be elevated on the totem pole and given both the funding and responsibility to create a pipeline of well-educated prospects for the land sales channel to work against. Also, marketing should have the responsibility for educating existing customers on new capabilities they should consider purchasing.

- **Support vertical solutions via outcome engineering and success science.** The organizational structure may need—depending on your product—to facilitate the development and selling of solutions that are designed to meet specific business challenges within specific vertical industries. To help customers achieve targeted business outcomes, technology providers need to better understand specific customer environments. This culminates in a requirement to create technology solutions that map to specific vertical industry requirements and the path customers will take to get to their outcomes. Pulling together marketing, product engineering, and service thinking into an outcome engineering function inside a success science organization to define and land vertical solutions moves beyond a "nice to have" capability. Back in 2014, John McGee, the chief marketing officer at GE Software, spoke at one of our conferences.[5] Backstage, after his presentation, we talked about the changing technology industry. John made a prescient comment to us: "At GE we realized that *all* technology needs to go to market vertically." Wow, what a statement from a company that has been selling technology since 1892!

We know this is not a short wish list. Companies will not be willing to apply all of these guiding principles right out of the gate. Hopefully, you can pick a few off this list to add to your current initiatives. At a minimum, keep these goals in mind as you design how your XaaS organization will operate.

Wave 2 Moves

Once the dust on Wave 1 restructuring begins to settle, you might end up with a few further enhancements and elaborations on the big blocks of your organization structure. It may look like this after a few years in the XaaS business.

- **Land sales segmented by vertical industry (if applicable).** There is a sales organization or sales overlay specifically focused on landing new customers by vertical industry, not region.

- **Customer success segmented by account size.** There is a customer success organization that applies coverage models based on account size. Larger, more strategic customers receive one-to-one coverage models. Customer success ultimately owns adoption, cost-effective renewal, and small-scale account expansion.

- **Big M marketing.** There is a marketing organization that owns three critical activities for the company: (1) lead generation for sales, (2) portfolio management for all the company offers, and (3) customer analytics that inform offer development and offer success. Success science may live here.

- **Global customer growth team.** This organization owns successfully delivering company offers at the best margin possible, having two parallel but highly integrated functions: customer success and service delivery. This organization is responsible for all the various service skills sets—from support technicians to technical educators to on-site project managers to adoption experts.

- **Big-picture product development.** This organization is responsible for developing products scoped by marketing in the most cost-efficient way possible. They don't stop at features. They build in the data streams, analytics, intervention capabilities, operating model requirements, customer outcome metrics—everything needed to make customers successful and minimize LAER costs.

- **Customer engagement platform infrastructure leader.** The leader of this team owns the platform and works with every department of the company to ensure that customer handoffs are minimized and the experience is great. This is an organization that has technical chops, embraces best-of-breed solutions (no "not invented here," please), and has incredible empathy for the customer.

Putting this all together, a target organization structure would look like Figure 4.7.

Here, you have added an executive who owns customer success, renewals, and expansions, as well as service delivery, and a senior vice president of infrastructure who owns the customer engagement technology platform.

We can also think about the funding for this organizational structure. Not only have the charters been altered for functions such as marketing, but how revenue is reinvested into these various organizations changes as well. Instead of the vast majority of revenue being spent on sales and product development, revenue is reinvested more evenly across these functions (Figure 4.8).

However, these are longer-term changes. We think you can start your XaaS journey without making all these huge moves.

Target Organization Structure

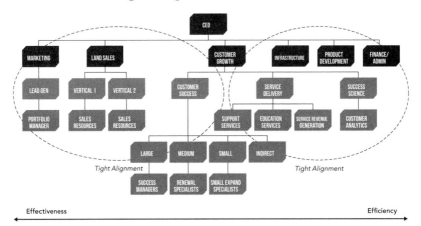

FIGURE 4.7 Target Organization Structure

Customer Engagement Organization

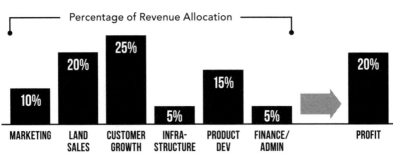

FIGURE 4.8 Funding Customer Engagement

But, you do need to begin taking many of the specific actions we have outlined in this chapter. On what timeline?

Timing

We will talk a lot about timing in the next chapter, but a few major factors can help box in the time you plan to take for building out your profitable XaaS organization—as well as when you make public announcements, as discussed in Chapter 5.

The first and easiest to understand is the search for talent. The people you need to empower the capabilities you want are in much demand. In this regard, traditional companies may have some advantages in that they can shop within their own ranks and within their vast external networks.

However, we think the speed advantages of traditional companies end there. That's because two other very important considerations can delay the speed with which traditional companies can address organizational challenges. Both challenges involve dealing with expectations—the expectations of your current employees and your current customers.

Traditional tech companies who are pivoting to XaaS have to "swallow the fish." They have to keep the traditional revenue and profit streams flowing while they stand up the new ones. They can't afford to send the entire company into organizational shock. They need to keep the plane in the air. Disruptive new companies don't have that problem. They are building organizations from scratch. They can build them to operate in the new model, not the traditional one. We think traditional companies must excel at communicating two central principles to employees as they make changes. The first is this is not about the new business versus the old business. Both the traditional offers and the XaaS offers are important. Customers need and want them both. Their job in the traditional business is still both financially and strategically important. After all, it is massively larger than the fledgling XaaS offers you are standing up. So, be big and proud about your role! The second point is that all these innovations will eventually reach scale, and they will get to play with the shiny new objects soon enough. Major innovations driven by XaaS will invade every offer. They will change every part of the company, not just the XaaS offers. Be patient and be a great operator. The new toys will be available soon.

The other internal struggle is going to be around existing organizational inertia and power bases—the human nature part. New companies don't have those legacies. It is up to the leadership of traditional companies to battle these evils. They need to rally everyone around the customer-led transformation of the industry and bring the shareholders along. They need to excite everyone about the possibilities.

But, we think that the really interesting drag on the timing of organizational changes at traditional tech companies is expectations of your existing customers. If they are used to you as a full-service supplier, how long will it be before they are willing to self-serve their way through much of the journey? If they are used to demanding that their global account manager appear on site rather than e-mailing their customer success manager every time they have a question, how long will those expectations be a drag on your new plays? You not only have to bring employees along on your XaaS journey, but you also have to bring along your existing customers.

It's a problem with a flip side to it. Some of your customers will *want* the new model. They will be disappointed that you are not moving faster. For those customers, you will need a road map. To have a road map, you need to make commitments. To offer commitments, some important decisions regarding swallowing the fish will need to get made. We discuss this further in Chapter 5.

However, those two customer expectations can help box in your timing decisions. The time when your big customers place ultimatums on your new capabilities sets the end date for your transformation. The time it takes for you to condition your early XaaS target market customers to consider you in a new light sets the earliest time that your go-to-market changes can take root.

You can start them earlier, but you can't scale them until your customers are ready for the new you.

So, in terms of the timing for moving to the new business organizational models, we think new companies get there first. But, here's the one thing to remember for traditional companies ready to make the pivot. For many of your largest, global customers, it's not about first to market; it's about first to *scale* and *breadth of portfolio*. That is where you have the advantage over disruptive new entrants. To do that, though, you need to get the existing organizations and customers through the knothole. You need to outline your organization's plans and incubate them so they are proven and debugged. In short, we think most traditional tech companies aren't moving fast enough. They need to get going on changes. Expectations need time to adjust.

A Suggestion: Disrupt from Below

AWS didn't start with a big sales force or a global service organization. They built a customer platform, started at the low end of the market, got it to work well, and then took it up-market. Their self-service model largely negates the need for sales and service motions at most of their customers. AWS focuses on trying to engineer the entire customer life-cycle experience into their platform. That was OK for SMBs. And today, AWS has low operating costs as a result. That is why they are so profitable and can still offer the lowest prices.

But the point is, they started at the low end of the market. In their case, it was start-ups that didn't want to build their own data centers. AWS figured out how to meet that need; then, they moved up-market. In 2016, more and more mission-critical, large enterprise applications are moving to AWS. We think that is a great approach to your XaaS transformation.

However, there is another big difference in the AWS lesson: They went to enormous lengths to engineer out complexity. In fact, that is their business. They cure traditional customer headaches by making complex computing tasks far simpler and cheaper to set up and operate. If you are a traditional enterprise application provider pivoting to XaaS, you didn't build your products with that thought at the forefront. You focused on winning the feature war and were willing to put many people in the field or require your customers to staff up to handle the complexity that you didn't engineer out.

Let's bring back this picture, seen in Figure 4.9.

If you remember, the rectangles are objects and the ovals are organizations, most of which interact with the customer. Those ovals could be staffed by your employees or those of your channel

XaaS Self-Service Business Model

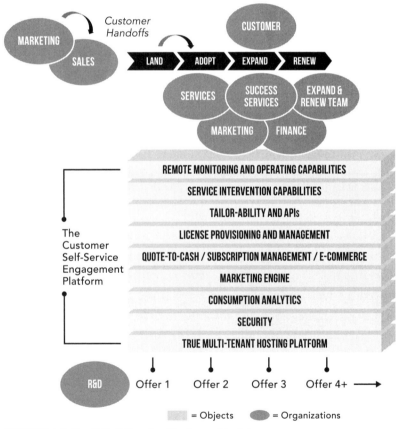

FIGURE 4.9 XaaS Self-Service Business Model

partners. In either case, here's the point: AWS has big rectangles and small ovals. The customer can get most of the things they need done on the engagement platform all by themselves. Most enterprise applications—even SaaS ones—have big ovals and relatively small rectangles. For example, they still require large professional services implementation projects to make the product work.

We are not going to debate whether enterprise applications can master complexity or remain a slave to it. Infrastructure companies argued the same thing. Now multiple IaaS companies are proving there is another way. Even SAP is on record saying that once they made it a priority, they were able to engineer out 70% of the services spending that was required of a customer to implement their products. It can be done; it just takes a commitment to mastering complexity. If you start as an SMB where the complexity is less, you stand a chance of building a platform that can host the entire customer experience for customers large and small. Get your XaaS organization to focus there first. Master the complexities they encounter. Then you can move upstream.

We are sure you've noticed that our answer to new organizational structure was not to throw a dozen guys into a nondescript warehouse, tell them to work together as a team, and not let them out until they have a $100 million XaaS business. That works great if you have the time. Apple does this pretty successfully, but it doesn't change anything we are saying. At some point, you have to scale that offer. You need the big company to on-board the offer that your incubator built. It's the same when a traditional company buys a XaaS provider. While your new offer is in the oven, how do you prepare the restaurant to offer and deliver it at scale? That's what we are addressing. If you have that luxury to incubate, if you haven't been sidelined too long and your large customers are still patient with you, then this is the way to go. But if not, or if you have done some acquisitions and the mother ship isn't doing much good with them, you may have no choice but to rattle the organization and move quickly.

In the end, tech is maturing. We don't think we will ever again see the high price points for technologies that were present when IBM, Oracle, and Cisco were built. In *B4B,*[6] we covered the four levels of supplier business models. Level 4 was for suppliers/providers who were willing to price as true services based on usage or outcomes. We described it as the most exciting and most dangerous of all the models, but led by Amazon, it is where much of tech is heading. As we leave this chapter on organizational impacts and before you attempt to make similar claims in the marketplace, we would ask you to keep the picture seen in Figure 4.10 in mind.

XaaS Self-Service Business Model

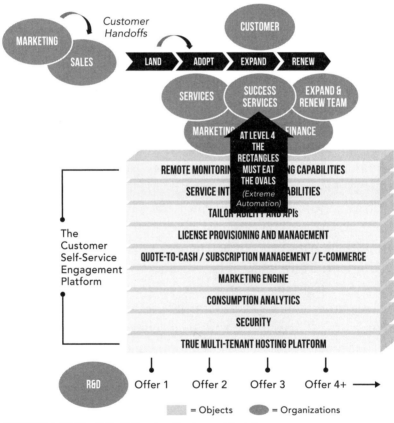

FIGURE 4.10 XaaS Self-Service Business Model

Playbook Summary

In this chapter, we put many concepts on the table regarding how the organizational structures of technology companies will change. However, in terms of working through how your XaaS strategy will impact organizational structure, we still believe the first play to run is assessing your capabilities gap.

Play: Capabilities Inventory

Objective: Determine what organizational capabilities will be required for your XaaS business to succeed. Understand which of those required capabilities already exists in the company. Determine who will be responsible for building up the missing capabilities.

Benefits:

- Helps you assess the capabilities gap. Organizational structure will not win markets—organizational capabilities will.
- Assigns ownership for specific missing capabilities.
- Starts the process of pivoting company capabilities toward supporting XaaS offers.

Players (who runs this play?): Executive leaders of all the main functions of the company, facilitated by a resource that can identify the inventory of organizational capabilities that will be required for the XaaS offer(s) of the company.

Play: Capabilities Gap Test

Objective: Determine what aspects of the current organizational structure will be most problematic in supporting your XaaS offer(s).

Benefits:

- Aligns executive leadership on the "why" of organizational changes.

- Has a set of design objectives that guide the structure conversation.

- Prioritizes organizational changes based on impact.

Players (who runs this play?): Executive leaders of all the main functions of the company, facilitated by a resource that can identify the inventory of organizational capabilities that will be required for the XaaS offer(s) of the company.

5 | Swallowing the Fish

For the past decade, incumbent market leaders in the technology industry have been grappling with two mega-trends:

1. **Commoditization.** Customers are less willing to pay a premium price for slightly differentiated technical capabilities. They are much more interested in value realization from technology solutions. Having lower-priced products makes that easier. This trend is putting downward pricing pressure on both hardware and software offerings.

2. **Acceleration of New Consumption Models.** Customers continue to explore new models for purchasing technology capabilities. Technology-as-a-service and managed service offerings continue to see double-digit revenue growth, while traditional hardware and software license revenues contract or remain flat.

During those 10 years, we have been analyzing public data to assess how incumbents are navigating the impact of these two trends. We track product revenues, product margins, service revenues, service margins, and overall operating income to place companies in one of four states:

- **State #1:** Traditional offerings are not yet under pressure from commoditization or new consumption models.
  - o Product revenues are still growing (10%+).
  - o Product margins are healthy.
  - o Operating income is stable.
- **State #2:** Traditional offerings have commoditized, and new, profitable offers that adhere to the new consumption models have not been put in play.
  - o Product revenues and/or margins are decreasing.
  - o Operating income is declining.
- **State #3:** New XaaS offers have been put in play, but they are not yet profitable.
  - o Service (and subscription) revenues are growing (10%+).
  - o Operating income is declining.
- **State #4:** New XaaS offers are in play and they are now profitable.
  - o Service (and subscription) revenues are growing.
  - o Operating income is stable or improving.

These four states are mapped in Figure 5.1.

Every quarter we map the financial performance of product companies in the T&S 50 index unto the 2x2 graphic seen in Figure 5.2. For the past year, they have mapped very closely to this distribution model.[1]

This tells us that a majority of incumbent technology companies are seeing their business models impacted by these industry transitions. Traditional product revenue growth has slowed or reversed. These companies have not yet navigated their business models through the transition and stood up enough new, high-growth offers. And as we will discuss later in this chapter, there is a second problem emerging where four out of five companies who do have high-growth XaaS offers suffer from a lack of stable profits.

Potential State of Tech Companies

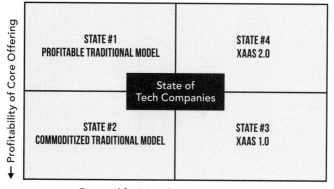

FIGURE 5.1: Potential State of Tech Companies

T&S 50 Financial Performance for 2015

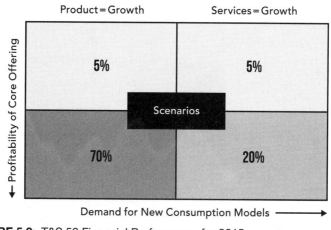

FIGURE 5.2: T&S 50 Financial Performance for 2015

The two megatrends of commoditization and new consumption models did not come out of nowhere in the past year. These forces have been actively in play and building momentum for a decade now. So why do so many incumbents seem to be caught flatfooted? We think it has a lot to do with "the fish."

In $B4B^2$ we introduced "the fish model," seen in Figure 5.3. The fish is what happens when a traditional company starts to shift its revenue mix from an asset purchase model to a subscription model. In this scenario, the company experiences a string of quarters where top-line revenues shrink as revenues from large, pay-up-front deals are replaced by recurring subscriptions without the big up-front payment. At the same time as revenues dip, the company must make investments in many of the new capabilities and structures that are required for profitable XaaS. The traditionally profitable and stable mix of more revenue than costs on the left side of the chart is replaced with a tumultuous period of costs exceeding revenue. Why would a company even consider swallowing the fish? It's because of the promise of the right side of the chart. Here, companies have built up enough recurring revenue to more than cover costs. Top-line growth has returned to the business. Not only that, but the positive effects of many of the new automated capabilities kick in, and overall sales and delivery costs actually begin to decrease.

No one likes the shape of the fish. It creates the classic innovator's dilemma challenge that has often been discussed in business

The Fish Model

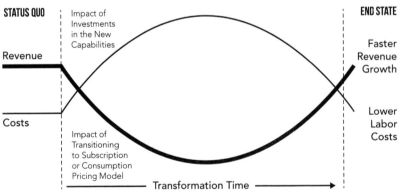

FIGURE 5.3: The Fish Model

literature. Profitable, incumbent players seem to stand still as new entrants disrupt a marketplace. They are reticent to disrupt their profitable economic engine—even as customers start to leave and revenues start to shrink.

Another challenge is that many executives believe they can reengineer the economic engine of the company without having to swallow this fish. For example, we presented this fish challenge to a CFO of a large public technology company. They were starting to experiment with XaaS offers. The response of the CFO was clear: "There is no fish in our transition." One year later, with the stock price going nowhere, that company was taken over by private investors, taken off the public market, and the entire executive team was replaced. Guess what? There was a fish.

More realistic executive teams know there is a fish to swallow when reengineering the economic engine of a company. But just because they know the fish is lying on the table staring them in the face, it doesn't mean they are ready to act on it. They are smart, capable executives who are able to lead the company through any transition. What is holding them back? Every executive team is terrified how boards and investors will react. "What will happen to our stock price if we tell investors that revenues will go down for several quarters? What happens when we stop generating this double-digit operating income? Will we be vulnerable to a takeover? Do we really need to swallow that fish right now?" As executive teams struggle with what to do with the fish, we hear these questions again and again:

1. How do we know when to start swallowing the fish?
2. How long should we take to swallow our fish?
3. How do we manage investor expectations?
4. How do we manage through the transition?
5. What companies have actually swallowed their fish successfully?

These are all legitimate questions. And we see public technology companies approaching this fish challenge in very different ways. In this chapter, we will cover the following ground:

- Three distinct approaches to swallowing the fish.
- Assessing each approach.
- Recommended approach for swallowing the fish.

Our objective with this content is to leverage industry lessons learned to provide guidance on at least one way traditional technology companies can navigate a dramatic change in their business model. At the end of the chapter, we are going to discuss a second fish that has emerged in the technology industry—one that is facing high-growth, born-in-the-cloud XaaS companies that are now trying to transition to slower growth with improving profitability.

Three Approaches to Swallowing the Transformation Fish

Our three XaaS profiles are very informative regarding how companies are currently approaching this industry transition. As XaaS offers have crept into market after market, we see the response of incumbent market leaders fitting into one of the three profiles.

Future Period Impact (FPI) Response

In this approach, the incumbent market leader seems to take the position that the impact of XaaS in their market is on the distant horizon. It can be dealt with in some future period. That assumption may be accurate or inaccurate—the important observation is that the company is behaving as if this assumption is accurate. As you will notice, Figure 5.4 reflects the same exact cost and revenue profile as the FVA we covered in Chapter 2. That's because the financial performance of an FPI is exactly the same. They don't know, or frankly care, how fast they monetize XaaS. They are prepared to make some investments now in case a few customers have

Profit Horizon

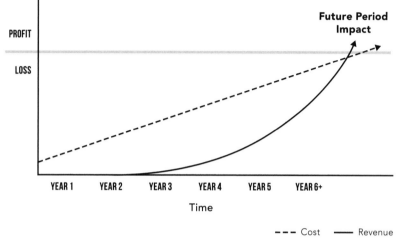

FIGURE 5.4: Profit Horizon: Future Period Impact

the XaaS "bug." But really they are doing the minimum, with no short-term expectations of meaningful XaaS revenue.

These companies will most likely have some type of XaaS offer in play—mostly as a defensive move against competitive XaaS offers. But even though these companies have their toe in the XaaS waters, they exhibit the following attributes:

- They are just beginning to mention cloud or XaaS.
- They may or may not have an actual XaaS offer in the market.
- There is little to no transparency on the financial performance of their XaaS offer.
- No specific growth targets for XaaS are communicated to investors.
- Customers still have the option to purchase the traditional products as assets (and, in fact, that is still the preferred way the company would like the customer to consume).
- The current economic engine of the company looks pretty much like it did 5 years ago.

As of the writing of this book, there are still many, many incumbent technology companies that fit this profile. In fact, this may be the most common profile for incumbents.

Mid-Term Wedge (MTW) Response

In this approach (seen in Figure 5.5), the incumbent market leader seems to have internalized that XaaS will be having a significant impact on their markets. Companies in the MTW are behaving as if they need to have successful XaaS offers in the next 3 to 5 years.

The response of companies in this profile is more aggressive because they are clearly on a journey to transition their business model. They actually want to build recurring revenue streams. Companies in this profile have more than their toe in the XaaS waters, and they exhibit the following attributes:

- Lots of public noise is made by these companies about the cloud and XaaS.

- They have one or more real XaaS offers in the market.

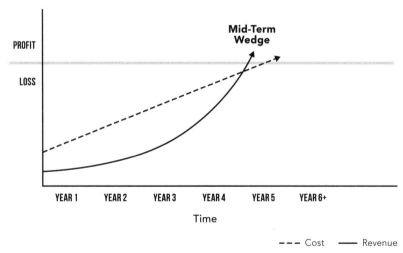

FIGURE 5.5: Profit Horizon: Mid-Term Wedge

- They may have acquired one or more XaaS companies.

- They are just beginning to provide investors with visibility to the revenue performance of XaaS offers, often because XaaS revenues are one of the few bright spots in the financial results. Press releases on quarterly financial results will often lead with the high growth being experienced with these new XaaS offers.

- However, it is still unlikely for these companies to provide complete financial transparency for the emerging XaaS business. *The Wall Street Journal* published an article titled "In Tech Services, 'Cloud' Can Be a Nebulous Term," which highlights how many tech companies are obscuring their true XaaS business performance in their financial reporting.[3]

- No specific growth targets for XaaS are communicated to investors. The company is not committing to when they believe a majority of revenue will be coming from XaaS.

- Customers still have the option to purchase the traditional products as assets.

- The current economic engine of the company has shifted slightly. Anywhere from 5% to 15% of total company revenue may now be coming from XaaS-related offers.

This is perhaps the second most common profile we see in the industry today. Many enterprise software companies fit this description. On the hardware side, companies may have aggressively built either cloud or managed service offers related to how customers can purchase some of its capabilities.

Current Profit Maximizers (CPM) Response

This is the most aggressive response. Here, the incumbent believes they need to transition their economic engine as quickly as possible. They are behaving like a CPM (Figure 5.6).

Companies in this profile have the following attributes:

- They have made a public commitment to subscription-based XaaS offers as their preferred or only purchase model.

Profit Horizon

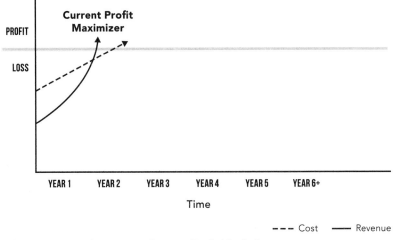

FIGURE 5.6: Profit Horizon: Current Profit Maximizer

- They provide investors with visibility to both the revenue and profit side of their XaaS business.
- Press releases on quarterly financial results will always lead with the financial status of the XaaS business.
- Specific growth targets for XaaS are communicated to investors. The company is also communicating profitability expectations.
- Customers may no longer have the option to purchase the traditional products as assets.
- The current economic engine of the company is aggressively shifting to XaaS. At the end of 3 years, a majority of revenue is coming from XaaS.

To date, this has been a very rare profile in the industry. However, three software companies quickly come to mind: Adobe, Autodesk, and Intuit.

Assessing Approaches

There are three distinct approaches for migrating a traditional, highly profitable technology business model to a new, still emerging XaaS business model. What is the best approach? For a public company, what are the metrics that define success? We would submit four that are hard to ignore:

1. Share price.
2. Market value of the company.
3. Revenue growth rate.
4. Operating income.

At the end of the day, every public company would like to make the following statement: "Our revenues are growing, our profits are healthy, our share price is up, and the market value of our company has increased." Yep, that's the opening paragraph every CEO wants to write for their annual report.

So what are the results companies are achieving with these three approaches related to these four success metrics? Well, before we analyze some of the data, we have to provide one piece of important context related to share price and market value. For "growth" stocks, these two metrics are typically driven by future opportunity. If investors *believe* a company has line of sight to a great market opportunity *and* the company has the ability to capture that market, then they invest. Stock price and market value go up.

This is important as it relates to XaaS in the technology industry. Many investors clearly believe XaaS will be the dominant consumption model in many technology market segments—even though XaaS is not the common model today in any segment. These growth investors that are bullish on XaaS have a view that is captured in Figure 5.7. XaaS is the next big wave. Companies that catch the wave have lots of opportunity for growth. Companies that miss the wave have diminishing opportunity for growth.

Assessing Approaches

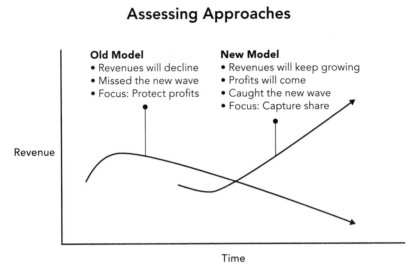

FIGURE 5.7: Assessing Approaches

If investors think the market is shifting to XaaS (the new model), the question becomes simple: Do investors believe a particular company is on the new curve? If the answer is yes, stock price keeps growing and the market valuation of the company can be outrageous. If the answer is no, the stock price languishes. "Value" investors looking for steady dividends move in. Market valuation may shrink.

With this context in hand, let us examine how these three approaches to managing the market transition are playing out for incumbent technology companies.

FPI Approach

Here are some real, current scenarios:

An enterprise software company lists the word "cloud" 36 times in their annual report. Yet, they mix any SaaS revenues they have with their historical subscription/maintenance revenues, effectively providing no visibility on how SaaS revenues are faring. Total subscription revenues are shrinking, indicating that their traditional subscription/maintenance business is on a faster decline than their new XaaS offers have been able to counter thus far. Here is the fish at work, even without the need to flip from license to subscription.

One network device company is signaling investors that XaaS is clearly impacting their markets. Yet, the company does not have any direct XaaS offers in play. They are limiting their cloud offers to providing technology to the companies that are building cloud solutions and only selling it as an asset purchase.

A big data storage and analytics company has "cloud" all over their website. In their annual report they state they can now offer their products as cloud services to customers. But they do not break out any specific financial information on this offer in their financial reporting, nor are they making any public pronouncements of XaaS financial targets or timelines.

How are these three FPIs faring on the four success metrics we identified? Figure 5.8 provides the CAGR on these four metrics from 2012–2015.

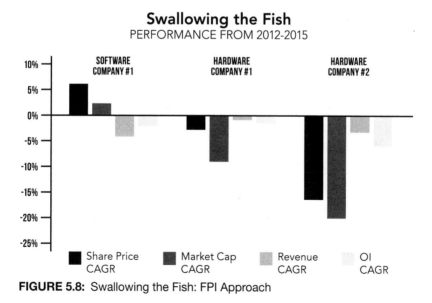

FIGURE 5.8: Swallowing the Fish: FPI Approach

There are a lot of negative numbers here! The software company has been able to hold on to their market cap, but their revenue and operating income are declining. The other two have not fared so well. All three face real pressures but are not willing to make aggressive moves.

MTW Approach

One large software company has clearly signaled the cloud is critical to their future. Currently, they are reporting that revenues from one XaaS offer are growing at 140% a year. However, investors are frustrated by the lack of transparency to the overall financial health of these XaaS offers.

Another large enterprise software company has just recently begun to aggressively signal they are serious about the cloud. Yet skeptics and their numerous cloud competitors argue this company does not truly have a competitive cloud offering. Nonetheless, they are marketing cloud hard now, committing to it as their future. Yet they continue to mix SaaS and traditional license revenue together in their financials. That total is shrinking, indicative of the fish at work. They are beginning to issue press releases about their XaaS business—including its size and growth rate—when its performance is strong.

A large data management company is embracing offers where customers can consume its technology as a service. It is definitely a real XaaS offer and it is doing well. Yet, their last annual report provides no detailed information on managed services or any other XaaS offer.

All three of these companies are aggressively talking about XaaS. All three have XaaS-related offers. But it is an opaque window that investors are forced to peer through when they attempt to understand the financial health of these businesses. No specific growth targets for XaaS are communicated to investors.

How are these MTWs fairing on the success metrics?

The first company on the left side of Figure 5.9 is facing a downward trend on profitability, but investors have been relatively

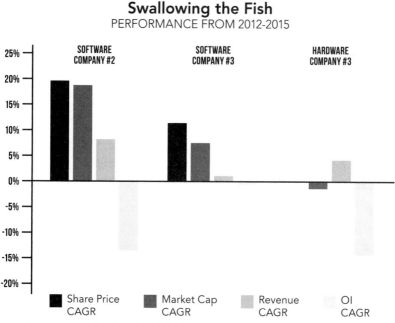

FIGURE 5.9: Swallowing the Fish: MTW Approach

kind to the stock. It appears they believe it has a chance to catch the new XaaS wave, even though it is not providing clear commitments on that business. The second company has done a phenomenal job of protecting an impressive operating income, but investors have been less kind with the stock. Perhaps this is why they are now becoming loud about the cloud. Finally, even though the third company has been growing revenues, the stock did not go anywhere with investors. Primarily a hardware company, they are the least loud about the cloud of the three.

CPM Approach

In this particular case, we will name the three companies that fit this profile in the past 3 years: Adobe, Intuit, and Autodesk.

On this topic of transitioning to XaaS, Adobe has been a trailblazer. In 2009, subscription revenues were only 2% of total company revenues for Adobe. In October 2011, the company announced their brand-new Creative Cloud offering. CTO

Kevin Lynch stated, "The move to the Creative Cloud is a major component in the transformation of Adobe."[4] By 2012, subscription revenues were 15% of total company revenues. In 2013, Adobe announced customers could only buy subscriptions from the company—the license offer was dead. In that same year, subscription had grown to 28% of revenues. In 3 years, the company went from almost no XaaS revenue to forcing customers to only consume technology as a service.

Intuit management closely followed the examples of Adobe. In 2000, Intuit was reporting that subscription revenues represented 14% of total company revenues. From 2000 to 2014, more of Intuit's revenue was migrating to subscription. Yet, they still had license software. Also, the company was wired to sell as many licenses as possible so they could recognize as much revenue up front as possible. But Intuit management approached the board in July 2014 and proposed a full cutover to subscription pricing. CFO Brad Smith had these comments on the decision:

> *"We began to find that when we talked to analysts and investors, on the surface they were seeing revenue growth that was perhaps slower than they expected. Internally, we knew it was because of the growing shift from desktop to online, but it was hard for an outside person like an analyst to see, understand, and verify.*
>
> *"For those reasons, the timing was right—the move would allow us to focus more as a company on software as a service, with accounting aligned strategically for Intuit's future. And it would let our desktop software look and feel more like software as a service, with ongoing services and enhancements provided year round."[5]*

Autodesk also followed Adobe's lead. In the 2013 annual report for Autodesk, they mention "subscription" revenues but don't break them out. In the 2014 annual report, the company made the following statement:

> *"In addition to sales of new perpetual use software licenses, we generate revenue through several subscription-based business*

models. The largest is our maintenance program, under which customers who own a perpetual use license for the most recent version of the underlying product are able to purchase maintenance that provides them with unspecified upgrades when-and-if-available and are able to download e-learning courses and receive online support over a one-year or multiyear maintenance service period."[6]

So by reclassifying traditional support contracts with emerging XaaS subscription revenues, Autodesk was suddenly able to report that subscription revenues represented 45% of total company revenues! In 2015, the company announced customers could no longer purchase software licenses starting January 2016.[7]

How did the three software companies that aggressively migrated to XaaS revenue models fare on the four success metrics? Well, the incredible reveal is seen in Figure 5.10. **Even though**

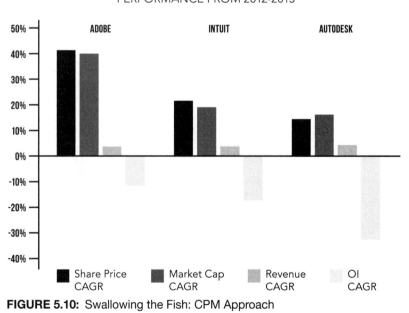

FIGURE 5.10: Swallowing the Fish: CPM Approach

all three of these companies decreased their operating incomes and barely grew top-line revenues during the transition, they demonstrated healthy growth in both stock price and market valuation.

Yes, you could argue that these three companies are all packaged software products that are easily converted from on-premise licenses to cloud subscriptions. Maybe you think it was not such a big deal because their customers don't have huge investments in surrounding infrastructure. In short, you rationalize that it was easier for them than it will be for you. We beg to differ. We think these were courageous early movers. They were able to overcome the historical DNA of customers, employees, and investors who may have preferred the comfort of the old model.

The results of all nine companies are provided side by side in Figure 5.11.

FIGURE 5.11: Swallowing the Fish: Approach Comparison

The Best Approach (and it is not just our opinion)

Yes, this is a sample of only nine companies we are analyzing, but we believe there is a powerful lesson to be learned. Revenue growth and operating income are not the critical metrics during a business model transformation. Investors will tolerate decreases in both of these metrics if they believe you have a viable plan to revise your business model and jump on a new market wave. From 2012–2015, the majority of investors clearly bought into the Adobe, Autodesk, and Intuit transitions. Why? They communicated their transition objectives very clearly and they committed to a firm timeline. They ran with an aggressive profit maximizer mentality. They were open and transparent in their financial reporting. They pressured their customers to make the shift. Even beyond these three companies, we would assert that the louder and more publicly aggressive companies seem to be about their pivot to XaaS, the better chance their stock price has of weathering the transition period.

If we return to the 2x2 state of the industry and we apply this lesson, we can overlay the following commentary:

- **You are in State #1:** Traditional offerings are not yet under pressure from commoditization or new consumption models.
    - o   Product revenues are still growing.
    - o   Product margins are healthy.
    - o   Operating income is stable.
    - o   *If investors believe your market is shifting to XaaS, stock price and market cap can flatline or go down (even though you are still a cash cow and top-line revenues may still be growing).*
- **You are in State #2:** Legacy offerings have commoditized, and new, profitable offers that adhere to the new consumption models have not been put in play.
    - o   Product revenues and/or margins are decreasing.
    - o   Operating income is declining.

o   *If your market is shifting to XaaS and you are not articulating a clear timeline to transition your economic engine, stock price and market cap WILL flatline or go down.*

- **You are in State #3:** New XaaS offers have been put in play, but they are not yet profitable.

  o   Service (and subscription) revenues are growing.

  o   Operating income is declining.

  o   *If you are actively shifting to XaaS but are very transparent with investors and have convincingly communicated a timeline for the transition, stock price and market cap can GO UP even if revenues and operating income are declining.*

- **You are in State #4:** New XaaS offers are in play and they are now profitable.

  o   Service (and subscription) revenues are growing.

  o   Operating income is stable or improving.

  o   *Now you will eventually need to pivot investor expectations from high growth to "growth + profitability." See the last section of this chapter for more on this challenge.*

If your legacy business model is on the brink of being pushed off of State #1, our recommendation is that the sooner a company can run the CPM play, the better. We don't think that the FPI approach is the smart play. We would assert that it is not the least risky strategy; it is the most risky strategy. Your investors will thank you for not eroding away valuation.

We are not the only ones who have given this advice. In his most recent book, *Zone to Win*,[8] author Geoffrey Moore makes the following observations on how the management team needs to communicate a business model transition to investors:

> *It is critical to prepare them (investors) for the upcoming changes before they impact the financial results and to control the ongoing narrative through which they are interpreted.*

You must not hope to skate through a transformational initiative keeping your traditional performance intact. That would take a miracle.

The new business has to be scaled to material size within a finite window of opportunity—typically three years or less—no matter what!

Best Practices for Swallowing the Fish

We have made this rather bold claim that management teams will serve their shareholders best by aggressively powering through a business model transition. In this section, we want to double-click into some of the specific tactics we recommend to manage through the transition. Be aware that the bar is getting higher. Early movers like Adobe blazed a trail and were afforded some latitude in their transition because investors really had nothing to compare it against. As more companies power through the transition, investors will have more data regarding what a good transition looks like. For example, Autodesk, which was a close follower to Adobe, faced more analyst scrutiny and investor headwinds than Adobe had.

When to Start

When XaaS offers started to gain more momentum about a decade ago, this was a common response we heard from large, established, enterprise technology companies: "Running your business in the cloud might be fine for small companies, but our customers would never let that happen." Well, we don't hear that comment quite so often today. As we write this book, our expectation would be that a majority of people reading this book work at companies that have already started the journey toward standing up XaaS offers. But just in case: How do you know if your specific market will truly be disrupted by XaaS? There are four obvious markers:

1. **Percentage of deals disrupted.** Even if the majority of your customers are still purchasing traditional offers, what

percentage of your deals were disrupted by a XaaS discussion? There could have been a competitive XaaS offer in play. The customer could have asked if you had a XaaS alternative. The customer could have asked if they could migrate to subscription pricing. In any of these scenarios, XaaS is disrupting the typical sales cycle. Is this 10% of the time? If it is more than 20% of the time, you need to get serious about XaaS.

2. **Noise from leading-edge customers.** You will know it when management gets an earful from strategic customer advisory boards or when your leaders and their leaders are having frank conversations about the future direction of the customer.

3. **Growth rate for traditional product and service offers.** This is the marker we have been tracking for 10 years in our T&S 50 data. When these two revenue streams go flat, there are only so many quarters you can attribute the decline to a late product release, a tepid global economy, or currency fluctuations.

4. **Stock price and market cap.** If these two numbers aren't growing, even if you are throwing off record profits, that should send a strong signal that investors believe your market is shifting away from your current offers.

It seems logical that if a company was facing the trifecta of deal disruption, declining revenues, and declining market value that the executive team would aggressively launch into business model transformation mode. But companies are not managed by Vulcans; they are managed by humans. For a host of reasons well discussed in the books *Innovator's Dilemma*,[9] *Zone to Win*, and *Seduced by Success*,[10] management teams do not proactively pursue change. They wait—like frogs in the ever-warming pot of water.

Our recommendation, actually our plea, is that companies start the transition process when a critical mass has been reached on the first marker of deal disruption. This is something that can be tracked through the sales team. Have sales reps start reporting for all deals (won and lost) if XaaS was a conversation. When X% of deals are being influenced for Y number of quarters, it is time to act. The executive team can assess what the right thresholds are for X and Y. Remember, this takes years to execute. Ideally you are planning well ahead of hitting this threshold. When you hit it, you need to go aggressively.

When the threshold is hit, the transition starts by investing resources and management cycles to experiment and pilot XaaS offers with these strategic customers or at the low end of the market. The company needs to start building the organizational capabilities required to support XaaS offers and start running some of the early-stage plays defined in this book.

This is the first bite into the fish. The investment curve (top of the fish) clicks up. Ideally this investment starts before the traditional revenues (bottom of the fish) start declining, and funding these investments without compromising short-term profits is nearly impossible. At this early stage, there is little to tell investors.

Setting Investor Expectations: Three Moves

After initial planning and piloting of your XaaS portfolio, it is time to put your shoulder to wheel for the business model transformation. This is where it gets real.

Again and again we hear the same statement from executives who are facing this XaaS business model transition: "Yeah, but we can't miss the quarter." In other words, they believe the expectation of investors is that despite shrinking legacy revenues and the need to stand up new offers, the company must sustain current profitability levels. Our data would say that is a false assumption. Once again, investors are less concerned with sustained profitability *if* they believe you have a viable plan for future growth. If you are not putting a believable plan for growth on the table, then, yes, they will most likely hold your feet to the fire on profitability.

In *Zone to Win*, Moore's recommendation is that management teams make three moves with investors during the transition. Here is our take on those three moves as it relates to XaaS:

1. **Announce XaaS initiatives.** Now that you have some piloting under your belt, you have a better sense of what XaaS offers make sense for your company. You publicly announce your intent with these offers. This is the second, bigger bite into the fish. You are signaling there are investments that need to be made to explore an exciting new growth opportunity. You may also announce your intent to do some strategic acquisitions to accelerate your traction in this area. By making this first public move, you accomplish two things. First, you signal to investors that you are serious about exploring XaaS. Second, it is a defensive move against new XaaS competitors. You have some type of XaaS offer for existing customers to consider. Be loud about your plans.

2. **Start the clock ticking.** This is the critical step—and it is gut-check time. After continued vetting and refinement of your new XaaS offers, you let investors know that the company is serious about transforming to a XaaS business model. You set clear expectations for investors. These expectations include:

   a. What will happen to revenue and operating income over the next four to eight quarters?
      i. Most likely both will go down for some period of time.
   b. What metrics are critical to watch during the transition?
      i. Number of new XaaS subscribers.
      ii. Renewal rate for XaaS customers.
      iii. Average dollar value for XaaS contracts.
   c. How long do you expect the transition to take?
      i. Ideally, no more than 3 years.

    d. How will investors know the transition is complete?

        i. What milestones will signal success?

       ii. What metrics can be used to assess success?

3. **Declare victory.** As the key milestones of success are achieved, you let investors know … over and over and over. At this point in time, you should be providing complete financial transparency to investors regarding your XaaS business. The business should clearly represent 20% or more of total company revenues and be rapidly climbing. And then, of course, pop the champagne.

Once again, the data supports this three-move strategy. Look at how Adobe, Autodesk, and Intuit have made these moves. Look again at how declining operating incomes and revenue growth in the short term did not adversely impact stock price or market value for these companies. In June 2014, *Fortune* published an article titled "For Adobe, Cloud Traction Leads to Record-High Stock Price."[11] The entire article is a supporting case study for the recommendations presented here. The following is an excerpt from the article:

> *Adobe's management team remains convinced that a bold and fast move to the cloud was the way to go. "Balancing the old and the new restricted how much innovation we could do on the new," Wadhwani says.*
>
> *Of course, educating Wall Street on the shift was another hurdle. Back in 2011 Adobe spent a full day with analysts, explaining the move to subscriptions and how that would change the model by which to value Adobe's future growth.*

Forcing the Issue

There is one attribute of the Adobe, Intuit, and Autodesk transitions that cannot be ignored. All three of these companies forced customers into the new business model. Is this an accelerator to success? Again, we are going to go big and bold here. We believe forcing customers to your future economic model is better than straddling two economic models for an extended period. If you don't turn off the old options, lagging customers will linger in the old model as long as they can. Will some customers be upset about being forced into a new consumption model? Absolutely. In 2013, Adobe had to face articles and blog posts with titles like, "Why Adobe's Subscription-Only Plan Sucks."[12] But remember the comment from Adobe's CEO: "Balancing the old and the new restricted how much innovation we could do on the new." Bifurcating resources across two distinct business models indefinitely hinders the transition.

How Long Does the Whole Journey Take?

This is a question our research team at TSIA keeps receiving. Companies want hard data on how long it is taking for incumbent technology providers to successfully transition to profitable XaaS business models. The key milestones across the entire life cycle would look something like Figure 5.12.

So how long is this taking companies? We have three challenges when attempting to answer that question definitively:

1. Nobody has a broad-based data set on when incumbent technology companies actually started their individual

Life Cycle Milestones

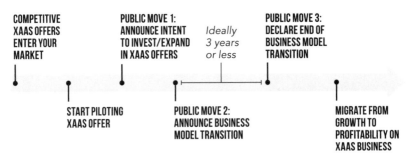

FIGURE 5.12: XaaS Life Cycle Milestones

investment activities into building XaaS offers, so it is hard to know when the clock started ticking for individual companies.

2. Very few incumbent companies have publicly declared they are attempting to make a significant business model transition, so are they on the timeline yet?

3. For companies like Autodesk, they have not entered and exited the final phase of migrating off of high growth and focusing more on a balance of growth and profitability—the true sign the transition is complete.

Having said all this, we can provide some big bumpers. Let's look at the bare minimum time requirement. A company should spend at least 1 year experimenting with XaaS offers before attempting to lock and load on the transition game plan they will take public. That year of pilots was probably preceded by a year of quiet internal planning. Estimate 3 years to migrate customers to the new model and roughly another 2 years to really optimize profitability of the new model. So all up and in, we believe this journey from start to finish is a minimum of 5 years. However, it could easily take 7 or 8. This is why we have been pleading with our TSIA members for the past 5 years to start these discussions internally. Mañana is not the operative word to use here. Every quarter that passes without being on this timeline simply reduces your odds of having enough runway to complete the timeline before the financial wheels start falling off.

We are well aware we have put some provocative recommendations on the table here. But let's go back to the three XaaS profile diagrams. The more "white space" between the revenue and the cost lines on those graphs equates to more total investment dollars over a multiyear period required to make your XaaS offer profitable. In other words, we think the FPI approach will ultimately require the most investment. For first-generation XaaS companies, the market has been willing to provide billions of dollars to cover that white space. For incumbent market leaders, we do not believe investors will be so generous. This means the CPM profile and an aggressive transition timeline is the optimal path to minimizing costs and protecting shareholder value in the long term. But this also means management teams will need to define and execute a successful transition plan. By no means, an easy task.

Another Fish to Swallow

Since writing *B4B*, there is a second scenario of swallowing the fish related to XaaS: The transition from high-growth XaaS to profitable XaaS. As we covered in Chapter 2, many first-generation XaaS companies are FVAs. They have been focused on top-line growth and not bottom-line profitability. And investors have been funding the losses. At some point, that music will stop for one of three reasons:

1. The stock market calls a "bubble" and FVAs without proven revenue and profit models are slammed.
2. Investors lose faith the company will ever make money.
3. The company has been wildly successful and it becomes difficult to sustain the high growth rate.

We all know the first scenario from the dot-com era. There are lots of stock market gurus at the time we are writing this book who are predicting another one now. The third scenario is becoming all too frequent. It is also unfolding in the marketplace as we write this book to highly successful first-generation XaaS companies.

But this second fish looks very different. We call it the "slow-down fish." Revenue growth is starting to slow. Costs are hopefully decreasing as a percentage of revenue, and the company is improving profitability or reversing losses rapidly. Figure 5.13 documents this pending inflection point.

The Slowdown Fish

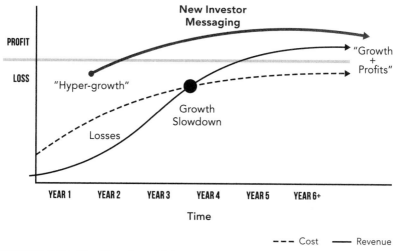

FIGURE 5.13: The Slowdown Fish

So what is the problem? The company is on a path to being more profitable! Yes, but top-line growth is slowing. Up to this point, investors have been hooked on the growth story. Here is a real-world example documented in an article titled "Why ServiceNow Inc. Stock Sank Today."[13] Here are a few excerpts from the article:

> *Shares of ServiceNow fell 19% after the cloud-based enterprise software company reported better-than-expected fourth-quarter 2015 results but followed with disappointing guidance.*
> *. . . the market was much less impressed with ServiceNow's full-year outlook, which calls for total billings of $1.6 billion, good for year-over-year growth of 33% to 34% at constant currency. ServiceNow also expects 2016 revenue between $1.34 billion and $1.37 billion, up between 33% and 36% from 2015 as reported and between 34% and 37% at constant currency. That includes subscription revenue between $1.18 billion and*

$1.20 billion and professional services and other revenue between $160 million and $170 million.

*By contrast, analysts' consensus estimates called for full-year revenue near the high end of that range, **and it appears Wall Street is concerned that the more modest growth in billings could be a harbinger of greater deceleration in ServiceNow's top-line growth.***

At the same time, it's not as though ServiceNow's full-year revenue and billings guidance were overwhelmingly negative. The company is still growing nicely and all the while anticipates demonstrating healthy operating margin and free cash flow margin of 12% and 24%, respectively. But with shares still trading above 60 times next year's estimated non-GAAP earnings, 13 times trailing-12-month sales, and ServiceNow still unprofitable on a GAAP basis, it's no surprise the market is bidding down ServiceNow stock at the first sign of imperfection.

So here is a XaaS company that has topped a billion dollars in revenue. It is continuing to grow at double-digit rates (unlike the incumbent technology companies we track in the T&S 50), and it is improving profitability. All that, and investors are pulling out? It's a perfect example of the slowdown fish. Successful XaaS companies, at some point in time, must transition their investors from a "high growth" story to a "growth and profitability" story. Waiting until you hit the growth slowdown point to begin shifting your message is not the best strategy. Trust us, this fish will need to be swallowed by every highly successful XaaS company. It is one thing to grow revenues annually at 40% when the company is $100 million. It is quite another to sustain that growth rate when the company is $1 billion.

When to Start

Here is the nub of the issue. Traditional companies have the markers previously listed to know when to start swallowing their fish.

The death of old revenue streams will eventually force their hand. High-growth XaaS companies have less visibility to when growth is truly slowing. You don't want to swallow the "high growth" to "growth + profit" fish until you absolutely have to. But ideally you would announce your transition before the slowdown. As long as investors believe you are a high-growth company, they will continue to fund the investments you need to capture more market share. So, what are the signs for a XaaS provider that it is time to swallow that fish?

There are three markers we would encourage XaaS companies to consider:

1. **Pipeline that does not support the current annual revenue growth rate.** The bar is high here. Currently, companies in the TSIA Cloud 20 index are growing revenues at an annual growth rate of 31%. If you do not have confidence you can support annual revenue growth rates north of 30%, it may be time to consider how the company is being positioned.

2. **Stock price and market cap.** Investor opinions do matter. If your stock price has stopped defying gravity, it may be time to adjust the messaging. Currently, TSIA Cloud 20 companies are enjoying market caps that are, on average, seven times greater than their annual revenues. If this multiplier falls below five, it may signal investors have stopped viewing you as a hyper-growth stock.

3. **Analysts and profitability.** If analysts are asking more and more questions about company profitability, there is a strong signal that it is time to put a "growth + profit" strategy on the table. Or, if you see a path to GAAP profits while you are still fast growing, it may be a good time to diversify your valuation messaging.

But once again, this is a very tricky transition. XaaS management teams may be faced with all three markers that are listed but still have conviction that the upcoming year will be high growth. You do not want to turn off the high-growth investor spigot prematurely. However, if the time has truly come to make this transition, how should it be managed?

Investor Expectations

What are the three moves in the hyper-growth to growth + profits transition? Once again, this is going to be all about setting investor expectations.

Here is our take on those three moves as it relates to swallowing the slowdown fish:

1. **Define the target financial model.** The most important step in this transition is to define a target financial model. How profitable will this business be in the end? We give you some target financial models to consider in Chapter 8. In an October 2014 presentation, Salesforce CFO Mark Hawkins stated that the company was facing headwinds for top-line growth, but the company would eventually be generating over 30 points of operating margin.[14] This is a great example of setting profitability expectations for investors.

2. **Start the clock ticking.** First, you tell investors how profitable the business could be. Then, when you are truly ready to make the transition, you set a time frame. You announce specific targets for the next 3 years:

   a. What will happen to revenue growth over the next 4 to 8 quarters?
      i. Most likely both slow down but continue to be positive.
   b. What will happen to operating profit over the next 4 to 8 quarters?
      i. Increase each quarter.

        ii. Culminate in achieving the target business model stated in Step 1.

    c. How long do you expect the profit transition to take?

        i. Ideally, no more than 3 years.

3. **Declare victory.** When the target business model is achieved, you let investors know. At this point, you should have migrated to true GAAP accounting principles to report profitability.

Unfortunately, it is still very early days on how to best navigate this particular transition. The best practices are yet to be proven. Having said that, we recommend readers go review the slide deck Salesforce published for investors in October 2014. You will see a solid example of how to educate investors on a pending transition. There is copy of the slides available at http://q4live. s1.clientfiles.s3-website-us-east-1.amazonaws.com/454432842/ files/doc_presentations/2014/Salesforce%20Analyst%20 Day%202014.pdf.

XaaS Playbook Summary

There are three plays that help a traditional company management team answer the question, "How do we swallow the fish?"

Play: Model the Fish (traditional companies)

Objective: Identify the approximate timeline, revenue, and cost impact of your transition.

Benefits:

- Helps determine the time you will require to create meaningful XaaS revenues, and what the effect on revenue and expenses will be during the transition.

- Helps formulate your talk track and guidance to employees, customers, and investors.

Players (who runs this play?): Core players: finance, product team, and marketing. Review team: CFO, CEO, and board.

Play: Set Transformation Public Milestone Dates for IR (traditional companies)

Objective: Identify the timeline for specific public transformation announcements.

Benefits:

- Sets a simple timeline the company can run to.
- Lists the three public moves that represent the beginning, middle, and end of the transformation (if applicable).

Players (who runs this play?): Core players: finance and IR. Review team: CFO, CEO, and board.

Play: Model Revenue Growth Rate Slowdown and Set Transformation to "Growth + Profits" Messaging Milestone Dates for IR (XaaS companies)

Objective: Identify the timeline for specific public announcements designed to begin introducing the move to a "growth + profits" company *before* you announce a revenue slowdown or downward revised guidance.

Benefits:

- Helps determine the rough time frame that you predict significant risk of slower growth rates.
- Begin messaging at least two quarters in advance that you have an eye on the long-term business model and will begin working toward a healthy balance of growth and profits.

- Stock may suffer initially but likely less and for a shorter time than a surprising announcement later on.

- Helps formulate your talk track and guidance to employees, customers, and investors.

Players (who runs this play?): Core players: finance and IR. Review team: CFO, CEO, and board.

6 | The Power of XaaS Portfolios

Some people working at XaaS companies today probably violently disagree with the friction curve. They may believe that the key to becoming profitable is to constantly reduce or eliminate friction and just keep adding customers until you cross the profit horizon line. But our perspective is that it will take years to do that. And, if you're successful during that time, particularly if you have weak economic moats, then you are going to have lots of competition. As we mentioned earlier, it's easier and faster to add software features today than at any other point in history—and it's just going to get easier as each year passes. At the same time, it's getting harder and harder to patent them. So, we think it's a risky management decision to simply put a XaaS offer into the market and assume you will use features to keep it differentiated long enough, with enough customers coming back dependably, to amass the gigantic volumes needed to turn profitable. So to be successful over the long term in the world of technology as a service, everyone needs to develop more sophisticated tactics to combat the three killer Cs of cost, churn, and commoditization that we mentioned in Chapter 2. We think that, in addition to product-market fit, these three topics should be in the forefront of management discussion day in and day out.

Building strong economic moats around your offer(s) is a strategic approach that can dramatically increase your probability of achieving GAAP profits, but these big thoughts need to be taken to the next level. They need to be operationalized. Tactics that ensure wise deployment of your strategies need to be developed. So, armed with the answers to your exercise around the economic moats you want to build, you can begin to answer the three simple—but critical—questions that represent the vertical dimension of our 3x3 of XaaS:

1. What is the offer portfolio and pricing model, and who are we selling it to?
2. What is the customer engagement model that we will use to sell and deliver this offer?
3. What are the financial keys that will allow us to make money with this offer?

These three questions compose the iron triangle of offer definition (Figure 6.1). In this chapter, we will be exploring tactics to answer the first question in that iron triangle: What is the offer portfolio and pricing model(s), and who are we selling it to?

Iron Triangle of Offer Definition

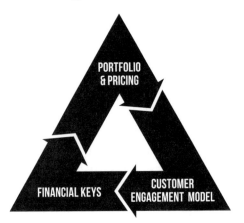

FIGURE 6.1 Iron Triangle of Offer Definition

Portfolio Categories

Building winning XaaS offers involves multiple considerations over both short- and longer-term time horizons. As we have already said, the first and certainly the most critical element of your offer is one with which we cannot help you. That is the question about your secret sauce—about the market acceptance of your value proposition. At the end of the day, no amount of packaging or pricing can overcome a weak offer that customers don't see value in purchasing. It is up to you to ensure that the core of your value proposition is strong and that customers will compensate you for it using either their money or their time. Over the next decade, tens of thousands of new XaaS offers will hit various enterprise technology markets. It is impossible for us to offer a single construct that will tell you whether your offer will gain market acceptance. It is up to you to get that part right. You must properly assess the needs of your target-market users and build the features and experience that will attract them and provide value (product-market fit). That could be in a completely new and never-before-seen market like ride sharing was, or it could strike out at a vulnerability among leaders in a traditional market. You might see an opening to use the cloud to lower price, remove risk, add new capabilities, reduce total cost ownership (TCO), or simply make it easier to do something other than the old offers available from the big incumbents. Either way, when you think you have that part figured out—when you think you have a strong product-market fit—then we can move on to structure the offer for short- and long-term success.

It's no secret that being first to market with an innovative value proposition is often a great tactic for success. But importantly, being first to market is not the only way to succeed nor is it a guarantee that you will. Apple didn't invent the cell phone; it redefined it along both technology (incorporating cameras, computers, and large screens) and offer lines (creating the App Store and iCloud services). The tech industry is littered with companies who were first to market but not first to success. It is also littered with companies who were first to market, first to succeed, and first to fail. Both Friendster and MySpace had the jump on Facebook but were not able to defend their early success. TIVO had the technology lead in DVRs, but succumbed to other market options that were good enough and were bundled and distributed by the cable providers. Despite these cautionary tales, it's still great to be first to market. And, given the recent enthusiasm of the markets for disruptive cloud companies regardless of their profitability, many future value aggregator start-ups may feel that the only time horizon they should be concerned with is initial trajectory. Once they have that, they may feel they can get "an exit" by selling to a larger company or to the public markets that will then assume the risk/reward of translating their units into profitable revenue. But, that is usually not an option for larger, traditional companies who are pivoting to XaaS. They must think not only about initial trajectory, but also about long-term defensibility against competition and commoditization. So, it makes sense, then, that your offer portfolio will not only be heavily influenced by your current profit horizon decision but also by whether you are willing to think and act now to benefit future phases as your profit horizon draws closer.

If your new XaaS offer represents either a simple, innovative capability or a narrowly defined best-of-breed solution, then your goal is to keep it very simple in the early phase (Figure 6.2). That reduces purchase or trial friction and encourages lots of people to get their feet wet. This way, you get more of the precious units of future value that are the key measure of the performance of your offer in the aggregator stage. However, over time, most of these simple offers can and should evolve. This evolution takes place for several reasons:

- Your customers want or demand a more complete solution.
- You are expanding your products and services to maintain competitive advantage.

The Friction Curve
PORTFOLIO PLAN A

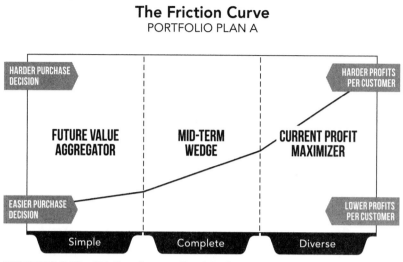

FIGURE 6.2 The Friction Curve – Portfolio Plan A

- You have ideas for adjacent offers or you are enabling an eco-system of partners who have them.
- You want to grow your revenue diversity and begin building multiple economies of scale.

We see this as a good and healthy progression. We have already argued for the benefits of diverse revenue stream as a key to strong financial performance. And if your new offer is a complex application or requires substantial technical support, you will need a more complete solution portfolio from day one in order for your early customers to be successful. However, there are other strong arguments to be made for planning a more diverse portfolio at the proper time in your offer's journey across the friction curve. One of the most powerful is how your portfolio can defend against competition and commoditization.

Usually, competition and commoditization go hand in hand. In the world of enterprise technology, however, that has not always been true. The preferred historic battleground for tech companies hasn't been price. It's been features. In the 1990s and 2000s,

SAP, Oracle, Peoplesoft, Siebel, and others competed furiously in enterprise software markets like ERP, CRM, and HRM. None of them were cheap. None of them developed offers with list prices that were 50% less or 90% less than the others. Even though software license revenue has legendary gross margins approaching 99%, these companies chose to wage feature wars, not price wars. Sure, they discounted. Sure, they would price match to get a deal. But they successfully avoided price commoditization for decades. Building and selling enterprise software was an expensive proposition, and the prices reflected that.

Many of the hardware companies were not quite as lucky. Moore's law saw to that. PCs, servers, UNIX, minis . . . a slow, steady, downward spiral of prices and margins. They tried to differentiate based on features. Some companies were able to do that for brief periods. But in the end, computers are about processing and storing information. The game was simply who offered the fastest processing and the most storage at the lowest price. Commoditization reigned supreme.

So, for the past several decades, enterprise technology has been a tale of two cities. Hardware companies faced intense competition that yielded commoditization in many market segments. Software companies competed head-to-head and feature-to-feature, but rarely based on substantially lower prices.

So, what about your XaaS offer? Which will it be? Will your competition maintain some price integrity in the market and battle you on features, or will they match you on features and use lower prices to gain market share? Is it to be high prices or rapid commoditization? Well, as we observed in 2009 in the book *Consumption Economics*,[1] the net impact on tech pricing of the cloud so far has been unarguably down. Unlike yesteryear's software reality, cloud competition is regularly using price to win market share. The most famous to date has been AWS's relentless use of lower pricing to challenge competitors like Rackspace and Microsoft Azure. However, it's not limited to infrastructure players. Many enterprise SaaS applications offer comparable features to competitors' products, but are offered at much lower prices. Think about web conferencing, where WebEx competes with half a dozen free or nearly free alternatives. Or think about personal productivity applications, where Google pits Google Apps against Microsoft Office 365 at per-user prices as low as $5 per month. Even classically expensive enterprise software categories like CRM and HRM can be purchased from among a huge range of prices with new, nearly always lower-priced competitors emerging almost monthly. Our point of view is simple: Feature functionality eventually commoditizes in XaaS markets. Unfortunately, you don't get to ask your competition to avoid this race to the bottom—but, it is important to anticipate what route they will likely pursue as you think about your portfolio tactics.

In short, we think your portfolio decisions (what do I offer at each point in my profit horizon phases?) are central to battling commoditization, ensuring customer success, and eventually achieving strong GAAP profits.

In Chapter 3, we introduced you to TSIA's latest technology services portfolio listing for cloud-based offers. Add those to your product offering options, sprinkle in a bundling approach we call "outcome services," and you get seven exciting offer categories to draw from for your XaaS portfolio:

- **Technology Subscription.** These are core technical capabilities the customer will access as part of the offer—in other words, simply offering better features as your secret sauce.

- **Adjacent Modules.** Offering complimentary modules or capabilities that extend or enhance the value of the core offer either directly or through third parties. This puts a halo around your core offer that competitors must somehow match.

- **Attached Services.** These are services designed to stand the customer up on the technology and maintain access to the technology. This category includes classic service activities such as professional services related to implementation and integration, technical education services, and technical support services. Especially for large enterprise customers, this is a must-have. Again, these services can be delivered directly or through a partner ecosystem.

- **Operational Services.** These are services designed to reduce operational complexity for customers. They include capacity management, remote monitoring, risk audits, and system administration. The main objective of these services is to minimize the cost and complexity of operating a technology.

- **Adoption Services.** These are services designed to help customers maximize their usage of technical capabilities. Unlike traditional education services, these "success" services involve usage analytics, user adoption monitoring and intervention, and intelligent feature provisioning. The main objective of these services is to maximize technology adoption.

- **Information Services.** These are services designed to help augment the value customers get from their use of the core subscription by providing data-based insights and other data-related activities. Your information services might add data into the customer's database or maintain the currency of the data that's already in there. It may compare their results to that of other users. The main objective of these services is to improve the customer's own data and insights by offering tools or supplemental data that has been aggregated by the technology provider.

- **Outcome Services.** These are where the provider has some or all of the customer's pricing tied to the delivery of a result. In these offers, a provider bundles all the technology subscription(s) and services required to deliver a targeted business outcome. Some or all of the pricing is then tied to the customer's achievement of that outcome. In other words, the provider is taking some or all of the risk away from the customer. If the outcome is not achieved, the customer doesn't pay. This could be as simple as pay-per-use pricing—if the customer doesn't end up using the solution, they don't pay. A more aggressive real-world example of this service category would be how red-light camera technology is sold to cities throughout the country. Cities do not pay for the cameras or the installation of the cameras. The provider is given a percentage of each ticket (the outcome) issued from the cameras.

Now let's take these categories and begin to think about how we will grow our offer portfolio as we move forward toward the profit horizon.

Portfolio Definition

The idea of a product road map is hardly new. However, we don't see enough XaaS companies developing full portfolio road maps that cut across all these categories—especially for those who are purposefully planning the evolution of their portfolio based on the profit horizon of their core offer and are beginning to engineer into the product all the capabilities they will need to deliver them profitably and at scale. Many of these offer categories are new or significantly revamped in the cloud (Figure 6.3). Being able to remotely drive user adoption, operate or manage technology, supplement data, use real-time analytics to compare customer performance levels, monitor and monetize actual outcomes . . . these are exciting and heady opportunities that can only be done profitably and at scale in the XaaS world. After all, the "aS" in SaaS, IaaS, PaaS, and so forth does mean "a service." That is what you are delivering. This exercise simply adds more and more services on top of your core offer. Capabilities in these categories can often be very cool, dramatically expanding the scope and value of the complete solution you offer and raising the bar for your competitors.

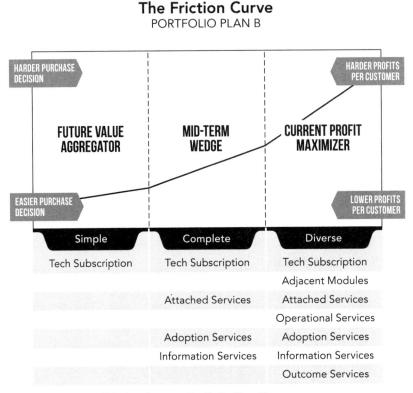

FIGURE 6.3 The Friction Curve – Portfolio Plan B

There are real-world examples. Salesforce has a set of "Premier Success" services that are designed to monitor usage and help customers accelerate adoption. Siemens Healthcare offers workflow optimization services for laboratories using Siemens equipment. LivePerson offers an outcome-based managed service designed to improve agent productivity in call centers. AWS has an automated "Trusted Advisor" service that monitors and optimizes cost-efficient usage of its offers. These capabilities are rapidly emerging in the marketplace. A complete XaaS plan determines which of these components makes sense for your offer at different stages in the profit horizon journey.

Let's do a short exercise to make sure we have thought through all the basic tenets of your portfolio. Let's see if we can define your offer in 1 to 2 pages based on Figure 6.4 and get everyone on the team to agree with it.

Below is an explanation of these basic tenets.

Core Offer or Portfolio Description. A few sentences that describe what benefit(s) the customer gets with the core technology subscription. Following are example descriptions for XaaS offers in the marketplace today:

- **Tableaux.** Hosted analytics platform that enables a company to connect and visualize data in minutes.[2]

- **LivePerson.** Enables online marketers to deliver the kind of rich, engaging customer experiences that drive results. Through advanced segmentation capabilities along with keyword-based targeting, LivePerson can help determine which customers to engage with and deliver a highly relevant interaction designed to lead the customer to conversion.[3]

- **Workday.** Workday Human Resource Management offers intuitive, self-service features to help you effectively organize, staff, and pay your global workforce. You can manage the full hire-to-retire life cycle in one simple, easy-to-use system.[4]

Target Buyer(s). Who will be interested in purchasing this XaaS portfolio? Senior target buyers could include:

- **CIO or IT Executive.** The offer reduces IT costs.
- **Sales Executive.** The offer improves sales productivity.
- **Marketing Executive.** The offer improves demand generation.
- **Engineering Executive.** The offer reduces development costs or accelerates time to market.
- **CFO.** The offer reduces overall company costs.
- **CEO.** The offer creates competitive differentiation.

ATTRIBUTE	DETAILS	FVA STAGE	MID-TERM WEDGE STAGE	CURRENT PROFIT STAGE
Core Offer or Portfolio Name	What will you call the core offer or portfolio?			
Short Description of Key Attributes	Describe the compelling value proposition of your offer or portfolio.			
Target Buyer(s)	Who is the buyer(s) you are aiming to attract?			
Financial Outcome				
Increase Revenue	How will this offer unlock revenue opportunities for the customer?			
Cost Savings	How will this offer help the customer save money?			
Risk Avoidance	How will this offer help the customer avoid business risk?			
Performance Metrics (KPIs) That Will Be Improved	Which key performance metrics related to the target financial outcome(s) will be improved?			
Target Customer Process	What are the critical customer processes that will be improved or innovated by consuming your portfolio?			
Key Customer Capabilities Enabled by the Portfolio Offer	What are the new or improved business capabilities your offer portfolio will provide to the customers?			
Portfolio Components	What components are included in your portfolio?			
Core Tech Subscription	Your central technology subscription offer.			
Adjacent Modules	Additional modules that are complimentary to the core offer.			
Attached Services	Services that help the customer implement or provide support on the solution.			
Operational Services	Services that will help reduce operational complexity for the customer.			
Adoption Services	Services that will help the customer become proficient with your solution.			
Information Services	Services that leverage unique data sets to provide business insights to the customer.			
Outcome Services	Will you bundle some or all of the above components into an outcome-based offer?			

FIGURE 6.4 The XaaS Plan Chart

- **Workgroup Manager.** The offer makes a team operate more effectively.
- **Individual Worker.** The offer makes someone more productive.

Financial Outcome. What is the economic outcome customers can expect to realize if they purchase these offers? There are three large categories of financial outcomes that will be of high interest to your potential customers:

- **Cost Savings.** Reduce operating costs for the customer.
- **Revenue Generation.** Increase revenue the customer can generate.
- **Risk Avoidance.** Prevent the loss of revenue or assets.

Figures 6.5.1 through 6.5.4 explode these three categories and document some potentially more specific outcomes within each one.

Business Outcomes
POTENTIAL BUSINESS VALUE

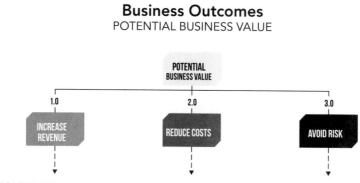

FIGURE 6.5.1 Business Outcomes – Potential Business Value

Business Outcomes
INCREASE REVENUE

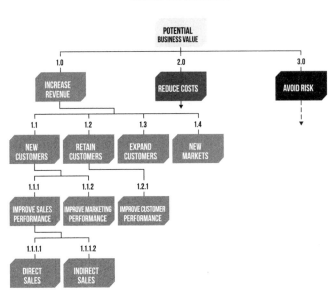

FIGURE 6.5.2 Business Outcomes – Increase Revenue

Business Outcomes
REDUCE COSTS

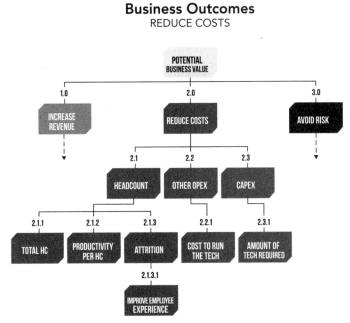

FIGURE 6.5.3 Business Outcomes – Reduce Costs

Business Outcomes
AVOID RISKS

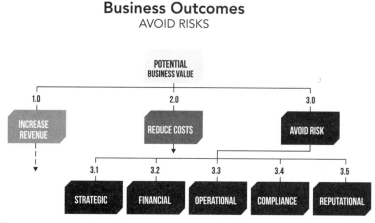

FIGURE 6.5.4 Business Outcomes – Avoid Risks

Ideally, you should be able to specifically identify the financial metrics the customer could improve by leveraging this portfolio. Examples of financial metrics include the following:

- Revenue per customer will increase.
- Profit per customer will increase.
- Cost to serve each customer will decrease.
- Labor costs will be reduced.
- Downtime will be avoided.

Key Performance Metrics. What are the key performance indicators (KPIs) or metrics the customer could improve by leveraging this portfolio? KPIs are the lifeblood of your customer's organization. They are how management sees whether the operational processes and tactics at work in the business are trending in a positive or negative direction. They are the prerequisites to achieving financial outcomes. For example, if a company could improve the acceptance rate of customer proposals (proposal hit rate), the company would expect company revenues to grow faster. Identify which KPIs will improve if your offers are adopted.

Customer Processes. What are the critical customer processes that will be improved or innovated by consuming your portfolio? Identifying the process allows the customer to understand not just what your product does but where in the business it applies. That helps crystallize which departments or employee teams will be affected and which ways of doing business will change.

Key Capability(s) Enabled by Your Offer. What are the new or improved business capabilities your offer portfolio will provide to customers? These are the sexy promises made by your offer description but in slightly more detail, maybe your top five or seven items. You might enable your customer to streamline product development cycles by shortening test phases. Maybe you can provide insights about end-customer behavior that help management target its marketing messages more effectively. The most exciting new or improved capabilities that the features of your offer portfolio can generate within the customer's business processes go here. Obviously, they need to really resonate with the target buyers you identified.

Portfolio Components. Once the targeted benefits and the outcomes are defined, the elements of the portfolio should be itemized. This is the exercise we just covered in the previous section. You will need to think about the surrounding products or value-added services that will help make the customer successful with the technology. At this point, you don't need to decide whether you will charge for these or how they might be bundled together. The objective is to simply identify what elements should and could be wrapped around the core technology subscription.

There is nothing earth-shattering about this exercise. Some of this is Offer Definition 101, but some of it is a little tougher. It is based on the work TSIA is doing on the concept of outcome engineering, a sort of mapping process that links technology capabilities to the customer's financial outcomes. It helps inform your sales and marketing messages and draws a clear line of sight for customers to understand why they should purchase your offer.

This is the correct starting point to crystallize your thinking about your XaaS offer. But yet, we have witnessed more than one management team forging ahead to stand up new XaaS offers with no clear agreement or understanding of all the elements in this form. Maybe it's because they are simply carrying forward their old playbook of offer definition. In the old playbook, differentiated feature functionality was all that mattered. In XaaS marketplaces, feature functionality is unlikely to keep offers differentiated in the long term.

This leads to one last step you need to complete, which is to turn your individual portfolio components into bundled offers that you will package and monetize within the portfolio. Again, you should not only be thinking about market acceptance, but also about how you will defend your offer from competition and commoditization. You must consider your offers now as well as how the portfolio will evolve as you move closer to the profit horizon. This is your portfolio road map.

Portfolio Road Map

ATTRIBUTE	FVA STAGE	MID-TERM WEDGE STAGE	CURRENT PROFIT STAGE
Portfolio Components			
Core Tech Subscription	Core Offer	Core Offer	Core Offer
Adjacent Modules		Module A	Module A
			Module B
Attached Services	Tech Support	Tech Support	Tech Support
		Implementation	Implementation
			Consulting
Operational Services			Managed Service
Adoption Services	Basic	Basic	Basic
		Premium	Premium
Information Services		Data Supplement	Data Supplement
			Advanced Analytics
Outcome Services			Pay for Performance
	Simple	Complete	Diverse
TOTAL NUMBER OF OFFER BUNDLES	1	5	10

FIGURE 6.6 Portfolio Road Map

In the portfolio road map example seen in Figure 6.6, the company starts off with a single, *simple* bundle in its portfolio. It is designed to be easy to purchase but includes all the offers necessary for customers to succeed. The provider has chosen to include tech support and basic adoption services as part of the bundle. But as the company proves its market fit and begins scaling its *complete* solution with an eye on hitting the wedge profit horizon in the mid-term, the portfolio grows into five bundles. Each is a separately priced offer. They can be sold to all existing customers a la carte, or they can be packaged into larger deals. Once the company nears turning a profit and wants to accelerate profits, it sets its sights on a *diverse* portfolio of offer bundles. Perhaps now the company is getting the attention of large enterprise customers who demand advanced consulting or managed services. Maybe it has learned to aggregate data from across multiple customers and has an advanced analytics offer that guides the customer to better performance. Finally, they may have enough confidence in their ability to make customers successful with the core offer that they have an outcome bundle that brings together essential product and service offers but bases the price of the bundle on usage or on making specific improvements in the customer's business outcomes.

This road map can be elaborated upon with timelines or created separately for key customer segments. You can get as fancy as you want. But what you are really doing is planning the portfolio journey from future value aggregator to current profit maximizer. Once that exercise is complete, you can move on to thinking about how each bundle will get priced to optimize its objectives.

Pricing Power

We are only going to spend a few minutes on pricing. In this chapter we will provide a simple overview of some key pricing considerations you will need to keep in mind for the offers in your portfolio. These are the high-level concepts we think all XaaS executives should think about in order to be able to effectively question and approve pricing.

In the world of XaaS, pricing is a conversation that gets interesting very quickly. Scanning the marketplace, there seems to be an incredibly wide variance of pricing models. Some seem (and probably are) overly simplistic. Others seem (and probably are) overly complicated. Even with companies that have long sold enterprise or consumer technology, there can be incredible consternation on how to approach the pricing of a new XaaS offer.

One way to frame the pricing discussion at a high level and further leverage the financial magic of your portfolio is to reach consensus among your team on the pricing power you may have. To do this, we built on the concept of pricing quadrants (Figure 6.7), which was first introduced to us by the firm Value and Pricing Partners.[5]

Every offer bundle in your XaaS portfolio can be placed in one of four pricing quadrants that are determined by two factors:

1. Is your offer generally accepted by the market as competitively advantaged and differentiated?

2. Is your offer one that is highly standard from customer to customer or is it highly customized?

The Four Pricing Quadrants

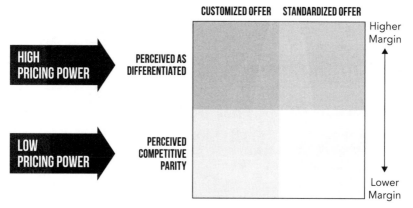

FIGURE 6.7 The Four Pricing Quadrants

Obviously, if the market accepts that your offer is competitively advantaged, then you have high pricing power. Conversely, if your offer is considered only to be at parity with, or worse, below your competition, then you are probably forced to stay very close to their prices (assuming you choose the same pricing anchor, which we will cover later). Let's call that low pricing power. It follows naturally, then, that where your offers have high pricing power, you should enjoy better margins or more volume than your competitors, depending on how you choose to play out your advantage.

This simple view allows us to begin framing some basic fundamentals of the pricing strategies we choose for our portfolio (Figure 6.8).

It's no surprise that everyone covets the upper-right quadrant. That is nirvana for XaaS. It means you have a standardized offer that requires little or no customization from customer to customer. You can achieve economies of scale quickly and more profitably than your competitors. You have the choice of charging a premium price or increasing your market share by keeping

The Four Pricing Quadrants
FUNDAMENTALS

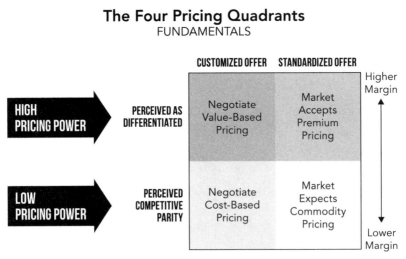

FIGURE 6.8 The Four Pricing Quadrants – Fundamentals

the price competitive while boasting a superior offer. Either path gives you the opportunity to have a higher-margin business than those other guys. If you don't enjoy high pricing power, then the market will expect your pricing to be the same or lower than the market overall.

If your offer is highly customized from customer to customer, it gets harder for the prospect to anticipate your price or to compare it to the competition. In that case, your pricing is probably not published anywhere and will likely involve an individual negotiation with each customer. For these kinds of offers, we have a very simple approach to thinking about your prices: You could set your price as low as your costs (otherwise, you will lose money), and you could set it as high as the financial value your offer creates for the customer (otherwise, they will lose money). As simple as that sounds, it's a great pair of numbers to set boundary conditions for pricing highly customized XaaS offers. These kinds of highly customized offers are very common in enterprise technology due to the complexity of certain solutions and the amount of professional services or consulting that accompany them.

So now that we have laid out the pricing power framework, we can begin to use it to smartly map our portfolio bundles to give us the best chance of reaching our profit horizon objectives.

The great news is that many new and market-making or highly disruptive XaaS offers begin their life in the upper-right quadrant (Figure 6.9). That means you have established a strong product-market fit and have built enough awareness of your value proposition that most prospective customers accept, or they can be easily convinced of your advantages.

As we said, that is a great place to be. Whether you were first to market or simply built a better mousetrap, you are in the enviable position of being differentiated and advantaged in your core technology subscription. Now comes the interesting part. In our work with many newer companies, it is rare to find that management doesn't believe they will be able to stay in the upper-right

The Four Pricing Quadrants
CORE OFFER

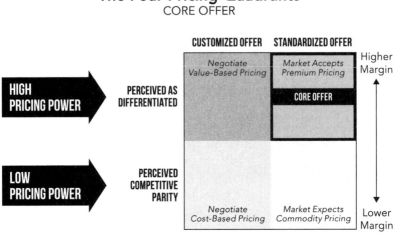

FIGURE 6.9 The Four Pricing Quadrants – Core Offer

quadrant in perpetuity. But in our experience, that's a very risky assumption. As we have said repeatedly, we think it's going to get harder and harder to stay in that quadrant just based on building better features. The reality so far is that as cloud markets mature, intense competition ensues.

We have already pointed out many examples of XaaS offers where markets went from new and in control of the early leader, to mature and crowded with several strong competitors. We have singled out examples of highly competitive markets, such as cloud computing, where AWS had the jump, and web collaboration, where WebEx had the jump. It's our view that the odds are against staying in the upper-right quadrant over time (Figure 6.10). At a minimum, we think it's a management error not to plan for the day when your core offer drops.

How do we best prepare for that day? Well, as you can tell, we see a great deal of magical power in the idea of portfolio thinking. So, how are we going to use portfolio thinking to help us here? We are going to create new and captive markets where our pricing power is high. Even when the core offer is commoditiz-

The Four Pricing Quadrants
CORE OFFER CHANGE

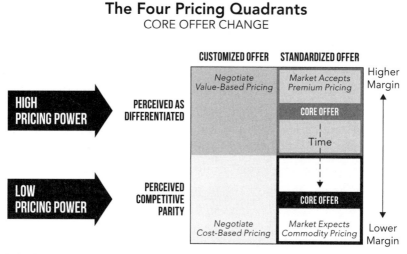

FIGURE 6.10 The Four Pricing Quadrants – Core Offer Change

ing and our pricing power is declining, there are complimentary offers to your existing customers where your competition simply can't compete for that dollar of customer spending. Why? Because once a prospective customer decides to purchase your core technology subscription, they move from one market—the general market—to another, far more captive market—your customer base. Once that happens, your pricing power with that customer goes way, way up.

This is a lesson that we think has been central to the high profit levels of the traditional tech companies. After all, customer lock-in was our number one economic moat, and diverse revenue streams was number five.

Just look at the history of the traditional enterprise software market! Not only was the software expensive; it was sticky. Once an enterprise customer had gone through the pain and agony of implementing one of these software platforms, switching vendors was not an option. No one in their right mind would sign up to repeat that journey. So, companies like SAP and Oracle were able to build huge maintenance and support franchises where nearly every historical customer was paying plus or minus 20% per year of list price to re-buy the software each year. Yes, there is lots of buzz today about the red-hot "subscription economy" in SaaS, but really, it's far from a new concept. Nearly every large enterprise software company today is living off its subscription annuity business and has been for years. These support and maintenance contracts are time-based and renewable. It's the ultimate wedge model. Once you can offer customer support globally at scale, the cost to take on one more incremental customer is minimal. Margins grow and grow as you put more customers on the pile. For these software companies and their shareholders, the ability to defend their prices and lock in their customers has been a thing of beauty. These services diversified the revenue streams of these companies, gave them a second economy of scale, and added to the completeness of the solution. Hardware companies were also able to build successful annuity businesses around break/fix services and operating system updates, but they were never able to match the franchises of their software brethren. After a few years, customers could and did switch vendors. Maintenance customers had comparatively short shelf lives and higher costs to serve, but it was still the highest margin business in the hardware portfolio of companies like HP and IBM.

Somehow, though, despite all this tribal knowledge, we don't see enough XaaS organizations building this thinking into their portfolio today. For many of them, the cultural mindset of the frictionless FVA became a permanent fixture, not simply a stage in the journey to the profit horizon. Their core offer just keeps growing and growing as more features are added. Services are given away for free or not offered at all.

We think the better approach is to create a broader portfolio of adjacent modules and services where you are the only game in town, where your pricing power with that customer is limited only by their ability to pay, not by your competition. That enables you to start building the multiple economies of scale that have generated outrageously attractive gross margins over the last several decades of tech.

In the example shown in Figure 6.11, the company's core offer has commoditized, and its pricing is limited by competitive offers. Its professional services are also often compared to the competition, at least their basic implementation services. To counter that, the company has announced four high-value offers where they have high pricing power and the potential to build multiple economies of scale. These additional services have far more pricing leeway than the basic offers. Creative pricing strategies can be brought to bear with little or no concern for competitive pressure.

Here is the key point: You need several pricing strategies inside your portfolio, not just one. You will have individual bundles that have different pricing power and where you can apply different pricing tactics to optimize margins.

As for the pricing tactics themselves, there are tons of great pieces of work for you to leverage. We aren't eager to try to top many of the academic and consulting firms that have spent years thinking about how to master the discipline of pricing. But we

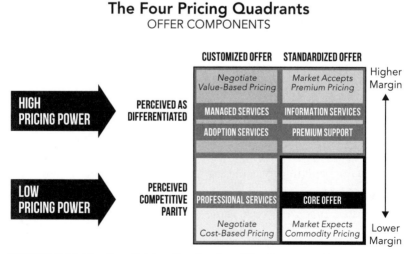

FIGURE 6.11 The Four Pricing Quadrants – Offer Components

do think there are a few key decisions and data points that are particularly important in setting XaaS prices. We have listed these in two phases you can follow to provide a solid rationale for the pricing of your portfolio.

Phase 1: Set Your Boundaries

1. Determine how much friction you can tolerate by placing your portfolio in the profit horizon framework.
2. Determine how you will bundle the offers in your portfolio using the portfolio definition exercise.
3. Determine whether any of your individual offers are limited by or must match your competition using the pricing power framework.
4. Calculate your actual unit cost (COGS) so you will know the gross profit at various prices.
5. Determine how much financial benefit your customers can achieve by consuming your portfolio. Ideally, this number should be readily provable and defensible. These last two steps frame in your boundary conditions.

Phase 2: Apply Pricing Tactics

6. Determine the pricing mechanism you will use for each bundle.
7. Identify what you will anchor the actual price to.
8. Apply a pricing model and set the initial price of the offer inside your boundary conditions.

Many valuable conjoint and regression models can be used to supplement this process, but we think these common-sense steps will help ensure that you cover some very important considerations:

- Do I know how much money we can make for customers, because that will probably determine the highest price of each offer and/or the entire bundle in my portfolio?

- Do I know what our unit costs are and what competitive limitation(s) we have, because one of them will probably determine the lowest price for each bundle?

- Did I consider how much friction I can or want to insert into the portfolio based on my profit horizon when I make my bundling decisions and set my prices? Do I have a plan for evolving my portfolio over time?

- Did I examine a reasonably broad number of pricing techniques rather than only one or two? There are many interesting ways to anchor pricing in XaaS. A creative anchoring strategy can make a huge difference in your margins.

The main objective of this chapter is to put forth some thinking that senior XaaS executives should consider as they evaluate the final pricing analysis and proposals made by their team.

One final observation on XaaS pricing strategy: It's easy to blow this off. It's easy to say we just price by the user by the month, and we will throw everything into that price. In an environment where investors are rewarding rapid unit growth and market share, pricing decisions can easily be weighted toward rapidly acquiring new customers. We can see the attractiveness and convenience of that decision. Some XaaS companies may even set the price at zero to really eliminate friction and encourage adoption. Although these approaches will certainly drive initial trial, they have rarely proven to yield consistent profits. It's going to take some effort and focus to work through the exercises we are advocating, but when your offer is the first in its category to achieve GAAP profits, you'll be glad you did.

Playbook Summary

Three plays are identified in this chapter:

Play: Portfolio Definition

Objective: Create and get agreement on a first-cut definition of the XaaS offer portfolio.

Benefits:

- Creates a common understanding among key stakeholders regarding what the XaaS offer portfolio includes.
- Identifies what technology and service components must be created before the offer can be taken to market.
- Identifies the value proposition of the offer.
- Identifies target buyers for the offer.
- Determines how these elements will evolve as you move closer to the profit horizon.

Players (who runs this play?): Core players: product development, product marketing, and services marketing. Review team: CEO, CFO, sales and services leadership.

Play: **Pricing Power Quadrant**

Objective: Determine how much pricing power makes sense for each offer bundle in the portfolio.

Benefits:

- Creates a simple model for communicating how the components of a XaaS model will be viewed in the markets they serve.
- Creates high-level framing for what pricing approaches are realistic for each component of the XaaS offer.
- Forces a management team to think about pricing in a more granular fashion, not as one single decision.

Players (who runs this play?): Core players: product development, product marketing, and services marketing. Review team: CEO, CFO, sales and services leadership.

Play: Frame XaaS Pricing for Core Offer

Objective: Follow Phase 1 and Phase 2 exercises on pages 180 to set pricing boundary for all the critical components of a XaaS portfolio.

Benefits:

- Provides a structured process for boxing in the initial price of a XaaS offer.
- Aligns the pricing of the XaaS offer with the strategy of the company.
- Minimizes the risk that the pricing of the XaaS offer will be misaligned with the attributes of the offer.
- Creates a documented XaaS pricing table.

Players (who runs this play?): Core players: product development, product marketing, and services marketing. Review team: CEO, CFO, sales and services leadership.

In Chapter 7, we continue the journey around the iron triangle of the XaaS playbook by double-clicking on this simple question: "So, how are we going to sell and deliver this offer?"

7 | XaaS Customer Engagement Models

When working on your XaaS strategy, you need to understand the journey you are undertaking with your customers—and the journey with a XaaS offer is very different from selling and delivering technology as an asset (Figure 7.1). You will be operating much closer to your customers. You will have many more touch points per year. You are going to have new plays—even new organizations that must work together seamlessly. In short, you will need a new engagement model aimed at growing customers successfully.

Why is this necessary? Well, if you are selling technology as an asset, meaning you are transferring ownership of the asset to the customer and getting paid up front, the critical milestone in your customer engagement model is convincing the customer to buy the asset. After all, once they make that decision, the asset is theirs and they assume the responsibility to leverage it. They don't just pay up front for the asset; they also pay for the associated implementation services. The revenue and the margin on the transaction are guaranteed for the supplier whether the customer gets much value or not. It's no wonder that the entire company celebrates when sales lands a big asset deal!

If you are selling technology as a service, the number of critical milestones on the revenue journey increases, and the

The XaaS Journey

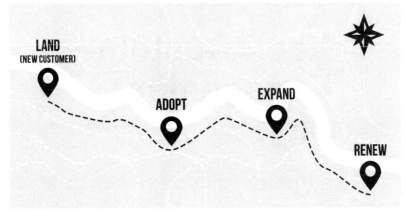

FIGURE 7.1 The XaaS Journey

trajectory changes shape. The spending level of the customer often starts off low and must build and build if the deal is to become profitable. If anywhere along the journey the customer does not like or use a service, they may stop using it and the revenue may stop flowing. To prevent that killer churn, new critical milestones must be achieved to ensure adoption, expansion, and renewals.

Thus, we divide this new XaaS customer engagement model into the four sequential phases called the LAER model that we introduced in Chapter 2:

- **Land.** All the sales and marketing activities required to land the first sale of a solution to a new customer, and the initial implementation of that solution.
- **Adopt.** All the activities involved in making sure the customer is successfully adopting and expanding their use of the solution.
- **Expand.** All the activities required to cost-effectively help current customers expand their spending as usage increases, including both cross-selling and upselling.

- **Renew.** All the activities required to ensure the customer renews their contract(s).

Traditional technology companies rightly focused on excelling at landing new customers and renewing maintenance contracts. However, they historically invested very little in activities designed to help customers systematically adopt technology capabilities. That responsibility was left mostly to the customer. Also, these companies were not usually optimized to cost-effectively identify and close the kinds of small-to-moderate opportunities for account expansion (more users and transactions, for example) that are essential to success in XaaS. Instead, tech companies focused on opportunities for large technology refreshes within the existing installed base. The traditional strengths that are the focus areas of asset-based supplier sales models are shown in Figure 7.2.

In these models, foregoing significant attention and investment in the adopt and expand aspects of the customer life cycle was an acceptable decision. However, being inattentive to adoption and expansion can crush the profitability of your XaaS business model.

The XaaS Revenue Waterfall

To begin our discussion on the logic behind this customer engagement model, we need to take a look at how revenue is

XaaS Customer Engagement Model

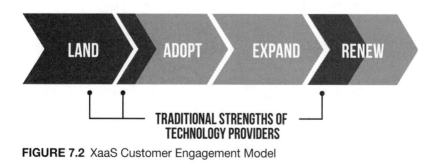

FIGURE 7.2 XaaS Customer Engagement Model

generated—and lost—in a typical XaaS company. Compared to traditional tech revenue models, the revenue optimization process is more complex in XaaS. Once customers are landed onto a new XaaS offer, the following revenue life cycle unfolds:

1. **Total Available Revenue to Renew.** In any given month (or quarter, or year), a specified number of customers are eligible to renew (or simply continue) their existing contracts. The value of all those customers' current spend levels is our starting point. It is expressed as a dollar amount, which equals, by definition, a current value of 100%.

2. **Churn Rate.** Some of these customers may decide to abandon the offer due to poor adoption or in favor of a competitor.

3. **Down-Sell Rate.** Some of these customers may negotiate a reduction in price or they may determine they need less of your offer. In either case, the customer renews but pays less than they did the previous year.

4. **Retention Rate.** This is the amount of current customer spending you are able to retain. (The total available renewable revenue you were able to achieve after any churn or down-sell [Item 1 minus Items 2 and 3]).

5. **Upsell Rate.** On the upside, some customers may decide they need more of your offer (more users on the platform, more features enabled, and so forth). These customers not only renew, but they also spend more with you for the same offer.

6. **Cross-Sell Rate.** You may successfully introduce some existing customers to other offers in your portfolio.

7. **Expansion Rate.** This is the total rate you are expanding—the spending of retained customers (Item 6 plus Item 7).

8. **Renewal Bookings Rate.** Add the retention rate (Item 4) and the expansion rate (Item 7). This is the net growth (or decline) of all renewal bookings. This can also be expressed as CVRR (contract value retention rate).

Figure 7.3 documents these break points in XaaS revenue streams. By moving left to right in the diagram, it becomes clear that simply landing a customer on a platform is not enough. For revenues to grow, the XaaS provider must be adept at driving adoption to improve renewal rates as well as identifying opportunities for account expansion. This is known as the XaaS revenue waterfall.

Revenue waterfall math is critical to the overall growth of the XaaS supplier. Because XaaS customers pay over time and payment can fluctuate, making an actual profit on that one customer is dependent upon continued spending over an extended period. Ideally, this spending level is also regularly increasing as adoption increases and adjacent offers are added. In many enterprise XaaS deals where land-selling costs are high and implementation costs are only partially subsidized by the customer, achieving profitability on the deal may not take place for years. So, it only goes to reason that playing an active role in helping the customer succeed is in your self-interest. The simple fact is that XaaS customer engagement models are different and must align closely

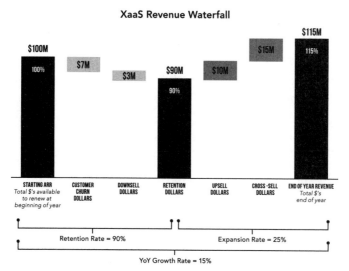

FIGURE 7.3 XaaS Revenue Waterfall

to these objectives. It's worth it to fund new touch points—even new organizations—if they materially improve your waterfall math. Even when customers sign up for a long-term commitment in exchange for more favorable pricing, there are still many moving parts to that deal. Some unhappy customers will "go to the mat" to get out of those contracts, and they frequently succeed. Often, they can dial down or simply never go beyond their minimum commitment. In all these cases, revenue waterfall math is impacted.

How much is at stake over subscription revenue waterfall math? Even more specifically, how costly is churn? Let's start with a bold statement. Assuming you have some product-market fit for your offer, churn is probably the most likely reason for your business to fail. Product-market fit means that customers are interested in your product, and it can do something of value for them. That's great. But if you are experiencing a high degree of churn for any reason, your economics break. That's because every single customer that churns has to be replaced just to stay where you are. Every dollar of revenue from that customer has to be earned from some new customer before your top line can grow. And the insidious thing is that the bigger you are, the greater the threat of churn. Why? It's simple math. A company with 20% churn and 1,000 customers has to replace 200 customers just to stay flat. They have to spend enough sales and marketing dollars to do that before they can grow. When that company grows to 10,000 customers, it has to replace 2,000 customers. Sure, you could grow your sales and marketing expenses linearly with revenue growth, but no one has that in their GAAP profit scenario. Just ask your vice president of sales how she would feel about having to replace 20% of the entire customer base each year before the company could even begin to start growing! The analogy that is often used is that of trying to fill a bucket with water when the bucket is full of holes.

We think churn of more than 20% per year will ultimately prove fatal. To be a profitable enterprise XaaS provider, we think churn really needs to be kept to single digits, with top performers experiencing less than 5% per year. Figure 7.4 describes the challenge in another way, in this case, time to profitability. Joel York, author of the blog *Chaotic Flow*,[1] shows how churn can significantly delay the profit horizon moment. That means more losses

Achieve SaaS Profitability with Churn

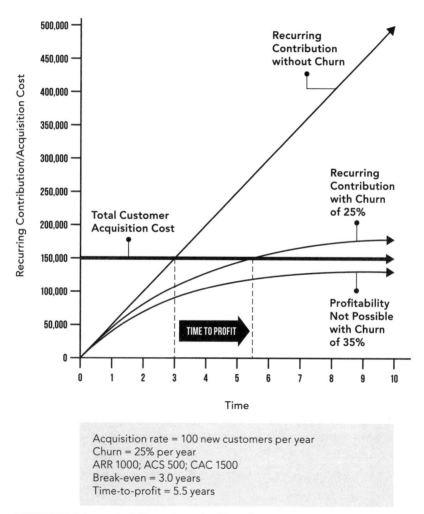

Acquisition rate = 100 new customers per year
Churn = 25% per year
ARR 1000; ACS 500; CAC 1500
Break-even = 3.0 years
Time-to-profit = 5.5 years

FIGURE 7.4 Impact of Churn from the Blog *Chaotic Flow* by Joel York

and greater cash burn. Although we think Mr. York's acceptable churn levels will prove more lenient than what you will want for your XaaS offer, his analysis is spot on.

So what causes churn? Poor product-market fit has to be at the top of the list. However, we assume in this book that you have proven that your core subscription offer has some degree of that. So, what are the other causes? Much detailed research and opinion have been offered on the causes of churn, but you can summarize them all into a few buckets:

- The competition is better than you are.
- You messed up.
- Wrong customer or a change at the customer.
- Lack of adoption.

This book is full of ideas to help outthink the competition far beyond features. As for messing up, there are a million ways to accomplish that, including billing problems, data breaches, bad customer service, and overselling. This book isn't about operational excellence in those areas. Just avoid them, and if you do have a problem, apologize, promise to fix it, fix it, tell them you fixed it, apologize again, and then move on to regaining their trust. Mess-ups as a cause of churn are universal. You could have these problems in any industry, so we won't spend much time on them here. And, if you sold your product to a customer who isn't a good fit, or sales overpromised what the product can deliver, you will probably churn those buyers. You fix that with good market segmentation and sales management.

But that last one—lack of adoption—is the unique killer in XaaS! It's unique in both its impact on churn and on your ability to solve for the problem. Poor adoption not only has negative short-term impacts, but it can even be a brand killer if it happens to enough customers and they get vocal about it. On the other hand, the positive impact of having high adoption is HUGE! It not only juices your revenue waterfall, but it also cuts your sales costs, builds your economic moats, and powers your social marketing. It's so big, in fact, that we are going to devote much of this chapter to the science of driving adoption at scale.

A Two-Sided Coin

With an understanding of revenue waterfall math and how important adoption is to underpinning expansion and renewal, let's get ready to begin our customer journey. But wait! The journey has two names. It's one coin but has two different sides (Figure 7.5):

- **Supplier Perspective.** Providers of XaaS solutions are motivated to drive adoption and expansion to reduce churn and grow customer spending systematically.
- **Customer Perspective.** Customers of XaaS solutions are motivated to drive adoption so that their company realizes the full potential financial impact of leveraging the technology within their business environment.

The Two Sides of the Coin

SUPPLIER SUCCESS

How much revenue can I get from each customer?

CUSTOMER OUTCOMES

How much business value can I generate for each customer?

FIGURE 7.5 The Two Sides of the Coin

Not only are the perspectives somewhat different, but the language and tactics we will use are also different.

Figure 7.6 illustrates both perspectives. LAER is the internal perspective and process you will use to maximize customer spending. However, you are not going to walk into one of your customers and tell them you want to land and expand them! That's your goal, not theirs. The customer wants better business outcomes. Making that happen involves four stages. We call them PIMO:

LAER and PIMO

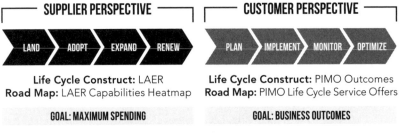

FIGURE 7.6 LAER and PIMO Business Outcomes

- **Plan.** All the pre-sales discussions, strategies, and agreements necessary to assure the buyer(s) that the involved parties have a considered plan to achieve the outcome that is promised by the solution.

- **Implement.** All the traditional technical and human implementation activities designed to stand up the solution as well as prepare the users and their processes.

- **Monitor.** The ongoing activities of the customer and the supplier to determine whether the solution is leading to the designated business outcome objectives. This should be a detailed data- and analytics-driven activity, and not just a feeling of satisfaction.

- **Optimize.** The interventions that optimize the outcome. That could include troubleshooting and correcting technical or adoption problems. It also includes identifying what is working well and taking steps to expand that success.

We will discuss PIMO in more detail later in this chapter. For now, just keep in mind that there are both your internal provider perspective and a customer perspective with slightly different objectives and tactics. We will approach these one at a time, starting with the internal perspective. Both of these approaches are designed to move customers rapidly across the stages of technology adoption, resulting in high renewal and expansion likelihood.

An Inside Look at LAER

Before we flash a picture of TSIA's LAER model and begin to unpack its components, we want to share a quick anecdote. While hosting a workshop on the LAER model with one company, we identified no less than 11 separate groups within the company that claimed they were working to drive customer adoption. That is commitment! But what were these 11 groups doing to actually drive customer adoption? No one was sure or could agree. This gets us to the crux of why you need a new customer engagement model: Everyone buys into the premise that customer adoption, expansion, and renewal are key steps to making XaaS offers successful. Yet, companies—both traditional and XaaS—often have little science or structure on how these can be systematically and organizationally optimized.

Detailed below and shown in Figure 7.7 is a high-level LAER framework that your company can customize and use to drive initiatives designed to build the customer engagement model for XaaS.

FIGURE 7.7 TSIA LAER—An Operating Framework

It's a fairly complex picture. So, we'll break it down by examining the new journey needed to take our customers from left to right in order to maximize their success and their spending. Let's take them on the road from no adoption to effective adoption.

Landing New Customers

One thing is still true in XaaS: You still have to land the deal. Now, just like in traditional tech, sometimes the XaaS deal is huge. It involves thousands of users, and it locks the customer in a multi-year contract. Those are great! But sometimes the initial XaaS deal is small—very small. It's a small pilot project or, in the extreme, only a single user.

In Chapter 3, we laid out seven tactics that we have seen in play in XaaS companies that you could experiment with to improve the results and/or lower the cost of your new customer land activities:

- Marketing-led selling
- Remote selling models
- Process-driven selling
- Land-only sales teams
- Automated sales
- Blended sales and service models
- Outcome-based selling

All seven of these are different from the traditional field sales model in some way. At TSIA, we are just beginning to explore the best practices of landing service deals of all types. We promise to put more meat on the bones of these and other tactics soon. But, the one thing we can say right now is that landing the deal in XaaS, as important as it is, is just the beginning of your customer engagement model. That's because XaaS is a service and, in the world of services, you get paid as you deliver, for what you deliver. The more you deliver, the more you get paid. As we just mentioned, many—maybe even most—initial deals are small pilots by a new customer or the trial of one or more individual users. They in themselves are not very financially rewarding. However, what they are is an opportunity to serve many users or high volumes of transactions. So, although land is still critically important, the real differences in your customer engagement model begin to appear now.

Disecting Adoption

As we have studied this challenge across multiple companies, we believe the following questions need to be clearly answered before your company can systematically drive customer adoption:

- What does good customer adoption look like?
- How do you assess the adoption rate of customers?
- Who is responsible for driving customer adoption?
- What practices accelerate customer adoption?
- How do you assess the ROI for investing in activities designed to drive customer adoption?

We will address most of these questions in this chapter. First, let's define three stages of technology adoption:

- **Low Adoption.** Customers are not using the technology, or a low percentage of potential users are leveraging the technology, or active users are underutilizing many of the capabilities of the technology.
- **High Adoption.** A high percentage of potential users are actually leveraging the technology. Many users are accessing at least some of the capabilities of the technology.
- **Effective Adoption.** Not only are a high percentage of potential users leveraging the technology, but they also are using the technology in the most efficient and effective ways possible. They are caught up in the sticky parts of the application.

To assess end-user adoption of a technology, technology providers can track two attributes to determine whether customers are moving from low to high adoption:

- **Who.** Who is logging on to use the technology? Are a high percentage of potential users actually logging on?
- **Quantity.** Are end users logging on frequently? How much are they using it?

But really, both you and your customers should be much more interested in moving from high adoption to effective adoption. Four attributes are helpful here:

- **Stickiness.** Is the customer leveraging features that lead to unique value and renewal? These are features proven to help customers improve productivity. Ideally, these are features unique to your technology.
- **Data Quality.** The ISO 9000 standards define data quality as "the degree to which a set of characteristics of data fulfills requirements. Characteristics are, e.g., completeness, validity, accuracy, and consistency." The higher data quality the customer is maintaining within the technology platform, the greater business value they will extract from the platform.
- **Efficiency.** Is the customer minimizing the time and expense associated with leveraging the technology? Is the customer completing tasks in a reasonable time frame compared to how long it takes other customers to complete similar tasks? Is the customer using more or fewer resources to execute tasks related to the technology?
- **Outcomes.** Finally, are the activities being performed with the technology impacting critical performance metrics for the customer?

Figure 7.8 shows all six attributes. Moving from assessing LOW versus HIGH to assessing EFFECTIVENESS should be part of

The Six Attributes of Adoption

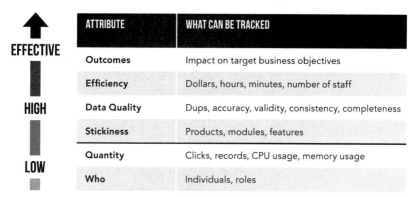

	ATTRIBUTE	WHAT CAN BE TRACKED
EFFECTIVE	Outcomes	Impact on target business objectives
	Efficiency	Dollars, hours, minutes, number of staff
HIGH	Data Quality	Dups, accuracy, validity, consistency, completeness
	Stickiness	Products, modules, features
	Quantity	Clicks, records, CPU usage, memory usage
LOW	Who	Individuals, roles

FIGURE 7.8 Six Attributes of Adoption

your customer data model strategy. You will need to be able to collect and analyze this data from each of your XaaS customers.

You can apply these six attributes to help assess the growing list of adoption tools and dashboards being offered by XaaS providers today. Here are a few industry examples:

- **Salesforce Adoption Dashboards.** Go to the Salesforce AppExchange and search for "adoption." Several apps appear. All are designed to provide insights on who is logging in to Salesforce, how often they are logging in (quantity), and what features they are using (stickiness). Most of these dashboards are designed to assess whether users are moving from low to high adoption. Some of these dashboards provide insights on data quality and effective usage of features.

- **Benchmarking by Zendesk.** Zendesk is a SaaS provider of IT help-desk software. As a service to customers, Zendesk provides various benchmarking reports. Zendesk customers can receive feedback on how they compare on critical operational metrics, such as customer satisfaction ratings, response time, and number of cases handled per staff. This benchmark data is designed to help Zendesk customers understand whether or not they are running effective IT help desks. If they are lagging on key performance metrics, the company will want to assess how IT help-desk staff can better adopt features of Zendesk to improve performance.

- **Amazon's Trusted Advisor Dashboard.** This is a tool driven by automated analytics that provides AWS customers with feedback on how to improve their adoption of AWS offers to maximize four areas of IT operations: cost optimization, security, fault tolerance, and performance improvement. The tool monitors more than 40 checkpoints and provides specific recommendations on how to implement improvements.

Figure 7.9 summarizes how these different monitoring examples provide different levels of insight related to the six levels of adoption.

If you are creating a dashboard to help customers with adoption, our recommendation is to assess your data streams in the dashboard against these six levels of adoption. The higher in the

Assessing Adoption Insights

ATTRIBUTE	CRM ADOPTION DASHBOARD	ZENDESK BENCHMARKING	AWS TRUSTED ADVISOR
Outcomes		IT help-desk satisfaction rating	Security risks
Efficiency		Tickets per staff, response time	Total monthly costs
Data Quality	Number of dups		Accounts, contacts, opportunities
Stickiness	Standard feature, custom features		
Quantity	Logins, number of contacts, number of opportunities, number of case records	Number of tickets in the system	Which AWS services, total usage (CPU, storage)
Who	Individuals, roles		

FIGURE 7.9 Assessing Adoption Insights

stack the insights from your dashboard move, the more business value it will provide you and your customers.

Although some technology providers are rapidly improving their ability to help customers along the adoption journey, the overall industry is still in the early days of successfully assessing end-user adoption. TSIA conducts an annual survey that explores what consumption data technology providers are actually tracking and leveraging. Here are some telling facts from our most recent survey:

- Sixty percent of survey respondents are tracking the total volume of logins to an application once it is purchased.

- However, only 43% of survey respondents track how many unique users logged in to an application once the customer purchased it. So, it is difficult to assess how widely an application is being adopted within a customer account if there is no sense of how many unique users are engaged.

- Sadly, only 14% of survey respondents have insight on what features are being used by specific users. This means it is very difficult for many technology providers to help customers move from low to effective adoption with such limited insight into what customers are actually using what features.[2]

As technology providers become more sophisticated with their ability to track adoption, providers are able to apply analytics to the adoption data. We observe that these analytical models move through a natural progression. First, companies start collecting consumption data to better *describe* what customers are actually doing. Then, the consumption data can be used to *predict* customer renewal and expansion. Ultimately, the consumption data can be used to understand if the customer is on track to achieve targeted business *outcomes*. Figure 7.10 provides the summary of our framework for the data streams required to effectively assess adoption.

Adoption Assessment Framework

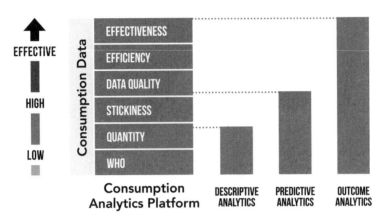

FIGURE 7.10 Adoption Assessment Framework

Analytics and adoption are concepts that go hand in hand in the world of XaaS. XaaS platforms have the ability to create a plethora of data streams. Analytics can be applied to these data streams to unlock business value for both the provider (renewal) and the customer (effective adoption). Of course, customers can be wary of vendors that want to capture and assess usage data. How do technology providers successfully respond to this concern? It's by linking usage analysis to business impact on the customer. If a technology provider simply asks to monitor usage activity, they will most likely be denied. If a technology provider ties the request to specific productivity improvements, the customer is much more willing to acquiesce.

The bottom line of this section is simple: It is hard to effectively drive customer adoption if you have no framework for assessing levels of adoption. Once you have defined an adoption framework, you can begin the journey of securing the data required to inform the framework. You will know what questions to ask of your data. As the data gets better, the analytics surrounding the data get more sophisticated and robust.

Who Drives Adoption, Expansion, and Renewal?

For many companies that are moving from traditional sales models to LAER, or for new XaaS companies that are trying to build a state-of-the-art customer engagement model, determining who does what, and where, is going to be a source of great internal debate. Before we try to answer those questions, let us consider the skills required to drive customer adoption.

To engage with a customer in the journey of effective adoption, expansion, and renewal, a team member will need some or all of the following skills:

- **Product/Technical Expertise.** Understands how the offer works.

- **Soft Service Skills.** Effectively works with customers to help them adopt.

- **Process Expertise.** Understands the critical processes that are common across many customers.

- **Vertical Industry Expertise.** Understands the language and challenges of a specific industry or market segment.

- **Opportunity Recognition Skills.** Can discern an opportunity to accelerate value to the customer, including adding additional products and services.

Figure 7.11 maps these skills against the levels of low, high, and effective adoption. Technical and soft service skills can help enable high adoption, but process and vertical industry expertise will more likely be skills required to help a customer truly achieve best-in-class, effective adoption.

So, who has all these required skills? The truth is not many of your current staff. Some excel at certain skill sets, but few are solid in them all. TSIA conducts annual compensation surveys for both sales- and service-related roles. As part of that research, we document job titles and descriptions used in the industry. Just ask us to see the list. There are no less than 27 customer-facing

Skills Required for Adoption

	SKILL	DESCRIPTION
EFFECTIVE	Opportunity Recognition Skills	Can discern an opportunity to accelerate value to the customer, including adding additional products and services.
HIGH	Vertical Industry Expertise	Understand the language and challenges of a specific industry or market segment.
	Process Expertise	Understand critical processes that are common across many customers.
LOW	Soft Service Skills	Can effectively work with customers to help them adopt.
	Technical Expertise	Understand how to offer work.

TABLE 7.11 Skills Required for Adoption

roles that are common in the technology industry. It's no wonder that customers get confused! Across all of these roles, where does technical, service, process, sales, and vertical expertise live? These distinct skill areas are probably sprinkled across the company. Often, deep vertical expertise does not exist in any of the roles. Service people are never told they need to recognize sales opportunities. Current positions are usually weighted toward managing technical complexity, not business process complexity. That all has to change.

Who *should* be chartered to drive adoption? Who is best positioned to take a customer on the journey from low to effective adoption? At this point in time, we have a two-part answer to that question.

First, we can report what technology companies have done so far. In 2015, we conducted a survey that asked technology companies to map customer-facing roles against the LAER life cycle. For each customer-facing role, respondents identified whether the role had any responsibilities for adoption. Based on the survey, we know that there are only two roles of the 27 that are regularly given the responsibility to drive customer adoption activities: customer success manager and technical account manager.

The role of customer success manager (CSM) is a relatively new one in the traditional tech industry, but it is already a mainstay in XaaS. This role is often given explicit responsibility for helping customers successfully adopt technology over time. Technical account managers (TAMs) have been around for years. These are virtual or on-site resources dedicated to specific customers. Traditionally, they have been targeted at providing comprehensive technical support but may engage in some adoption activity. Often, the customer funds the TAM role. There is no doubt that the CSM role is the dominant and fastest-growing alternative, but TAMs may offer traditional companies who do not yet have a customer success function to accelerate adoption for their largest customers.

For the second part of the answer, we can comment on where we think the puck will move regarding adoption responsibilities.

The Customer Growth Team

There is no question that sands are shifting between traditional sales and service roles. The lines are blurring, and we think that is OK. We are all part of a customer growth team. Adoption will certainly be the top focus for the customer success team, aided by lots of attention from R&D. This frees up field sales resources such as account executives, product specialists, and sales engineers to be better deployed toward landing new customers or doing big expand deals. But customer success is not enough.

Service- and product-related roles such as TAMs, client engagement managers, and product adoption specialists will also have responsibility to drive customer adoption. So will traditional service roles such as technical consultants, technical instructors, and technical support specialists, who will also need to diversify their skill sets so they can better assist customers through the adoption journey. Adoption will not be the domain of one group or one role—adoption will be the charter of every role that touches the customer before or after the initial sale. To say it another way, if you are thinking that the only organization that has responsibility for driving adoption is your customer success team, we would suggest you reconsider.

Figure 7.12 updates the adoption framework by adding the concept of customer growth roles being responsible for leveraging adoption data to drive adopt, expand, renew (AER) activities.

We believe that although customer success will own the primary responsibility for monitoring adoption and running the plays that promote it, we think it's a responsibility that will be shared across all traditional services lines like customer support and field services. We also think there will need to be new consultative offers around the concept of outcome engineering that are likely to be delivered by the professional services organization. Outcome engineering (OE) is a new concept that TSIA is advancing. In essence, OE is about making sure that all of the prerequisites to high customer success are present at a single customer. As we will discuss shortly, this means that you know what the prerequisites are because you have studied the science of success for your

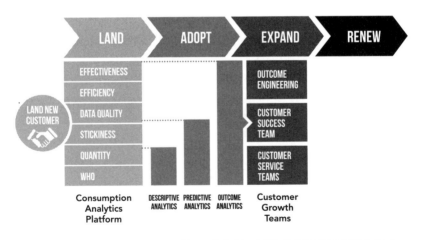

FIGURE 7.12 Customer Growth Teams

XaaS offer. You know what separates top-performing customers from average customers both in your terms and in the business outcome terms meaningful to them. And you have the ability to assess and remedy the situation at individual customers to ensure that the critical success factors are in place and working well. Because it's project-based work, it seems likely it will be housed in professional services.

The point is that it's going to take a village to drive high adoption but, as we have said many times, it is incredibly powerful to fuel your XaaS business.

So, let's switch to the dicey subject of where the customer success team should report. Looking out at the industry, we see three patterns for how companies are situating customer success inside the company:

- Customer success is a service function.
- Customer success is a sales function.
- Customer success is an independent function reporting directly to the CEO/COO/CCO/CRO.

In some ways, it should be no contest. Customer success motions are more like service motions than anything else. So, why the debate? It's simple. Most companies are fearful that services management and staff can't be relied on to spot sales opportunities or meet expansion quotas. No one wants to say that out loud, but it's a common concern and hardly unfounded. Many service executives have traditionally bristled at the thought of having their teams be even tangentially involved in selling. In their minds, that would break the holy vow around being the unadulterated trusted advisor. As we are already on record as saying, we think that's a false conclusion. We would like to stress that generating expansion and renewal dollars should be a process—not a heroic event. If done correctly, it is in the best interest of the customer. It is helping, not selling. We think the organizational debate is highly secondary to the skills debate. If the processes, data, and skills are there, then who cares where the function reports? Ultimately, we think most companies will settle on customer success being part of services, which is where most of the other customer-facing touch points reside that help the customer through their experience of succeeding with the offer.

Where most employees in success and service roles need help is on opportunity recognition. It is this skill weakness that is wreaking havoc on the organizational decisions regarding the customer success function. If that could be fixed and opportunities could be reliably identified and handed off to sales, then the fear might be abated. However, based on what we have seen so far, the fear is legitimate. Now the question is, will services management learn to introduce opportunity identification and sales skills into their workforce without violating the trusted advisor status? It needs to happen soon; otherwise, customer success organizations will find themselves in the unfortunate scenario where the more revenue they own, the more worried the senior leaders are about them carrying such a huge number, and the more likely they are to put it under sales. The same holds true for traditional service functions. How many sales opportunities flash right before the eyeballs of a field service technician? What about a professional services engagement team? And, who can count how many discussions customer support has where the best answer to the customer's issue is to add products or services? It's up to you to get them the training they need. We simply need more diverse skills in the customer growth team of the future than we did in our traditional technical service teams.

However, the most important point is this: Your LAER processes and analytics can surface 80% of the expansion opportunities and renewal threats. You definitely want the opportunity recognition skills to catch the other 20%, but if you run the right plays and collect the right data about each customer, you will be delighted with your customer engagement model. You will have a customer growth team, and you will have a process that you can rely on to achieve great results for you and your customers.

Plays to Drive Adoption

We are now ready to talk about some of the tactics you can use to make LAER work. As we just said, effective plays can do amazing things to optimize expansion and renewal. TSIA published a Service Insight titled "Defining the Customer Engagement Life Cycle."[3] The paper documented a map of the key capabilities and practices that must be in place to manage a customer throughout the entire life cycle of adopt, expand, and renew. Within these capabilities, there are three classes of practices related to driving adoption:

- **Enabling Practices.** Practices designed to motivate and enable the customer to use the technology.

- **Monitoring Practices.** Practices designed to understand how the customer is actually adopting the technology.

- **Intervention Practices.** Practices designed to address specific gaps in adoption that have been identified through monitoring or benchmarking.

There are 26 individual capabilities or plays that TSIA has identified so far across these classes. But we suggest you prioritize these 10:

- **Enabling Practices**
  1. Account Segmentation: The act of segmenting customers by their ability to consume specific products and services.
  2. Relationship Mapping: Identifying customer contacts that will be key in driving adoption.
  3. Customer On-Boarding: Effectively starting the adoption and value journey with the customer.

4. Value Visioning: Documenting what business value the customer hopes to achieve with your solution.

5. Benchmarking: Baselining the customer's current performance on key KPIs related to your technology solution and their target business outcomes.

- **Monitoring Practices**

6. Adoption Framework: A documented framework for assessing customer adoption levels.

7. Adoption Monitoring: The process of monitoring customer adoption levels on an ongoing basis.

8. Adoption Analytics: Analyzing customer adoption data to drive customer interventions.

- **Intervention Practices**

9. Predictive Analytics: Analyzing customer data to predict renewal challenges or expansion opportunities.

10. Adoption Playbooks: Documented plays your employees can run with customers to accelerate adoption.

Throughout all the many steps in your customer engagement model, you need a closed loop where actual customer consumption data guides ongoing adoption efforts. What you are really doing is creating a customer data model that underpins your customer engagement model. The adoption framework documented in Figure 7.13 captures the closed loop.

The concept of the outer ring in Figure 7.13 is simple, but profoundly important. Growing customers successfully relies heavily on driving adoption. To drive adoption, you need a customer data model that is full of the current, critical data about the customer and their use of your XaaS offer. That data will be analyzed to determine what action needs to be taken. That means it has to integrate with tools that the actors who own the action use every day. It can't just sit in an analytics tool or, worse, in some data warehouse. It has to work with the customer relationship management (CRM), professional

TSIA Adoption Framework

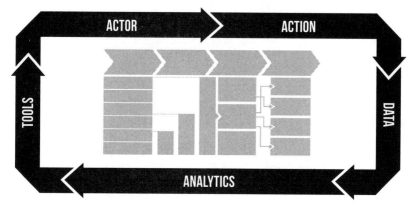

FIGURE 7.13 TSIA Adoption Framework

services automation (PSA), case management, or customer success tools. That's where the actors will learn that an action must be performed on a particular customer. And, those actors are not always the customer success managers. Once the actor has been assigned a specific action, they (generally) follow a well-defined process. Once that action has been taken, the customer's data should change as the results of the action take hold. That change will alter the profile of the customer's health, and analytics will determine the next action. Then, the cycle repeats until you have a top-performing customer.

Early in this chapter, we noted that the journey with your XaaS customers will look a lot different from the journey of traditional tech—that there will be many more touch points for both new and existing organizations. This loop explains how those touch points get triggered.

Expand and Renew

All that effort just to drive adoption? Is it really necessary? What's the payback? Well, the time has arrived. The payback is in customer expansion and incredibly high renewal rates. These are the keys to your revenue waterfall math. They combat the killer Cs. They help build your economic moats. Expansion and renewal rates are lifeblood to a profitable XaaS offer, the raison d'etre of your customer engagement model.

But who does that expanding and renewing? Does the sales rep who landed the account own the expansion and renewal? Or do we have specialized teams designed to do that? Figure 7.14 is our perspective.

We believe two things in this regard. The first is that the leads for expansion can and should come from every touch point we have with the customer. That means expansion leads should flow not just from marketing and customer success, but also from services. Services has far more touch points per year than sales. If helping the customer means that the customer should spend some money, then there is nothing untrustworthy in making that recommendation. Stopping short of that would be like a doctor who didn't recommend a life-saving drug because he didn't want to be accused of upselling.

The second thing that our data supports is that purpose-built sales teams can often outperform general field sales in expansion

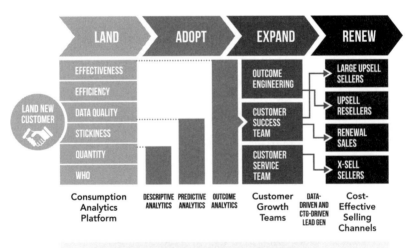

FIGURE 7.14 TSIA LAER—An Operating Framework

and renewal conversion rates and do so at a lower cost of sales. Because they are optimized around their purpose, they are often faster to engage, have more data and tools at their disposal, and are more process driven. These sales channels can lead to the highest margin revenue a XaaS business can secure. Investment firm Pacific Crest conducts an annual survey for privately held SaaS companies. One of the questions they ask is, "How much do you spend on a fully loaded sales and marketing costs basis to acquire $1 of actual cash value (ACV) from a customer?" Figure 7.15 contains data from the 2014 survey. It documents how, on average,

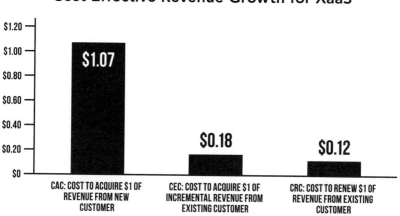

FIGURE 7.15 Cost-Effective Revenue Growth for XaaS

XaaS companies report they are spending more than $1 to land $1 of revenue from a new customer.[4] However, they are spending less than $0.20 to secure $1 of expansion revenue from an existing customer. Also, XaaS companies are spending even less than that to secure $1 of renewal revenue from an existing customer.

Data, staff, and practices that are driving adoption can and should be linked to the successful renewal and expansion of existing customers. Securing higher margin revenue through the customer base will become paramount for XaaS companies when they are eventually tasked to become profitable. Figure 7.16 draws

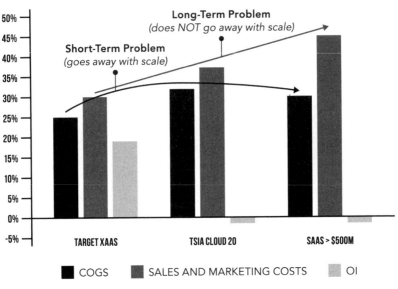

Customer Acquisition Costs for SaaS

FIGURE 7.16 Customer Acquisition Costs for SaaS

data from the TSIA Cloud 20 index, which suggests the XaaS industry still has a long way to go. This analysis shows that SaaS companies are spending a greater percentage of revenues on sales and marketing costs as they grow. This is an unsustainable model. At some point, SaaS companies will need to leverage higher margin renewal and expansion revenues to balance the books. Investing in purpose-built sales capabilities today will prepare XaaS companies for the day profitability becomes the requirement.

To reduce overall sales costs, they need different revenue streams with different sales cost profiles. Their land sales costs will be high. What they need are bigger and bigger expand and renewal revenue streams with dramatically lower associated costs. As the business grows, the balance of revenue growth shifts from the high-priced land stream to the lower-cost channels. Overall, cost of sales begins to decline in this blended mix. However, this only works if you are not relying on your expensive field sales teams to do all the expansion and renewals. So, we think purpose-built renewal and expand specialists make a lot of sense. We have implemented this model at TSIA with great success.

However, there are smart limits to this approach. We recommend segmenting renewal and expansion opportunities according to complexity and growth potential.

The first segment is large renewals. For many customers, their renewal sequence is the best chance to add on more products and services. We definitely believe you should pick a number—a renewal dollar amount that defines your larger transactions—and make sure your sales team is part of the renewals process. But we don't mean in place of the CSM or renewals specialist. It's AND, not OR. You want all the customer success and renewal processes that are proven to drive great results *and* you want the sales team in there trying to upsell.

The second segmentation strategy is to separate expand sales opportunities into three buckets:

- Large cross-sell opportunities
- Large upsell opportunities
- Small and standard upsell/cross-sell opportunities

It just makes sense that significant cross-sell opportunities be treated as new land opportunities and be passed to field sales. By cross-sell, we mean a new and different part of your portfolio, not more of the same offer. Because it's a cross-sell, it means more education and probably even new buying influences. We think you should simply treat it as a new lead and pass it to sales.

Similarly, we think you should pass large upsells of the same offer on to sales. If there was a successful pilot of your XaaS offer at one division of a company and now they are ready to go global, you probably shouldn't be letting a CSM or expand specialist go after that deal and walk it through the procurement cycle. It's going to be a long and complex negotiation with lots of new service requirements. It needs the full attention of your sales account team. So once again, just as you did with renewals, pick a threshold for upsell and invite sales to join the CSM and expand specialist to get the job done.

But, for all those other upsells . . . more user licenses, small expands, information services, and so forth. let the CSM or sales specialist do the deal or let the customer self-serve. They represent the majority of the transactions, but they are not overly complex. That will free your precious and expensive field teams to pursue their highest and best purpose—landing big deals.

LAER Performance Metrics

Another age-old business adage is, "what gets measured gets managed." Selling and delivering XaaS offers break glass. It forces a company to rethink roles and responsibilities. It forces the creation of new processes. And yes, it creates a new set of success metrics.

When selling traditional CapEx deals, technology companies relied on success metrics such as product revenue growth, product margins, average deal size, and maintenance renewal rates. If revenues are growing, deals are large and profitable, and customers are renewing their maintenance contracts, then life is probably pretty good. Of course, other metrics need to be managed, but they were always secondary.

In the world of XaaS, the success metrics shift from a focus on land and renew to a focus on adopt, expand, and renew. Yes, landing new customers is assumed to always be critical. But as the XaaS waterfall demonstrates, landing alone will not guarantee long-term success. In Chapter 8 when we discuss the financial keys to the XaaS business model, we will itemize the overarching financial metrics to manage, such as total cost of sales and monthly recurring revenue. At this step in the planning process, you want to identify the performance metrics that will be used to evaluate effectiveness during each phase of the LAER journey. Figure 7.17 provides another sampling of the list of performance metrics required to measure the performance of your XaaS capabilities and why these metrics are important to track.

Performance Metrics for LAER Phases

LAND

Metric

CAC: Customer Acquisition Costs

Definition

Customer acquisition cost equals sales and marketing (S&M) costs tied specifically to landing new customers.

This cost can be viewed in three different ways:
1. CAC in absolute dollar amount.
2. CAC for every one dollar ($1) in incremental revenue growth from new customers.
3. CAC as a percentage of total company revenues.

Business Insight

How much are we spending to acquire revenue from new customers? Largest expense bucket for most XaaS companies and the one that could sink the financial ship.

Metric

Revenue Growth

Definition

Growth or decline in total annual recurring revenue. Total annual recurring revenue (ARR) equals subscription revenue plus fee-based support/adoption services plus value-added recurring services. Use most recently completed fiscal year or a rolling 12-month period. Use the 12-month value of each active subscription plan (even if the plan has multi-year terms). Include subscription revenue plus fee-based support/adoption services and closely related value-added services (for example, custom report creation). Exclude managed services and project-based revenues. Year-over-year growth/decline rate equals most recent year revenue MINUS year prior revenue DIVIDED BY year prior revenue multiplied by 100.

Business Insight

Obviously, the rate at which your subscription revenues are growing. Recommend using the calculation as stated so growth rates can be benchmarked in apples-to-apple comparison.

Metric

Support/Adoption Services Attach Rate

Definition

Premium support/adoption services attach rate: This metric measures how often fee-based support bundles are sold at point of sale of new subscription plans. It measures the effectiveness of your subscription salespeople to sell fee-based support and adoption services along with new subscription plans. Support attach rate equals number of new subscription plans sold with premium and/or platinum support bundles at point of sale divided by total number of new subscription plans sold within the fiscal year multiplied by 100. Use most recently completed fiscal year or a rolling 12-month period.

Business Insight

This is all about how successfully you are diversifying your revenue streams beyond the core subscription. See Chapter 3 on economic moats.

LAND (CONTINUED)

Metric

Services Margin

Definition

Services margin: gross margin (support and adoption service revenue minus cost to deliver services) DIVIDED BY support and adoption revenue multiplied by 100. Support and adoption service revenue equals expense allocations or revenues carved out of subscription revenues plus fee-based premium and platinum support revenue plus annuity-based value-added service revenue plus standalone adoption service revenue. Exclude project-based revenue and managed services revenue. Cost of services equals direct costs incurred to deliver above services, including direct labor plus subcontracted labor and travel. Exclude corporate allocations. Use most recently completed fiscal year or a rolling 12-month period. Use recognized revenue.

Business Insight

Understand the profitability of the services being wrapped around the technology subscription.

Metric

Subscription Discount Rate

Definition

There are two key metrics, frequency and depth of discounting: (1) What percentage of your subscription plan renewals have a discount off the intended list price for the renewal? This metric is assessing the FREQUENCY of renewal discounting. Use most recently completed fiscal year or a rolling 12-month period. Count the number of subscription plans renewed in the 12-month period that had a discount. (2) What is the average discount off the intended list price on renewals of subscription plans? Average discount equals sum of discount percentages for all subscription plan renewals that have a discount DIVIDED BY total number of subscription plans renewed. Enter percentage. Use most recently completed fiscal year or a rolling 12-month period.

Business Insight

High discounting rates are a warning signal the XaaS is commoditizing.

ADOPT

Metric

Customer Adoption Rating

Definition

Customer adoption rating equals number of "effectively" adopted users divided by total number of users. Effectively adopted means customer achieves threshold score based on the specific adoption framework defined by the company.

Business Insight

Hard number to rate how customers are adopting on average or across different market segments.

Metric

Second-Year Renewal Rate

Definition

For new subscription plans in their first year, how many renew into the second term? With this question, we are assessing how many new customers are retained early in their relationship with your company. Second-term renewal rate equals number of new subscription plans renewed into the second term in this year divided by total number of new subscription plans sold in the prior year multiplied by 100. Start with the new subscription plans that were sold in the year PRIOR to the fiscal year you are benchmarking. How many of these plans renewed into the fiscal year that you are benchmarking? Use most recently completed fiscal year or a rolling 12-month period. Enter percentage.

Business Insight

Did we really deliver value and drive adoption? If not, second-year renewal rates will be low.

Metric

Accounts per Role

Definition

This metric equals number of accounts assigned to customer success manager. Larger accounts may have one dedicated CSM. Smaller accounts may share CSM with hundreds of other accounts.

Business Insight

Recommend this number is benchmarked against industry datasets to determine if coverage models are in line. Too few accounts per CSM equals opportunity for process and technology. Too many accounts per CSM should create discussions on funding.

EXPAND

Metric

CEC: Customer Expansion Costs

Definition

Customer expansion cost equals sales and marketing (S&M) costs tied specifically to generating new incremental revenue growth from existing customers. This cost can be viewed in three different ways:
1. CEC in absolute dollar amount.
2. CEC for every one dollar ($1) in incremental revenue growth from existing customers (ExS).
3. CEC as a percentage of total company revenues.

Business Insight

Expand costs should be much lower than customer acquisition costs. At the same time, this selling motion should be funded and managed.

Metric

Cross-Sell Rate

Definition

Incremental recurring revenues gained in the past 12 months due to cross-selling. Cross-sells include (1) customers who purchased access to additional cloud computing applications or technologies beyond what was renewed in the prior year, (2) managed services that were newly purchased within the year, (3) project-based value-added services. Use most recently completed fiscal year or a rolling 12-month period. Use the 12-month value of each cross-sell that occurred in this fiscal year. Include only the incremental order value. Cross-sell rate equals dollars cross-sold in prior 12 months DIVIDED BY total subscription dollars available to renew at beginning of year multiplied by 100.

Business Insight

Way to assess the effectiveness of CEC spending and how effective company is at selling complimentary offers to existing customers.

Metric

Upsell Rate

Definition

Incremental recurring revenues gained in the past 12 months due to upselling. Upselling includes (1) customers who were upsold to at least one support tier higher than the prior year, e.g., from free basic support to premium support, or from premium support to platinum support, (2) increase in number of users, (3) increase in system compute time utilized, (4) price increases or unwinding of prior discounts, (5) standalone adoption services that were newly purchased within the year and that are not bundled with the support offering, (6) value-added services that are sold separately from the support services that were newly purchased within the year. Use most recently completed fiscal year or a rolling 12-month period. Include only the incremental order value. Upsell rate equals dollars upsold in prior 12 months DIVIDED BY total subscription dollars available to renew at beginning of year multiplied by 100.

Business Insight

Way to assess the effectiveness of CEC spending and how effective company is at moving customers up to higher value-added offers.

RENEW

Metric

Down-Sell Rate

Definition

Erosion in recurring revenues due to down-selling within the year. These customers renewed their subscription plan, but there was a reduction in the amount renewed this year versus the prior year. Examples of down-selling could include (1) applying a new or deeper discount to the renewal, (2) reduction in number of users, (3) reduction in system compute time utilized, (4) removal of products from the subscription plan, (5) down-sell from fee-based support services to free support services, (6) non-renewal of value-added recurring services, etc. Use most recently completed fiscal year or a rolling 12-month period.

Business Insight

Warning sign that customers do not value various features in your offer.

Metric

Contract Renewal Rate

Definition

This metric measures the number of subscription plans renewed during the 12-month period (not the dollar amount). Use most recently completed fiscal year or a rolling 12-month period. Include subscription revenue plus fee-based support/adoption services and closely related value-added services (for example, custom report creation). Exclude project-based revenues. Total recurring revenue (ARR) equals subscription revenue plus fee-based support/adoption services plus value-added recurring services. Contract renewal rate equals number of subscription plans renewed at end of year DIVIDED BY total number of subscription plans available to renew at beginning of year multiplied by 100. Enter percentage.

Business Insight

The classic metric tracked by all XaaS companies. If renewal rate is falling, the business is going in the wrong direction.

Metric

Revenue Renewal Rate

Definition

What were the total recurring revenue dollars renewed with existing customers at the end of the year? Total recurring revenue dollars booked at end of year DIVIDED BY total recurring revenue dollars available to renew at beginning of year. This metric is inclusive of the effects of attrition, down-selling, upselling, and cross-selling.

Business Insight

Customers may have renewed, but after discounting and down-selling, there may be fewer revenue dollars left on the table.

RENEW (CONTINUED)

Metric
CRC: Customer Renewal Costs

Definition
Customer renewal cost equals sales and marketing (S&M) costs tied specifically to renewing existing customers. This cost can be viewed in three different ways:
1. CRC in absolute dollar amount.
2. CRC for every one dollar ($1) in renewal revenue from existing customers.
3. CRC as a percentage of total company revenues.

Business Insight
Renewal costs should be much lower than customer acquisition costs. At the same time, this selling motion should be funded and managed.

FIGURE 7.17 Performance Metrics for LAER Phases

Industry Examples

Here are a few real-world examples from 2015 of XaaS and traditional tech companies who are implementing these LAER concepts.

WebEx

WebEx provides collaboration software. Originally an independent software company, WebEx was acquired by Cisco. In their coverage model, customer success is not involved in landing or renewing the customer. The customer success organization stays squarely focused on helping customers successfully adopt the WebEx platform. Customer success managers have a combination of technical and process skills required to help drive adoption.

In all of these LAER coverage models, it is important to engineer for scalability. Customer success staff resources are finite, not infinite, so they must be applied to where they have the greatest financial impact. Cisco/WebEx does detailed account segmentation to drive the customer success coverage model. Accounts at the top of the segmentation pyramid are assigned a dedicated customer success manager. Accounts farther down the pyramid may have coverage models where one customer success manager is working with 50 customers. Finally, WebEx will leverage technology to enable the smallest customers to self-help.

Infor

Infor has established a customer success team that is responsible for adoption and renewal. To accomplish this, the company established three distinct roles:

- **Account Relationship Manager.** Responsible for the renewals of small to midsized accounts. May be responsible for 100 to 200 individual accounts. Focused on keeping the renewal process on track with these customers.

- **Customer Account Manager.** Responsible for the renewal and adoption in larger accounts. Typically, responsible for 10 accounts. Focused on adoption and utilization assistance. Owns the actual renewal transaction with the customer.

- **Customer Success Manager.** Fee-based account resource a customer can invest in to help drive adoption. Oversees multiple implementation activities across several accounts. Focused on the largest customers.

In this coverage model, it is clear the services organization has primary responsibility for not only adoption but renewing the account as well.

Salesforce

A few years ago, Salesforce went beyond the Infor coverage model. This is the model that was in play when Maria Martinez, the president of Customers for Life at Salesforce, presented at a TSIA conference in 2012. In this model, after a customer is landed onto the Salesforce platform by the sales organization, the Customers for Life organization is responsible for serving, renewing, and expanding that customer. This coverage model has two roles in play that we have seen in the previous examples:

- **Customer Success Manager.** Responsible for helping the customer adopt technology.

- **Renewal Manager.** Responsible for running the renewal process with the customer. Interestingly, this role reports to the customer success manager. This means the customer success manager is ultimately responsible for adoption and renewal, but Salesforce has bifurcated those responsibilities into two distinct positions.

However, this coverage model identifies several new roles that are designed to both support the customer and drive account expansion:

- **Support Specialist.** Classic technical support. This capability is usually carved out of subscription revenues and may live in a different services organization chartered to provide technical support.
- **Account Executive.** Responsible for identifying new opportunities to expand the Salesforce footprint within the account.
- **Solutions Advisor.** Specialists in specific Salesforce solutions. Works with account executives to land new solutions within existing Salesforce customers.

In this coverage model, the traditional sales organization is chartered to find new customers and get them on the platform. Once they are on the platform, the Customer for Life organization is applying resources to adopt, expand, and renew those customers.

Endgame Coverage Models

So companies are clearly experimenting regarding the roles and responsibilities engaged to drive XaaS customers through the LAER life cycle. So, what does the endgame look like? This is in the very early days, so the proven LAER coverage models are still emerging. But, there is a strawman model we would like to put on the table. Envision a customer coverage model that breaks down the traditional roles and responsibilities between sales and services—one that is segmented and optimized based on the LAER life cycle. Note that we are reversing the expand and renew phases in the figures to make it easier to map roles to them. First, there would be a role focused on landing new customers (Figure 7.18).

Then, once the customer is using the XaaS offer, there would be a role focused on helping that customer adopt (Figure 7.19). That role may also be responsible for renewing the customer's

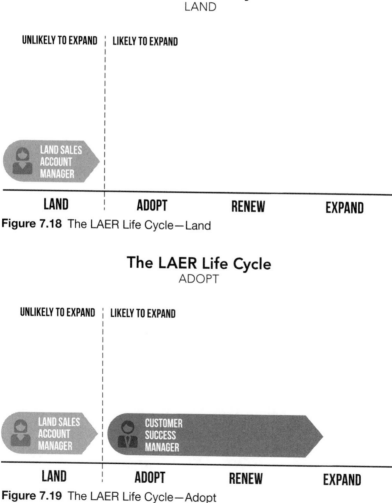

Figure 7.18 The LAER Life Cycle—Land

Figure 7.19 The LAER Life Cycle—Adopt

current XaaS subscription. Why? Because the renewal of highly adopted customers should be a process, not an event. Do you need a salesperson to renew a happy customer?

However, if the customer success manager responsible for adoption and renewal runs into renewal challenges, they may need assistance in landing the value proposition again. A renewal specialist may need to be engaged (Figure 7.20).

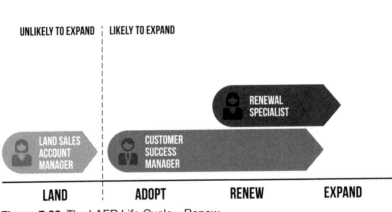

Figure 7.20 The LAER Life Cycle—Renew

Now that we have all these highly adopting customers using our XaaS offer, there is clearly an opportunity for expansion within the install base. We expect our customer success managers to look for these opportunities, but we may want to create some dedicated resources focused on identifying expansion opportunities (Figure 7.21).

Finally, what if an existing customer wants to really up their game and dramatically increase spend on our solutions? This probably requires a hard-core sales resource to be reengaged (Figure 7.22).

So, take a look at Figure 7.22. Does that customer coverage model look anything like what you have in place today? Based on

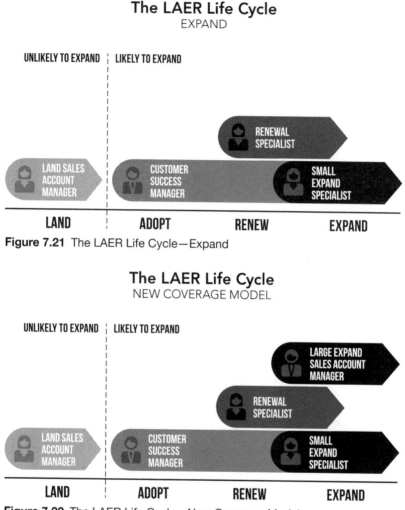

The LAER Life Cycle
EXPAND

UNLIKELY TO EXPAND ┊ LIKELY TO EXPAND

RENEWAL SPECIALIST

LAND SALES ACCOUNT MANAGER

CUSTOMER SUCCESS MANAGER

SMALL EXPAND SPECIALIST

LAND ┊ ADOPT   RENEW   EXPAND

Figure 7.21 The LAER Life Cycle—Expand

The LAER Life Cycle
NEW COVERAGE MODEL

UNLIKELY TO EXPAND ┊ LIKELY TO EXPAND

LARGE EXPAND SALES ACCOUNT MANAGER

RENEWAL SPECIALIST

LAND SALES ACCOUNT MANAGER

CUSTOMER SUCCESS MANAGER

SMALL EXPAND SPECIALIST

LAND ┊ ADOPT   RENEW   EXPAND

Figure 7.22 The LAER Life Cycle—New Coverage Model

our research, the answer is no. But this figure is a perfect example of how the current sales and service roles will be blurring into new coverage models optimized to drive a customer through the LAER life cycle.

LAER Coverage Models and the Profit Horizon

The profit horizon for an offer will heavily influence how a company invests in the different LAER phases.

Future Value Aggregators

Future value aggregators are focused first and foremost on acquiring and retaining units of future value. That is the anchor of their stock valuation. This means companies with this long-term profit horizon will invest heavily in marketing or sales resources to land users/customers. Figure 7.23 documents where this profile will

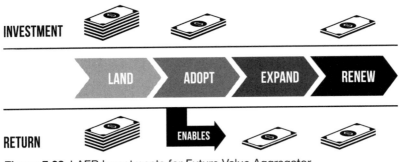

Figure 7.23 LAER Investments for Future Value Aggregator

invest across the LAER model and what returns that investment will generate. For many FVAs, returns are measured in units of future value more than dollars and cents. New customers are costly to acquire but are central to the company's story. Existing customers are cheaper to renew, so they will actually drive a higher financial return for the company; the definition of "return" is unique for this kind of company. The key for future value aggregators is to make sure they put enough investment on the adopt phase of LAER from the very beginning. Investing all of the dollars in land will result in churn numbers that are challenging to overcome.

Mid-Term Wedge Model

Companies that are getting close to running a mid-term wedge model will find themselves moving toward traditional financial measures of "return." They will begin decreasing their land investment as a percentage of revenue, further increasing their investments in adopt, and adding investments in expand and renew (Figure 7.24). This will accelerate revenue in these lower-cost channels and have the desired effect of reducing the overall cost of sales percentage. The returns will be highly profitable renewals and expansion revenue.

LAER Investments for Mid-Term Wedge

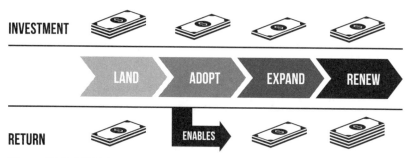

Figure 7.24 LAER Investments for Mid-Term Wedge

Current Profit Maximizer Model

Finally, companies that are focused on making their XaaS offer profitable in the short term will have a very balanced approach to LAER investments (Figure 7.25). Yes, they will invest in sales resources to land new customers. However, they will invest just as

LAER Investments for Current Profit Maximizer

INVESTMENT

LAND | ADOPT | EXPAND | RENEW

RETURN | ENABLES

Figure 7.25 LAER Investments for Current Profit Maximizer

much in making sure they take customers through the journey of adoption, expansion, and renewal. In this approach, the majority of revenue is now coming from renewals and expansion at a low cost of sales. We would expect overall cost of sales and marketing for companies in this mode to be in the 20% to 30% range. For companies that are employing advanced land tactics, it may be even lower.

PIMO

As we mentioned earlier, you can't walk into a customer and say you want to land and expand them. You can't walk in and talk about *your* success metrics. You need to talk to them in a language that they recognize and appreciate. They need to hear about their customer journey to the outcome, not your journey to deal profits. That storyline must be recognizable and, even more importantly, it must be executable by them. We just pointed out that your journey to profits and the customer's journey to the outcome will be highly correlated and synergistic (Figure 7.26). But, nonetheless, the customer perspective requires its own language.

We introduced PIMO in *B4B*,[5] and many companies have adopted this or a similar taxonomy. It is not intellectually

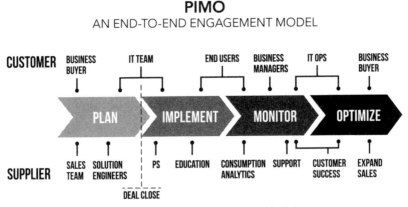

Figure 7.26 PIMO—An End-to-End Engagement Model

groundbreaking. But like LAER, we find that most traditional tech companies limited their conversation mostly to the plan and implement phases. They were light on the monitor and optimize phases. In XaaS, that just doesn't work. You need to have serious customer attention to all four phases if you are going to optimize your internal adopt, expand, and renewal metrics as well as the business outcome metrics you promised to your customer. We read a study conducted in 2009 about how top-performing IT organizations were measuring end-user adoption. Unfortunately, the percentage doing that was abysmal. You can't afford to have customers who have not bought into the key activities that your success science research proves are essential. They need to apply resources and focus along with you to monitor and optimize the business outcome. Far too many IT projects have been poorly implemented and then been largely just maintained in that weak state. You can't afford that for your XaaS offer.

What is most interesting about Figure 7.26 is the huge number of players in the ecosystem of engagement across both the provider and the customer. It gives you a basic idea of how many individual players and organizations may be needed to achieve success. This is the orchestra. Each team needs to play their parts in concert with one another. Although your LAER strategy will guide most of your standard, repeatable activities in the customer engagement model, specific actions will also be needed for specific customers. The PIMO approach includes documenting those unique activities so that your CRM or customer success systems can be informed and people can take action.

It is an interesting question as to which organization on the provider side should own the creation of the PIMO road map on a given deal. Is it sales or sales engineering? Is it professional services? If so, is it a paid engagement or is it free (considered a cost of sales)? What about the customer success organization? Should it be reaching into the pre-sales motions to help prepare the PIMO road map that it will ultimately inherit?

Here are some TSIA perspectives on this evolving topic:

- Every deal should include a PIMO road map. It is central to a successful LAER strategy.
- Your goal should be a highly automated road-map creation process. Ultimately, the success science team will probably own the road map templates and the tools to create them.
- There should be two levels of PIMO:
  - o Free, automated PIMO road maps for SMB, which are automatically applied to deals.
  - o Fee-based, consultative PIMO engagements for large enterprises. They should *want* your consultative expertise. They should be willing to pay for your experience and your success science. They should be willing to put real skin into the creation and execution of the plan. If they aren't wiling to pay, then sales and services marketing have not done their jobs correctly.
- These paid engagements need cross-functional involvement:
  - o Provider side: Sales engineering who knows what the customer is trying to accomplish, professional services who will oversee the implementation, customer success who will own the monitor and optimize phases.
  - o Customer side: Technical owners, business owners.
- Is there a single owner on the provider side?
  - o We think customer success should own the road map ultimately because they will be held accountable for the eventual renewal and expansion performance of the customer. We think they will often leverage the PS organization that has the field resources, tools, and techniques to be able to deliver project-based work that involves on-site activity. If there is no on-site activity, perhaps customer success could own both the creation and delivery.

Our friends at Gainsight tell us they are often surprised at how infrequently customer success organizations are handed a solid PIMO-type road map when a new customer goes live. Often, there is little documentation of the business outcomes that were discussed during the pre-sales process and, even more rare, that a complete PIMO road map is documented and agreed to by both the provider and the customer. That forces the customer to re-state much of what they already told the sales team, a frustrating experience for them. It can also mean there is not much specific commitment on the customer side to implement best practices and a clear measurement of outcome success. In these cases, it is up to the customer success manager to build the monitor and optimize plans on the fly and plead with the customer to commit the resources necessary to execute. That is a problem for both parties.

Just like convincing your customer to use your XaaS offer in the first place, getting them to commit to PIMO means it must be seen as a valuable endeavor. They must understand that it is the powerful combination of your XaaS technology and PIMO that lead to the business outcome they covet. To do that, we have to be conversant in the language of outcomes.

Outcome Chains and Outcome Engineering

Success science, which we will cover next, will help you understand what customer conditions you should seek to replicate so that every customer is a top performer. You will seek to uncover the factors that optimize what you care about (adopt, expand, renew) and what the customer cares about (business outcomes). Your team will have no problem grasping the concepts and language of LAER, but many times providers struggle to speak the language of their customers. They don't really know much about the industry in which their customers operate. They can't draw the connections from their products and services to the specific business outcomes that resonate with buyers. They are far more comfortable talking about their features or technical capabilities than they are about the customer's income statement. That capability gap can put a XaaS deal at risk or fail to convince the customer they should implement some of the practices that other top-performing customers have embraced.

TSIA has partnered with SaaS provider Outcome Chains, Inc., to build a structure for this discussion with the customer. It is a map to answering the simple question: How will your solution translate into a measurable business outcome for the customer? Communicating these outcome chains in the pre-sales process or as part of an outcome engineering service engagement gives a chance for the provider to demonstrate that they understand the science of translating their technology and services offers into tangible business value. This is so critical in XaaS because business buyers, as opposed to the IT department, are making or heavily influencing so many technology decisions today. These business buyers don't care about speeds and feeds; they care about improving business outcomes. Your sales and service teams must be able to speak that language to win their wallet. You want them to be seen as a strategic supplier, not a parts provider. Outcome chains are how companies can answer that towering question from the customer in a consumable fashion.

Basically, business outcomes are achieved by mastering a chain of activities that involve an ecosystem of players and technology. The outcome chain itself is broken into three sections:

- The Outcome(s)
- The Synch
- The Execution

It's relatively easy to imagine what some of the elements in the outcome or execution sections might be. But the tricky thing is how to synch up the execution to the outcome. We believe the answer to that problem lies in the operating KPIs of the customer. That is where the rubber of the execution meets the road of the financial outcomes. They are the leading indicators of financial improvement. Let's go a step further to see what that means. Here is a slightly more detailed view of the parts or rows in the outcome chain:

- The Outcome(s):
  - o Targeted outcome(s)—what the customer can attain.
  - o Financial results—what the financial impact will be.
- The Synch:
  - o Operating KPIs—the critical KPIs that will be targeted for improvement.
- The Execution:
  - o Customer processes—the processes that will be affected and improved.
  - o Capabilities—the new organizational or technical capabilities that will be added.
  - o Products—the technology products that will enable the new capabilities.
  - o Services—the services required to plan, implement, monitor, and optimize the outcome.
  - o Players—all the players required in its execution (customer, provider, third parties).

This simple logic chain, starting at the top with the outcomes and working down, is what business buyers want to understand. They want providers who know these answers—who can teach them what is possible because they know how other companies in their industry have benefited. We have seen it work. This is the business case and the achievement plan rolled into one. It's not so short that it looks like marketing fluff. It's not so long that the customer's eyes roll back in their head. We overheard one CIO who sat through a briefing using this methodology say, "If you had just wanted to show me a demo, I would have sent you to someone in purchasing—but I will have this conversation all day! Can I get a copy of that outcome chain? I need to go talk to our CFO.”

Laying out this complete outcome chain is a great structure to gain the attention of senior business executives and to get to objections far faster. You can now pinpoint where the buyer has concerns or is skeptical. You can see what excites them. After all, you have just built the business case for them! You can build outcome chains for all your top solutions and, if it applies, build them for all the major vertical industries you serve.

Once we have our outcome chain story ready to tell the customer, we can prepare to talk to them about the next steps in their PIMO outcome journey. You can talk about what happens after they have signed up for your XaaS offer . . . how you are going to make this all real. They will have confidence you can deliver that outcome!

Success Science

Central to the success of a solid LAER and PIMO strategy, as well as compelling outcome chains, is a modeling of what a successful customer looks like at various stages of their life cycle and what activities underlie that success. We unveiled the concept in *B4B*, and it is still in its nascent stage. Developing this model, something we call success science, is therefore new to most tech companies, but it's a skill on which companies should be placing a high priority. By studying high-performing customers, XaaS providers can uncover the conditions required for success and what data must be collected to assess the performance of individual customers against the success model. Defining success is itself a non-trivial activity. As an example, let's start with what *should* be a simple question: Who are our top-performing customers? Is it by total spending? Growth rate? Profitability? Customers who use all your latest and greatest offers? The most satisfied and referenceable customers? Just that basic task of defining successful customers may throw your team into an intellectual tizzy. Then consider that your answer is just defining customer success in internal terms, not in the business outcome terminology and metrics that the customers use. Yes, the goals are highly correlated, that is, if the customer is highly successful at achieving their outcome, then the spending of that customer with their XaaS supplier will systematically increase. If that happens at enough customers, then the XaaS supplier becomes successful. That is why we say that the ability to systematically grow customers will become a defining element of a XaaS supplier's engagement model. But if the tactics to achieving both sides of the coin are not surfaced, both you and your customers will be highly inefficient at achieving success. It may seem like rocket science at first, but the best way to think about optimizing a XaaS provider's selfish success is to think somewhat unselfishly about the end customers' success. Grow *their* revenue and your XaaS business revenue will grow. Grow *their* profits and your profits will grow.

This is a critically important chore. First you need to find those high-performing customers; then, you need to get them under a microscope. You need to discover why they are such great performers. Next, you need to figure out how to replicate those best practices for as many customers as possible. That is success science in a nutshell. Somewhat remarkably, many enterprise tech companies have not made a priority of building a deep understanding of the conditions that lead to successful business outcomes from their products. As we have discussed in our previous books, success science is going to become a side-by-side partner to both technical innovations like new features and the business levers like a big sales force. Success science will become the road map for your LAER and PIMO strategies, as well as your outcome chains. As we mentioned in *B4B*, it's the sheet music for the orchestra, and we will continue to stress its importance.

R&D Engagement

One final observation has to be stressed with regard to the tactics of driving adoption, expansion, and renewal: The product R&D organization MUST be a critical enabler. Without the required data streams and analytics coming from the platform, it is difficult to understand whether the customer is effectively adopting the technology or ready to expand. The R&D organization needs to be a close partner when attempting to implement this framework. To improve how R&D is engaged in enabling adoption, we have seen the following tactics employed successfully:

- **Adoption Quarterly Business Review (AQBR).** The service organization that has primary responsibility for driving customer adoption hosts quarterly sessions with product engineering resources to review adoption trends and discuss initiatives to improve adoption.

- **Adoption Portfolio Board.** Services engineering and product engineering representatives serve on a board that is responsible for identifying and prioritizing product enhancements that will help accelerate adoption.

- **R&D Resources Allocated to Service Enablement Features.** In this approach, a specified amount of R&D budget or head count is allocated to product features prioritized by the services organization. The services organization focuses their R&D cycles on features that make it easier for customers to implement, integrate, and use the technology.

The logic may feel intuitively correct enough to get R&D to the table. However, we can actually put more financial support behind the case for these investments. TSIA has been benchmarking members that track various data points related to customer adoption. Also, we have been begun analyzing the impact of leveraging consumption data on the growth of overall services revenue for tech companies. Figures 7.27.1 and 7.27.2 show some of the early results. Companies that collect information on the specific

Capture Feature Purchase Information

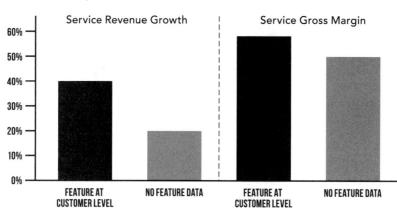

Figure 7.27.1 Impact of Tracking Consumption Data: Capture Feature Purchase

Leverage Purchase Information

Measure Consumption Information

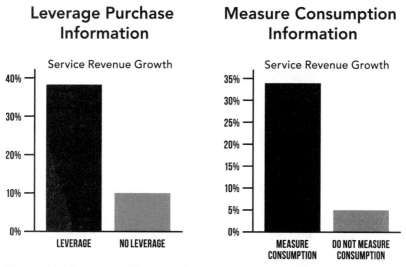

Figure 7.27.2 Impact of Tracking Consumption Data: Leverage Purchase and Measure Consumption Information

features customers have purchased are growing overall service revenues twice as fast and experiencing service margins that are 10 points higher than companies not capturing this data. Companies that actively leverage that information in their customer engagements are growing service revenues 4 times faster than their peers in the industry. Companies measuring consumption information have service revenues growing over 3 times higher than peers not measuring consumption data. Clearly, tracking and leveraging adoption data seems to impact revenues and margins.

In short, we think there is a simple but powerful conclusion that can be reached about XaaS: The definition of a completed product is different. Each product is made up of not just a set of features that the users and administrators experience, but it is also an operations platform. It collects and analyzes data and it has end-user intervention capabilities. It is a vehicle through which marketing can communicate with users. It is a platform to enable all the value-added services we have discussed. It is a self-service selling platform for customers who want to expand. The list goes on and on. We love the tagline coined by entrepreneur and Netscape founder Marc Andreessen that "software is eating the world." In XaaS, the product needs to eat most of the functions of the company. It's the key to keeping costs under control and enabling exciting customer capabilities. It is simply a profoundly different scope than we thought of in traditional product development.

XaaS Playbook Plays

Five high-level plays are identified in this chapter. Each is significant in determining how you will keep customers on the platform and make your XaaS offer profitable in the long term.

Play: Model the XaaS Revenue Waterfall

Objective: Understand and set goals for detailed XaaS revenue components over time.

Benefits:

- Documents critical expectations regarding renewal rates, discounting, and account growth.
- Sets expectations for the importance of investments in adoption, expansion, and renewal.

Players (who runs this play?): Core player: finance. Review team: CEO, sales and services leadership.

Play: Draw Your LAER Diagram

Objective: Identify the analytics, responsibilities, and hand-offs that will make you successful at driving high adoption, expansion, and renewal.

Benefits:

- Identifies what data and analytics are required.

- Documents the organizations and roles that will be involved in each phase of the engagement life cycle.

- Forces the conversation about how each type of renewal and expansion opportunity will be pursued.

Players (who runs this play?): Core players: sales, services, and R&D. Review team: CEO, CFO, sales and services leadership.

Play: Draw Your PIMO Diagram

Objective: Identify the key steps that you will take with the customer to ensure success for both parties.

Benefits:

- Lays out the success cycles from a customer perspective.

- Documents the organizations and roles on both sides that will be involved in each phase of the engagement life cycle.

- Teaches the customer what best practices they must adopt.

Players (who runs this play?): Core players: sales, services, and success science. Review team: CEO, CFO, sales and services leadership.

Play: Whiteboard a Success Science Function

Objective: Conceptualize how a success science organization would look. What would its objectives be? What skills would be in residence? How would you define top-performing customers? How would this function interface with R&D, sales, and services?

Benefits:

- Identifies the skills and data required for success science.
- Documents the organizational relationships to other key functions of the company.
- Defines objectives for the organization.

Players (who runs this play?): Core players: product marketing, sales, services, and R&D. Review team: CEO, CFO, sales and services leadership.

Play: Create an Outcome Chain

Objective: Make sure you can tell the business outcome story that links your XaaS offers and services to tangible value for your customers. Use this to anchor your marketing, sales, and service activities.

Benefits:

- Structures your sales and marketing messages.
- Becomes the IP for your outcome engineering service offer.
- Helps frame in what role(s) channel partners might play.
- Allows you to integrate multiple offers into a single overall solution.
- Is the basis of your ROI model.

Players (who runs this play?): Core players: product marketing, sales, services. Review team: CEO, CFO, sales and services leadership.

8 | The Financial Keys of XaaS

There is no doubt that XaaS offers can generate substantial revenue. After all, it was a proven business model long before the cloud came along. Just look at ADP, D&B, or your cellular service provider—companies that have offered technology as a service for decades. Today's hot cloud companies are also racking up impressive revenue stats. Unlike the dot-com companies of the late 1990s that were virtually all FVAs, the revenues at companies like Salesforce and AWS are big and getting bigger. Figure 8.1 documents the incredible growth in combined top-line revenues for the 14 XaaS companies that have remained in our Cloud 20 index for more than 12 consecutive quarters with a CAGR of 26.6%.

These 14 companies have collectively doubled their revenues in just 3 years, but top-line growth is only one sign of financial success. Bottom-line profitability is the other. This is where XaaS providers have clearly struggled. In the Q4 2015 snapshot, publicly traded XaaS companies tracked in the Cloud 20 were generating an average operating income of −0.8%. Of the 20, 8 reported a loss.[1] In the same snapshot, Salesforce, which has now grown to more than $1.7 billion in quarterly revenues, barely cracked into profitability with a reported GAAP operating income of 2.5%.[2] In the following quarter, announced February 2016, management

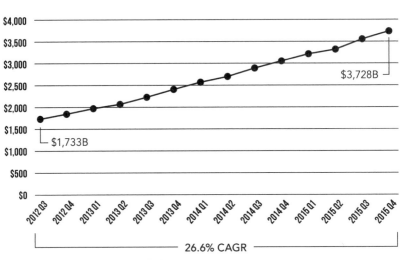

FIGURE 8.1 Growth of XaaS Companies

was predicting its first full-year GAAP break-even. CFO Mark Hawkins commented, "We are certainly excited about continuing on the path of raising profitability. And the top-line [revenue] is happening, too."

It is interesting to contrast Salesforce's financial trajectory with Oracle's historical performance. In 1986, Oracle went public with $55 million in revenue. They were profitable that year. They grew revenues to more than $500 million in 4 years. They were profitable every quarter along the way. In the third quarter of 1990, they reported their first and only loss, and then quickly corrected and continued the trajectory of increased profitability over 2 decades. Today, they are generating an operating profit north of 35%. No enterprise application SaaS company can make a similar claim. Clearly, there is something different in the financial model.

Figure 8.2 compares the operating expenses of present-day SaaS companies in the TSIA Cloud 20 that have revenues over $500 million to the current cost structures and profit performance of the license software companies in the Technology & Services

Cost Category Comparison
of T&S 50 versus Cloud 20 (>500M)

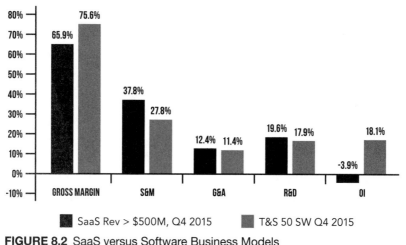

FIGURE 8.2 SaaS versus Software Business Models

50 (T&S 50). As can be seen, these larger SaaS companies are still not profitable on a GAAP basis, and the traditional license companies are exhibiting superior financial performance on all five key indicators. This could lead you to question the logic that SaaS grows into a profitable business model over time. What they do really well is grow revenues. What they do not do so well (so far) is throw off GAAP profits. That is the reality of the XaaS 1.0 financial model.

As we have repeatedly pointed out, SaaS companies in the Cloud 20 are currently spending an astronomical average of 39% of revenues on sales and marketing. In fact, companies like Log-MeIn, Salesforce, and Vocus are all spending more than 50%. This percentage is much higher than the 28% of revenue being spent by license-based software companies on sales and marketing. It is perhaps the largest single cause of low GAAP profits for many SaaS companies.

So, why would any company want to pursue a financial model that can be so prone to losses? Let's explore the pros and cons of XaaS economics.

On the upside, there are lots of things to love. Four reasons in particular jump to the top of the list:

- Customers like the consumption model.
- Investors are keen to reward the revenue growth potential.
- Recurring revenue is a beautiful thing.
- Free cash-flow generation can be very strong.

Let's explore these four benefits of the XaaS economic model in a bit more detail.

From a customer perspective, there is no debate as to whether XaaS concepts like subscription/pay-for-use pricing and simple-to-consume technology have become permanent fixtures on the tech landscape. Both consumers and enterprise tech buyers—particularly buyers and users on the business side of enterprises (as opposed to the IT side)—LOVE these models. XaaS reduces their risks and speeds their results. They can start with small pilots and short-term commitments (monthly, annual, even NO commitment) and grow if and when they succeed. XaaS also allows them to side-step many of the perceived delays and hassles that are associated with large IT-driven projects. They can just sign up and start consuming. And, most importantly, there are some pretty cool XaaS technologies out there . . . some with features and benefits that can only be achieved in the cloud. So let's not spend any time defending XaaS as a permanent alternative to buying technology assets. It is here to stay, and suppliers should learn to love it or risk losing customers.

The second reason that XaaS is a great place for providers to be right now has to do with the incredible valuations currently being bestowed on pure-play XaaS companies by the financial markets.

This part of the story can be frustrating if you are a traditional, asset-based company. That is because tech-stock valuations as of early 2016 are a tale of two formulas. Traditional tech-company stocks are still valued the old-fashioned way, as a multiple of GAAP earnings. But pure-play XaaS company stocks are being priced based on a multiple of revenues driven by the revenue growth rate.

It would have been hard to imagine just a decade ago, but many traditional tech stocks are anchored almost entirely by their profits, not their growth. This is especially true of consistently profitable, divided-yielding tech stocks like Microsoft, CA, Symantec, and Cisco. If these kinds of companies went through an extended period of deteriorating profit, their stock prices would be imperiled. It follows that the management of these businesses must focus each and every quarter on sustaining and growing profits. That's the fish model problem we covered in Chapter 5. Clearly, revenue growth remains very valuable to these companies but NOT at the expense of profits. They often know some growth levers they would like to pull—i.e., significant investments that could lead to more growth but result in lower profits during the investment period—but that trade-off is not one that many of their shareholders are willing to tolerate.

At least until recently, the executives who lead pure-play XaaS companies have found themselves in exactly the opposite situation. It seemed perfectly acceptable to the investors in these companies to not have any GAAP profits as long as they have a great revenue growth rate. For some companies, the measure of growth may not even be of actual revenue. As we have already covered in this book, some FVAs are free to discuss growth rates in terms that may have little or no current economic value, like users, downloads, or page views. Investors are betting that, at some point, those assets will be translated into economic value, but for right now, it is a game of capture, not monetize. This has been particularly true for consumer applications like Pandora or Twitter. But the phenomenon is not exclusive to them. Many B2B XaaS companies today will often lead their financial reviews with user growth statistics. For these companies, management decisions are often made with a different mind-set: Will this investment help our growth rates continue or accelerate? In early 2016, some financial analysts have criticized a few XaaS companies who keep extending their profit horizon or are reporting sales slowdowns. If this noise in the system increases, it will put more pressure on XaaS executives to prove their financial model sooner rather than later. But for now most are still free to pursue growth investments as long as the cash lasts.

Another case for higher sales and marketing spending by SaaS companies in particular can be made by arguing that these companies may have a larger total addressable market (TAM) than traditional companies. That's because cloud-based solutions reduce the number of investments a corporate customer has to make (they don't have to buy more hardware, they pay less for implementation services, and so forth—often things that they purchased from other vendors). That means budget dollars can be aggregated and focused on buying more of the XaaS provider's offer. Also the XaaS company can tap into both IT and departmental budgets. It can derive revenue not only by charging for basic access to the offer but also for actual use. The more the customer uses, the more they pay. That is not the case with most traditional software products. Finally, depending on what the SaaS offer is, the provider may actually be able to expand their TAM by opening up entirely new cloud marketplaces that make users out of people or companies that never would have been able to access a traditional, on-premise software product. Just think about how Apple and Salesforce make money off their market platforms. Arguing that the XaaS TAM is larger helps support the notion that spending more to develop and access it makes sense. The logic is that the XaaS company can ultimately be larger than a traditional competitive counterpart.

So there are two different stock price formulas: one based on profit growth, and one based on revenue growth. The impact of this difference on the ways that these businesses are managed is huge. Traditional tech companies face the daunting challenge of swallowing the fish. What's frustrating for many of them is that they actually have sizable XaaS businesses growing within their four walls, but they simply can't get the markets to value them in the same way that they value the pure-play cloud stocks. That logic would give the management of these businesses a clear path forward. They could grow their SaaS businesses by reinvesting some of the profits from their traditional businesses. They could report them separately. The higher valuation of the SaaS revenues would more than offset the reduction in valuation due to lower profitability. The stock price would remain the same or higher during the transition. Both management and investors would have a straightforward and transparent way to transform the financial model for the XaaS epoch. This is part of the path we recommended in Chapter 5, but we see very few companies doing it effectively.

It is safe to say that running a pure-play XaaS company today is a simpler task than transforming a traditional systems or software company. Investors support and reward their simple message: growth.

The third leg of the XaaS stool that everyone loves is its recurring revenue nature. XaaS is, after all, technology as a *service*, and services are typically purchased as subscriptions the same way cable TV or cellular service is. If you look at the financials of most enterprise XaaS companies, you see two wonderful things: one item on the balance sheet and another item off of it.

Though often priced "by the month," most enterprise XaaS companies have adopted the practice of getting customers onto annual contracts that are billed and paid at the beginning of the contract period. The company then has a liability of actually delivering the service over the life of the contract. In accounting terms, this is known as *deferred revenue*—revenue that has been contracted for, billed, and even paid—but not yet delivered. This figure is recorded as a current liability on a XaaS balance sheet. This liability is balanced by the assets of accounts receivable or cash for these "pre-billed" services. The beauty of deferred revenue is that it is already committed and paid up front. The XaaS company doesn't have to worry about building revenue from zero each month. It has revenue that is already committed, billed, and prepaid. All they have to do is deliver it. That's great.

A second item that is frequently reported by XaaS companies but not carried on the balance sheet is something called "unbilled deferred revenue." Unbilled deferred revenue represents business that is contracted but unbilled and off the balance sheet, meaning that customers are contractually committed to subscribe to the services for future periods. This is true for enterprise XaaS companies like Salesforce and wireless carriers like AT&T. Enterprise XaaS companies will often grant price incentives for their customers to sign multiyear contracts. That means a customer will commit to use the service at a particular minimum volume level for 2- or 3-year periods. In return for that commitment, they will pay a price that is more favorable than similar customers who only sign monthly or annual agreements. In this case, the XaaS company bills in advance for each year of the contract period on the anniversary date of the contract. The first year's revenue is treated as deferred revenue and placed on the balance sheet as described earlier. The future years are tracked as unbilled, deferred revenue but not placed on the balance sheet until they are actually billed.

Why is all of this so important? First of all, deferred and unbilled deferred revenues give visibility and confidence to a company's future financial performance. When Salesforce finished its 2015 fiscal year, it reported $5.4 billion in revenue. It also reported deferred revenue of $3.2 billion and unbilled deferred revenue of $5.7 billion. That means as the company entered its fiscal year 2016 period, it had guaranteed revenue of more than 60% of its previous year. To grow, it just needs to add another 40% from new bookings and non-committed renewals. Anything over that number will represent true incremental growth. So, management and analysts gain confidence that Salesforce will grow strong again, not only this year, where there is a committed revenue baseline of $3.2 billion, but also for the next couple of years, where there are committed customer revenues of another $5.7 billion for the company to draw from. This is supplemented in the XaaS model by highly likely renewals. Even when there are no committed future bookings, high renewal rates assure investors that future revenue growth is extremely likely.

Combining committed and uncommitted renewals, companies like Salesforce and Netflix can head into a future year with the confidence that they just need to build on the 85% to 90% of recurring revenue from last year to achieve real growth. It's a heck of a lot easier than starting over from scratch every year! Very powerful!

Recurring revenues offer an enticing allure of high profits. The magic occurs when a company's recurring revenue base grows at a faster rate than its recurring expense base. It's the wedge model we described in Chapter 2. Hit that inflection point, and XaaS businesses should turn into money-making machines, because the incremental unit economics are very favorable. If XaaS management can achieve this state, then they can deliver both high-confidence revenue and high-confidence profits. Everyone is on the lookout for that point—both investors and management.

The other beauty of recurring revenue is its predictability. Wall Street loves predictability. It allows management to set fixed cost and profit targets with confidence. It reduces the risk of wide swings that spook investors. If you took two companies with similar growth and profit rates, one with high predictability and the other with low predictability, the former would receive a higher valuation. Maybe a MUCH higher valuation.

As we previously mentioned, we know this can work in enterprise tech because we not only have famous historical examples like ADP, but we also have a great living example of the power of the recurring revenue business model in the form of customer service/support and maintenance agreements. For decades enterprise tech companies maintained a pile of annual customer-service contracts. They have added service agreement after service agreement after service agreement—tens of thousands or hundreds of thousands for many companies. These are renewable annual subscription contracts, just like XaaS agreements. Once the company has enough service-agreement revenue to cover their foundational service delivery and software maintenance costs, the good times begin. Because the incremental unit cost to serve one more contract customer is low, the margins are huge.

Get enough of those agreements on your contract pile, and you have a brilliantly performing P&L. Software companies like Oracle report maintenance and support margins of over 80%.

We have also seen it start to happen among XaaS companies. We mentioned that Rackspace was achieving very solid profits—for a time. More recently they have been under pressure from the killer Cs, but Amazon's AWS is now unveiling surprisingly impressive growth and profit numbers.

So we know the subscription financial model can work. It can be big, profitable. and growing. It has worked in other industries and it has worked in tech.

The last (and certainly not least) thing we love about XaaS financial models is their ability to generate free cash flow. What often gets lost in most people's criticism of XaaS economics is that free cash flow often occurs before and at a higher rate than GAAP profits! That's because the revenue recognition rules force the company to defer the revenue ratably over the entire year, but the cash often comes in up front. After a SaaS company has enough cash coming in from its current customers to pay its expenses and pay off the costs of acquiring new customers, the cash should start to flow. Many larger XaaS companies report free cash flow gains that are much stronger than their GAAP profits.

These four defenses of the XaaS business model are legitimate, and they are frequently cited by top executives of leading SaaS and managed services companies. Many even articulate a fifth defense based on redefining the market's view of "true profits." This argument, also known as "non-GAAP profits," maintains that certain expenses like stock option costs and acquisition goodwill should not be imputed into a company's operating expenses. This can make XaaS profit numbers skyrocket. As we mentioned, we are not focusing on that debate. We are focused on GAAP profits because it's the current financial standard. Achieve GAAP profits and your non-GAAP profits will be breathtaking.

Although the model can indeed work, the reality is that many XaaS companies today are not being pressured to prove it. They are currently free to pursue the theory that market share and top-line revenue growth are the only two success metrics that matter. Thus, they are heavily investing in sales and marketing to grab customers. The logic is that the platform with the most customers will ultimately be the winner, the wedge inflection point will be reached, and—with market dominance and a large base of customers—profitability will come.

But XaaS has its critics, too! There are plenty of skeptical tech executives, accountants, and analysts who rally around the lack of GAAP profits. They wonder what will happen to the FVAs and MTWs who are short of the profit inflection point when Wall Street enthusiasm wanes and investors begin demanding profitability.

This leads us to perhaps the most controversial financial aspect of the subscription business model. Let's call the problem the "current cost of acquiring future revenues." In the world of subscriptions, revenue comes in over time but sales costs are incurred up front. According to GAAP, you have to recognize that expense when it occurs, not match it over time to the recognition of revenue. So that means you are paying in this fiscal period for the revenue growth you are going to have in future periods. If you cut back too far to ensure current period profits, you can risk future period revenue growth. So many XaaS companies argue that spending 1 to 3 times current bookings on sales and marketing expenses makes sense because they are "buying scale." The logic makes total sense, but GAAP accounting doesn't make it look pretty. The argument that there will need to be some adjustment in sales cost accounting rules, along with setting aside stock option and goodwill expenses, continues to rage on. The reality is that both sides are right. Service-based businesses have been dealing with the current cost of acquiring future revenue problems for decades. Somehow they have survived and made GAAP profits along the way. But they have not been hyper-growth XaaS companies. Their up-front sales costs could be absorbed, and they could still turn a GAAP profit. But today's "unicorn" XaaS companies simply can't absorb that much sales expense. They will continue to argue it's the best use of capital—better than paying out profits. If they are able to build large revenue streams where sales costs can ultimately be dialed down as a percentage and profits extracted, they could be right. But that has not yet happened, as we have previously pointed out.

No matter which side of the fence you are on and regardless of the profit horizon you have in mind, a successful XaaS provider must have a clear understanding of how real profitability will be achieved and in what time frame. That understanding begins with an inventory of the various ways XaaS providers can make money.

Gears of the XaaS Economic Engine

Although the concept of technology as a service seems to introduce an overwhelming number of creative ways to monetize with customers, the economic engine of a XaaS company is typically composed of up to five potential revenue streams:

- **Asset Revenue.** This is when the customer pays for the right to own and use a copy of the software or hardware product. Some XaaS providers may sell some of their technology up front as an asset as part of a large deal. Many traditional companies offer hybrid solutions comprised of a mix of on-premise assets and cloud services. And, we are all familiar with paying for a smartphone up front and then agreeing to a 3-year cellular service contract.

- **Technology Subscription Revenue.** This is when the customer pays for access to technology as a service. That is the XaaS offer. Companies may have one core offer or a broad portfolio of them.

- **Annuity Services Revenue.** This is when the customer pays for ongoing premium services wrapped around the technology subscription, usually in an annual or multiyear contract. Premium support or success services, information services, and managed services fall into this revenue category.

- **Project Services Revenue.** This is when the customer pays the XaaS provider for specific deliverables such as implementation or user training. These services may be a fixed fee or charged on a time-and-materials basis.

- **Transaction Revenues.** These are revenues that occur per customer transaction. For example, every time a customer clicks a certain feature, they are charged a small fee. Hopefully, these services collect small fees at large volumes.

Each of these revenue streams has a unique financial profile in terms of margin and profitability. We can review these revenue streams using the four traditional components of any business model:

- **Cost of Goods Sold (COGS) and Gross Margin (revenue minus COGS).** These are the costs associated with making, installing, and warranting the specific offer that is driving the revenue stream.

- **Sales and Marketing (S&M).** These are the costs to acquire and retain customers for this offer.

- **Research and Development (R&D).** These are the costs of developing the capabilities the customer is purchasing as part of this offer.

- **General and Administrative (G&A).** These are the operating and overhead costs allocated to the offer by the company that underlies it.

We track publicly reported data related to these revenue streams. For example, traditional technology companies reported the gross margin associated with selling hardware and software assets in Q4 2015. This is shown in Figure 8.3.

The average gross margin for these technology-as-an-asset companies is as follows:

- Software company average gross margin is 87% and the median is 89%.

- Hardware/systems company average gross margin is 50% and the median is 58%.

Technology Product Margins

COMPANY	TICKER	PRODUCT MARGIN
OpenText	OTEX	94.78%
Mentor Graphics	MENT	94.22%
VMware	VMW	93.25%
CA Technologies	CA	92.41%
Adobe Systems	ADBE	91.45%
MicroStrategy	MSTR	90.26%
Intuit	INTU	89.30%
Parametric Technology Corporation	PTC	86.07%
Oracle	ORCL	85.56%
Citrix Systems	CTXS	83.10%
Symantec	SYMC	82.42%
Autodesk	ADSK	81.13%
IBM	IBM	73.99%
Brocade	BRCD	68.52%
Cerner	CERN	67.47%
Juniper Networks	JNPR	65.14%
Cisco Systems	CSCO	60.86%
Unisys	UIS	59.25%
Teradata	TDC	59.17%
EMC	EMC	57.82%
Agilent	A	54.01%
NetApp	NTAP	49.94%
Xerox	XRX	37.30%
ABB	ABB	27.45%
NCR Corporation	NCR	25.58%
Diebold	DBD	16.42%

FIGURE 8.3 Technology Product Margins

We aren't going to focus very much on traditional product margins, but we put it here for reference because employees from many hybrid companies will be reading this book. They will be using asset margins to blend into their overall financial model.

As for publicly traded XaaS companies, the Cloud 20 snapshot reveals a wide range of gross margin associated with technology subscription revenues. As shown in Figure 8.4, these

Subscription Margins

COMPANY	TICKER	TECHNOLOGY SUBSCRIPTION MARGIN
LogMeIn	LOGM	87.53%
Qualys	QLYS	79.37%
Medidata	MDSO	77.90%
LifeLock	LOCK	77.63%
Salesforce	CRM	75.25%
Constant Contact	CTCT	73.22%
Intralinks	IL	72.26%
LivePerson	LPSN	72.12%
Demandware	DWRE	70.66%
Cornerstone OnDemand	CSOD	68.78%
ServiceNow	NOW	68.64%
Workday	WDAY	67.43%
Rackspace	RAX	66.36%
NetSuite	N	65.72%
Veeva Systems	VEEV	65.38%
Jive Software	JIVE	63.60%
Google	GOOG	62.32%
Ultimate Software	ULTI	61.45%
Athena Health	ATHN	59.82%
RealPage	RP	56.51%

FIGURE 8.4 Subscription Margins

margins ranged from 56% to more than 87% in Q4 2015. Part of the margin variation is driven by each company's decision on where certain specific costs should be accounted for. We know that there are lots of apples and oranges in comparing these numbers, but at least it offers us some visibility into actual performance. For XaaS companies, hosting costs are typically the major component of COGS, followed by basic customer support costs. We will kick out the outliers for our work ahead.

The average subscription margin for these XaaS companies is 69.60%, and the median is 68.71%. We will come back to these numbers soon.

As we move past basic subscription gross margins, we run into a limitation with the public data. We need to analyze all the revenue streams for the play we want you to run. However, not all the benchmark numbers we need for our financial model are widely available. The margin profile of things like project or annuity service revenue streams are often hidden from the public data. Therefore, we will supplement our data set with some TSIA industry benchmark data. As an example, Figure 8.5 provides an

Business Model of Project Revenues

BUSINESS MODEL FOR PROJECT-BASED SERVICES	INDUSTRY AVERAGE	HARDWARE	SOFTWARE	XAAS PROVIDERS	LARGE	SMB
Project Margin	39.6%					
% of Revenue Spent on Non-Billable Resources Regionally	12.1%					
Direct Sales Costs	5.5%					
Direct Marketing Costs	0.7%					
Direct Service Development Costs	2.0%					
Direct G&A	6.2%					
Operating Contribution	13.8%					

FIGURE 8.5 Business Model of Project Revenues

example of the financial data TSIA tracks related to project-based services. It shows the industry average and itemizes some of the peer groups we maintain related to project revenue performance. (Yes, we are teasing you with the average data, but not the peer-group breakouts.)

We will use these averages in the exercise soon to come. If you are a TSIA member company, we will be happy to provide you with your peer-group averages. We can also explain how we calculate each line.

So, pulling together the public and proprietary data streams, we can create tables that provide a trimmed-range snapshot of the financial performance that is currently reasonable to expect for each revenue stream. In a trimmed range, we drop the bottom 25% and top 25% of data points. We look at companies performing within the 25% to 75% range of expected performance. This approach eliminates outlier performers on the high and low ends. Of course, these financial results are moving targets and shift over time. You could argue with this data source or that one. That is why we continuously benchmark the performance of these revenue streams so the database gets bigger and the trends get more apparent. However, what is important is the model. Figure 8.6 provides a sample readout we provide to TSIA members when they are working with us to model target economic engines.

As we have said repeatedly, in establishing a very clear path to XaaS profitability, we think the question of setting the target revenue mix is a central topic. Diversifying into a profitable project services business is just one example. The answer to what the optimal mix is varies greatly based on the profit horizon being applied to the XaaS business. But, in general, we see portfolio mix as a critical tool that management has on its journey to profitable XaaS.

This brings us to the important part of this chapter. We have been studying both the public data and our TSIA research data. We think we are starting to see some patterns in revenue mix,

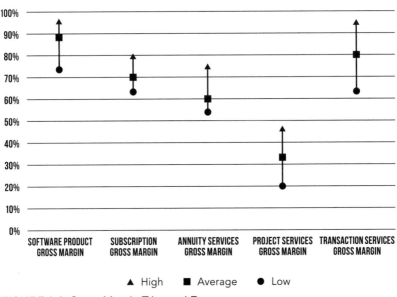

FIGURE 8.6 Gross Margin Trimmed Ranges

margins, and profitability. Admittedly, it is still pretty foggy out there, but things are finally beginning to take shape. The key is to marry some of the data about what is currently occurring in the pure-play XaaS world with other things that have been proven possible in the traditional tech world. The major breakthrough and the exercise we encourage each company to do is to financially model your XaaS going forward, armed with four weapons from this book:

- A knowledge of what state your XaaS business is in today and what other states remain for you to go through before you become a full-fledged current profit maximizer (CPM).

- A target financial model for each state that is rooted in some reality. The reality will be boxed in by a range of actual industry performance data from one of the sources we mentioned earlier.

- A target financial model exercise that forces you to think through the evolution of your offer portfolio and its accompanying revenue streams as you move from state to state.

- A timeline to journey from your current state to the CPM state that is also based in some reality.

The bottom line is that we think XaaS can be a 20% EBITDA (GAAP) business or better. Here is where we begin to model the financial and portfolio journey to get there.

Financial Keys for the Future Value Aggregator

Future value aggregators are focused on demonstrating that they can capture the high volumes of units that will lead to future success. The unit of future value (UFV) can be almost anything:

- Number of visitors

- Number of page views

- Number of subscribers

- Number of logins

- Number of customer logos

- Number of project plans under management

This means the first metric of financial success for FVAs is the raw number of UFVs being acquired and retained over time. They will track how many units they have captured and make those gains the lead in their financial reporting story.

The second slate of financial metrics—and often the more challenging achievement for FVAs—reflects their ability to actually convert the UFVs into paying customers. Are customers willing to pay for the core offer or its premium version? The relevant metric here is monthly recurring revenue (MRR) or annual recurring revenue (ARR). Investors will want to know how much customers are willing to pay for this offer and the dollar amount that grows over time. XaaS companies will also report:

- Number of paying customers
- Average subscription price or average revenue per user (ARPU)
- Monthly recurring revenue/annual recurring revenue
- Churn rate

To optimize the acquisition of these UFVs, the FVA will seek to minimize any friction linked to attracting and retaining them. FVAs will eventually need to prove a business model that acquires new customers in a way that does not break the bank. Customer acquisition costs (CAC) should become a relevant metric early on for most XaaS providers. The financial model of an FVA can collapse under the weight of unwieldy CAC. As we pointed out, there are public XaaS companies running with sales and marketing expenses over 50% of revenue. Some companies have been over 100% at points in their development. Of course, this is not likely to be sustainable in the long term, but the bar for FVA spending is pretty high and forgiving at the present moment.

In summary, here are six metrics that are typically highly correlated to the success story of future value aggregators:

- Growth in units of future value
- Growth in number of paying customers
- Average revenue per user
- Monthly recurring revenue (total recurring revenue from all paying customers)
- Customer acquisition costs (the amount of money spent, on average, to acquire a new customer)
- Churn rate (percentage of paying and non-paying customers who stop subscribing or using the core offer each month)

FVAs will be heavily weighted toward subscription or transaction revenue streams. They will focus very little on monetizing project or annuity services. These revenue streams are more complex to sell and simply slow down the momentum of acquiring units of future value. In this profile, where the focus is on growth, the only revenue stream that is likely to be profitable is the premium annuity subscriptions. Any professional services required to get the customer up and running are likely to be bundled or absorbed into the cost of the subscription. Figure 8.7 models the revenue streams for a XaaS provider in the FVA profile.

This sample model shows a negative operating profit. Many FVAs will run negative operating profits as they invest heavily in sales and marketing, experience lower gross margin on the core subscription offering, and throw services or basic access in for free to secure new customers.

Scanning the industry, we can easily find real-world examples of companies successfully executing the FVA financial profile. To define successful FVAs, we would look for companies that have the following attributes:

- Double- or triple-digit top-line growth in UFVs
- Double- or triple-digit revenue growth (albeit sometimes from a small number)

FVA Revenue Streams

REVENUE STREAMS	TECHNOLOGY SUBSCRIPTION	PREMIUM ANNUITY ACCOUNT SERVICES	PROFESSIONAL SERVICES	TRANSACTION REVENUES	AGGREGATE BUSINESS MODEL
% of Company Revenue	90%	10%			100%
COGS%	40%	40%			40%
GM%	60%	60%			60%
S&M%	60%	15%			56%
R&D%	20%	20%			20%
G&A%	15%	15%			15%
OI%	-35%	10%			-30%

FIGURE 8.7 FVA Revenue Streams (Note: All costs are expressed as a percentage of revenue for that specific line of business/revenue.)

- High percentage of revenue spent on sales and marketing
- Majority of revenue coming from the core offer
- Quarterly losses
- Company valuations that are typically 10 times (or higher) their annual company revenues

DocuSign is a perfect example of a company that successfully ran the FVA profile claiming over 50 million users and is now pivoting toward the mid-term wedge. They are moving from the value of electronic signatures offered in various fee and free combinations to offering digital transaction management for enterprises. As they make the pivot, they are beginning to offer professional services as well. Founded in 2003 and beginning sales in 2005,[3] DocuSign has spent the better part of a decade in FVA mode. They have raised more than $400 million[4] to help subsidize the operations in those years and lay the foundation for a profitable wedge model.

LinkedIn is another interesting example of an FVA that is moving toward an MTW player. The company exhibits all of the classic attributes. They grew members from 20 million in 2006 to 400 million by 2015.[5] The company has been growing revenues at a double-digit pace and has exceeded $2 billion. However, most of that revenue is not coming from the 400 million people they aggregated, most of whom take advantage of free membership. The company has learned to monetize its units of value (members) by offering talent solutions to corporate HR departments and advertising solutions to marketers. This is in addition to its premium subscription offers to members. The company has been profitable on a GAAP basis, but only marginally (it publishes a non-GAAP EBITDA calculation that reflects much more favorable profits). Even after 10 years in the market, the company is still spending almost 37% of revenue on sales and marketing. We would expect it to begin to show the GAAP profit power of its model soon, but it may come at the same time as revenue growth slows. We got a taste of the market's reaction to that in early 2016, when LinkedIn's stock dropped 40% in value because the company revised growth guidance down to "only" 20% to 30%. The company's market capitalization dropped from $25 billion to $13 billion, from a 10-times multiple of revenue to a 4.5-times multiple. This is a classic case of the challenge that FVAs face as revenues slow, and they must begin to transition their stock valuations from high growth to solid growth plus profits.

Financial Keys for the Mid-Term Wedge

XaaS providers that have been aggregating paying customers and believe they can now turn the business model toward profitability have a longer set of financial metrics to manage. In the mid-term wedge profile (MTW), subscription growth and MRR are still critical metrics. However, companies in the MTW profile must now also focus on costs. Are the costs to acquire new customers (CAC) and to serve existing customers (COGs) coming under control? Is the company expanding and renewing customers (CEC, CRC) in the most cost-effective way possible? Simple churn rate metrics get replaced by more sophisticated measures. In addition, the MTW must pay close attention to commoditization and discounting. Some of the basic numbers reported by FVAs may actually drop below the radar as the company becomes larger and these more sophisticated metrics take precedence. Pulling these thoughts together, there are nine financial metrics the MTW should watch and improve:

- **Monthly Recurring Revenue (MRR).** Average amount of money a customer is spending with the company.
- **Customer Acquisition Costs (CAC).** The amount of money spent, on average, to acquire a new customer.

- **Unit Renewal Rate (URR).** The percentage of customers that are renewing their subscriptions.

- **Contract Value Renewal Rate (CVRR).** When renewal contracts come up each month, does that pool of customers spend more or less money with the company? Ideally, CVRR is over 100%. When CVRR is below 100%, customers may be churning or customers may be securing discounts during renewal.

- **Discount Rate on New and Renewal Deals.** If discount rates are high, it is a sure sign the offer is commoditizing.

- **Technology Subscription COGs.** The percentage of subscription revenues spent on the technology and support related to delivering the offer.

- **Annuity and Project Revenue COGs.** The percentage of annuity and project revenues that are spent to deliver those services. In the FVA profile, these services may have been free or break-even. Now, these revenue streams should be achieving at least industry average gross margins.

- **Cost to Renew Customers (CRC).** What percentage of sales and marketing dollars is spent on the process of renewing customers? If this percentage is high, it will be difficult to tamp down overall S&M spending.

- **Cost to Expand Customers (CEC).** What percentage of sales and marketing dollars is spent on securing incremental revenue from existing customers? The cost to secure expansion revenues should be much lower than the cost to secure revenue from a new customer. If this is not true, it will again be difficult to tamp down overall sales and marketing expenditures.

MTWs are still heavily weighted toward technology subscription revenues. Yet, they should now be diversifying. That could come in the form of multiple core offers, but they may also begin offering project and annuity services that create the following financial benefits:

- Bring incremental revenue and higher-margin dollars into the financial model
- Help reduce the cost of renewing customers (CRC) by delivering fee-based services that drive adoption and stickiness
- Become a cost-effective channel for identifying expand selling opportunities (reduce CEC costs)

There are likely to be three revenue streams in play for the MTW, at least in enterprise markets: the technology subscription, premium annuity services, and fee-based, project-based professional services. In this profile, where the focus is turning toward profitability, all three revenue streams should be profitable or close to reaching profitability. Also, a slightly greater percentage of revenue will be coming from the annuity and project services. Figure 8.8 models these three revenue streams for a XaaS provider that has crossed the line into profitability.

MTW Revenue Streams

REVENUE STREAMS	TECHNOLOGY SUBSCRIPTION	PREMIUM ANNUITY ACCOUNT SERVICES	PROFESSIONAL SERVICES	TRANSACTION REVENUES	AGGREGATE BUSINESS MODEL
% of Company Revenue	70%	20%	10%		100%
COGS%	35%	35%	65%		38%
GM%	65%	65%	35%		62%
S&M%	45%	12%	8%		35%
R&D%	18%	10%	5%		15%
G&A%	12%	12%	12%		12%
OI%	-10%	31%	10%		0%

FIGURE 8.8 MTW Revenue Streams (Note: All costs are expressed as a percentage of revenue for that specific line of business/revenue.)

This sample model shows a positive operating profit of 2.5%. We would expect MTWs to be running quarterly operating profits anywhere from negative 10% to positive 10% as they approach and pass the profit horizon. We would also expect a year or two where the MTWs have operating profits that bounce from positive to negative, quarter to quarter, as they dial-in the operating model.

To identify real-world mid-term wedge examples, we would look for companies that have the following attributes:

- Healthy top-line revenue growth, but it may be slowing
- Slowly trending toward spending less money on sales and marketing as a percentage of total revenue
- Slow but steady improvement in gross margins as scale is reached
- Positive and stabilizing trend in operating income (whether or not it is currently profitable)
- Majority of revenue still coming from a core offer (subscriptions or transactions) but growing a diversified portfolio
- Company valuations are typically 5 to 10 times (or higher) annual company revenues

Workday is a MTW SaaS company that is beginning to exhibit these trends. Figure 8.9 documents the incredible revenue growth rate of Workday, which has been hovering between the 60% to 75% range. It also documents the high spend on sales and marketing, which is fortunately stabilizing, and the double-digit negative (but improving) operating income quarter after quarter. In early 2016, Workday was sporting a market capitalization that was 11 times annual revenues! Impressive. But, alas, the journey from FVA to MTW has also impacted Workday and its stock price. As the company begins to signal a slower growth outlook and GAAP losses alternate between improvement and decline, the market is reacting by shaving its valuation premium.

No conversation about the MTW is complete without a discussion of Salesforce. Everyone in the industry seems to be waiting

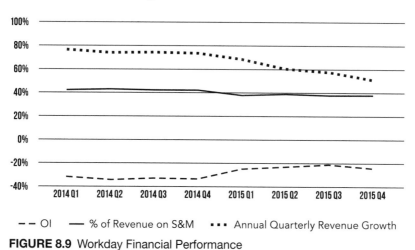

FIGURE 8.9 Workday Financial Performance

for them to hit the profit inflection point. Would it be at revenues of $500 million? $1 billion? $5 billion? Will it be at $10 billion?

There is no doubt that Salesforce could be very profitable on a GAAP basis when and if they need to. They just have to turn the sales and marketing dial a bit to the left. But their stock is doing just fine, so the pressure to demonstrate profits is tolerable. They will orient toward growth and market share through high sales costs for as long as they can. But they are clearly messaging that they are making preparations to demonstrate strong profitability. The recent analyst briefings have them on record as saying they are going to take a more balanced approach to financial management. They are the epitome of an MTW sitting on the edge of the profit inflection point, waiting to be pushed into green territory. In early 2016, they had a market cap of around 9 times annual revenue.

Financial Keys for the Current Profit Maximizer

As we mentioned, most large enterprise tech companies that have established a history of producing rich margins are finding it hard to convince profit- and dividend-oriented investors that unprofitable XaaS offerings, even if they are growing rapidly, are a good thing for business. Take this quote from a *Forbes* article titled "Why the 10% Drop in Software Sales Is the Most Important Number in IBM's Q2 Earnings Report"[6] as an example of market reaction to the fish model:

> *"We are concerned that IBM's software business may see increasing pressure from the transition to a SaaS business model," wrote Jefferies equity analyst James Kisner. "Recall, Oracle ORCL +0.00% reported very light license revenues driven largely by an accelerating transition to cloud (SaaS)."*
>
> *Meanwhile, Credit Suisse's Kulbinder Garcha last week reiterated an underperform rating in part because software revenue would need to come in above trend to boost earnings above consensus, something he sees as highly unlikely. He added, **"Following a thorough analysis of their cloud, we believe it may ultimately be margin dilutive for IBM, even if the company drives revenue."***

Established technology providers are being forced to optimize XaaS business models as rapidly as possible. When pursuing this current profit maximizer (CPM) profile, management teams must immediately focus on the financial metrics that predicate a profitable XaaS business model. Many of these are the same exact metrics that are critical in the MTW profile:

- Average monthly recurring revenue (AMRR)
- Customer acquisition costs (CAC)
- Unit renewal rate (URR)
- Contract value renewal rate (CVRR)
- Discount rate
- Technology subscription COGs
- Annuity and project revenue COGs
- Cost to renew customers (CRC)
- Cost to expand customers (CEC)

However, the CPM have additional financial focal points:

- Revenue mix
- Revenue line profitability
- Upsell rates and COS
- Cross-sell rates and COS
- Focused R&D and G&A expense targets
- Platform investments eating away at sales, service, and G&A labor costs

Out of the gate, most CPMs should be adept at monetizing additional revenue streams beyond the core technology subscription offers. This includes all the new types of value-added services we identified in Chapter 6. Ideally, they would have healthy revenue in most if not all of the revenue streams we identified at the beginning of this chapter:

1. **Annuity Revenues.** The customer pays for the service in an annual or multiyear service contract.

2. **Project Revenues.** The customer pays for the service on a project-by-project basis.

3. **Transaction Revenues.** The customer pays every time they execute a specific activity, such as processing a report or submitting an inventory.

In addition, these companies should have become very proficient at getting sales costs under control. As we have often pointed out, one key to doing that is having a healthy balance of growth coming from adding new customers at a high CAC while strongly expanding existing customers at a much smaller sales cost (CEC). Combined with a high renewal-rate revenue stream at a low sales cost (CRC), the company's overall COS drops to a manageable 20% to 30%. We are not saying that all XaaS companies at this level will have COS of 30% or less. Some companies may choose to continue to spend lavishly on CAC to perpetuate their land grab, thus driving overall COS up. What we are saying is that it is POSSIBLE for a XaaS company at this level to balance very respectable growth rates with very manageable overall sales costs.

Figure 8.10 models the optimized economic engine of a profitable CPM that has established multiple revenue streams.

As shown in this figure, even though the core technology subscription is only generating an OI of 9.8%, the overall economic engine is generating an excellent operating profit of 20.2%.

There are examples of companies that are leveraging multiple revenue streams to maximize the profitability of their XaaS offer or to manage their swallowing of the fish. These companies are working hard to remain profitable through this significant industry transition. The telling attributes of the CPM profile would include:

- Still solid but not spectacular growth in revenues.
- Profitable growth in fee-based annuity and project revenue streams.

CPM Revenue Streams

REVENUE STREAMS	TECHNOLOGY SUBSCRIPTION	PREMIUM ANNUITY ACCOUNT SERVICES	PROFESSIONAL SERVICES	TRANSACTION REVENUES	AGGREGATE BUSINESS MODEL
% of Company Revenue	55%	20%	15%	10%	100%
COGS%	25%	25%	60%	10%	29%
GM%	75%	75%	40%	90%	71%
S&M%	42%	10%	5%	5%	26%
R&D%	20%	10%	5%	8%	15%
G&A%	10%	10%	10%	10%	10%
OI%	3%	45%	20%	67%	20%

FIGURE 8.10 CPM Revenue Streams (Note: All costs are expressed as a percentage of revenue for that specific line of business/revenue.)

- Operating incomes that remain positive quarter to quarter.
- Company valuations that are typically a multiple of 3 to 10 times (or higher) annual company revenues.

The first example of a CPM is Veeva Systems, a company specializing in SaaS applications for the global life sciences industry. There are plenty of SaaS companies with annual revenues north of $500 million but still with negative operating incomes. Veeva is bucking that trend. With annual revenues half that amount, the company is solidly profitable. In the second quarter of 2015, the company generated an operating income of 23%. More importantly, the company is generating over 20% of revenues from value-added services at a margin of 24%. Service offerings listed on the Veeva website include:[7]

- Transformation Consulting
- Professional Services
- Managed Services
- Environment Management as a Service
- Veeva Code-Based Custom Development
- Administrator Training

In early 2016 Veeva had a market cap of around 8 times annual revenue.

The company went public in 2011 with 33% of revenues coming from fee-based services as a critical source of revenue and some margin. By 2015, services was generating almost $20 million a year in margin. Figure 8.11 documents the financial performance for Veeva from 2013 through 2015. As can be seen, unlike many SaaS companies, Veeva has doubled operating income dollars while growing revenues from $129 million to more than $300 million.

Perhaps one of the more instructive examples of companies pivoting from selling technology as an asset to selling technology

Veeva Financial Performance
CONSOLIDATED STATEMENTS OF COMPREHENSIVE INCOME (USD $)
IN THOUSANDS, EXCEPT PER SHARE DATA, UNLESS OTHERWISE SPECIFIED

	12 MONTHS ENDED:		
	JAN. 31, 2015	JAN. 31, 2014	JAN. 31, 2013
Revenues:			
Subscription Services	$233,063	$146,621	$73,280
Professional Services and Other	$80,159	$63,530	$56,268
Total Revenues	$313,222	$210,151	$129,548
Cost of Revenues:			
Cost of Subscription Services	$55,005	$36,199	$18,852
Cost of Professional Services and Other	$60,653	$46,403	$38,164
Total Cost of Revenues	$115,658	$82,602	$57,016
Gross Profit	$197,564	$127,549	$72,532
Operating Expenses:			
Research and Developement	$41,156	$26,327	$14,638
Sales and Marketing	$56,203	$41,507	$19,490
General and Administrative	$30,239	$20,411	$8,371
Total Operating Expenses	$127,598	$88,245	$42,499
Operating Income	$69,966	$39,304	$30,033

FIGURE 8.11 Veeva Financial Performance

as a service is the Canada-based software company OpenText. A public company since 1996 and with revenues now over $1 billion, this company is an established software provider. OpenText has embraced a philosophy of allowing customers to consume technology the way they want to consume technology. If OpenText customers want to continue to purchase software licenses, they can. If customers want to migrate to subscription pricing, they can. If customers want OpenText to provide their software as a managed service where OpenText manages the software on the customer's site, that is an option as well. This philosophy has led to a diversified economic engine. Here are notes from the company's 2015 annual report:

During fiscal 2015 we saw the following activity:

- *Total revenue was $1,851.9 million, up 14.0% over the prior fiscal year.*

- *Total recurring revenue was $1,557.7 million, up 18.1% over the prior fiscal year.*

- *Cloud services and subscription revenue was $605.3 million, up 62.1% over the prior fiscal year.*

- *License revenue was $294.3 million, down 3.8% over the prior fiscal year.*

- *GAAP-based gross margin was 67.5% compared to 68.5% in the prior fiscal year.*

- *GAAP-based operating margin was 18.8% compared to 18.5% in the prior fiscal year.*

- *Non-GAAP-based operating margin was 30.9%, stable year over year.*

- *Operating cash flow was $523.0 million, up 25.4% from the prior fiscal year.*

- *Cash and cash equivalents was $700.0 million as of June 30, 2015, compared to $427.9 million as of June 30, 2014.*

License revenue is shrinking and represents less than 16% of total company revenues. Technology subscription revenues are growing rapidly and now represent 33% of total company revenue. Total recurring revenues, which include multiyear managed services and support services contracts, now represent 84% of company revenue. Most importantly, the company has remained profitable throughout this transition in revenue mix.

In early 2016, OpenText had a market cap of around 3 times annual revenue.

Rackspace is another MTW that has proven profitability. Before they got caught up in a price war led by AWS, the company generated an operating income as high as 29% by focusing on "fanatical support." Perhaps this is a proof point that differentiated services can help unlock higher profits. In fact, one of the company's newest tactics to battle against AWS's aggressive price-cutting onslaught is to refocus its offers and messaging to "Managed Cloud." The lead paragraph on their website in February 2016 read:

> *"Experience our highly specialized expertise and best-in-class service across the world's leading infrastructure technologies, databases, and applications."*

They position the technology second and their expert services first.

As we made clear in Chapter 5, Adobe is one of our favorite examples of a traditional license software company that has transitioned to a profitable subscription business model. By May 2013, Adobe was no longer licensing its popular Creative Suite software. Customers could only consume the software through a subscription.[8] A majority of Adobe revenues are secured through the technology subscription. As of 2014, only 11% of Adobe revenues were related to any type of value-added services. The company has proven they can live on the profitable side of the wedge model—but barely. As shown in Figure 8.12, the transition from a big license engine to a big technology subscription engine has resulted in almost halving the operating income of the company. There is a lesson to be had here that we will explore more in the chapter on churn, costs, and commoditization.

In early 2016, Adobe had a market cap of around 9 times annual revenue.

But the one example that everyone loves to talk about most right now is Amazon Web Services. More than any other company we know of, they have successfully passed through all three phases in a remarkably short period of just 10 years.

Adobe Financial Performance
Since Migrating to Subscription Pricing

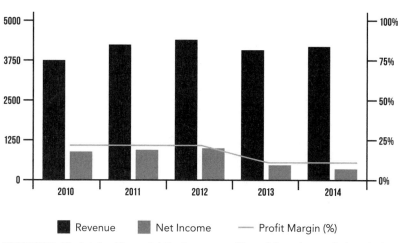

FIGURE 8.12 Adobe Financial Performance Since Migrating to Subscription Pricing

Although the company has just recently started to break out the financial profile of this business unit, Amazon is reporting the following financial statistics:[9]

- AWS is generating $2 billion in quarterly revenues.
- AWS revenues are growing at 78%.
- AWS is generating 25% operating income.

The AWS offering is incredibly service light from a revenue standpoint. We think this is a risky move for most companies. Betting the farm on features or scale alone can work, but is not often sustainable. For every Google search business, there are dozens of troubled XaaS companies that were driven into the ground by lower-priced or better-featured competitors. For AWS, revenue and profits are generated through a big technology transaction gear of renting computing cycles at very low rates. Their strategy is based on portfolio diversification. As their capabilities grow, customers expand their average MRR. For this wedge model to be so profitable, it is clear that Amazon must keep S&M and G&A expenses in check. It must also ensure that revenues are growing faster than COGS.

Because AWS is part of Amazon, we cannot place a specific stock value on it. However, many analysts speculate it to be worth more than $100 billion, which would give it a market cap of around 13 times annual revenue.

By comparison to these great XaaS company examples, in early 2016 most of the large, traditional enterprise hardware and systems companies were trading at around 1 times revenue. Most traditional enterprise software companies were trading at revenue multiples in the 2 to 3 times range. For those companies, it is easy to see why getting through the fish and potentially achieving multiples of 5 times or 8 times is of extreme interest to management and boards of directors alike. That is why we wrote this book—to gather up our reading of the tea leaves (and the data)—to begin formulating some road maps for the journey. Some road maps are for traditional companies moving into the subscription economy, and others are for companies born in the cloud era that need to begin pivoting their story from remarkable revenue growth to profits and solid growth.

Profile Traps

The other thing we are learning on these journeys is that there is real potential for XaaS offers to fall into traps in these three profiles. This is going to be especially dangerous if financial markets become more conservative. There are scenarios where actual company performance does not align to the strategy keys of the profit horizon. There are three very recognizable scenarios of disconnect:

1. FVAs that are spending like a drunken sailor on acquiring units of future value, but have no effective strategy to monetize them.

2. MTWs that have accumulated a large mass of paying customers but are not yet demonstrating improving economies of scale or efficiency, especially in sales and marketing.

3. CPMs that need current profits but are afraid to make some of the hard decisions to rapidly build scale by forcing customers onto their platforms, charging profitable prices, or diversifying their revenue mix.

What is the consequence of these mismatches? For public companies, the price will be paid in the company valuation. Just look at cloud storage and file sharing provider Box. Their valuation began a descent before their IPO and it has continued. We would argue they did not manage effectively from FVA to MTW.

The bottom line is this: There are specific management and financial objectives for each phase in the profit horizon journey. Start-up XaaS providers need to understand—if they are on an FVA or MTW profit horizon—what their financial keys are and what time frames they will accomplish them in. Legacy technology companies need to transition to XaaS on a path that accelerates them quickly into CPMs. We strongly believe aligning your XaaS strategy decisions with the profile you are attempting to execute increases your ability to improve shareholder value.

Timeline Planning

The notion of the three states of XaaS offers (FVA/FPI, MTW, CPM) is especially helpful as you think through the number of years in your financial transformation journey. Central to this part of the exercise is seen in Figure 8.13.

Although there are certainly some exceptions, the companies we have studied seem to spend a predictable range of years in each of these three states of management focus. The left column represents the shortest amount of time we have seen anyone in each state. The right column represents the longest. The "+" sign means

Financial Transformation Journey
YEARS IN EACH STAGE

	MINIMUM TIME	MAXIMUM TIME
Future Value Aggregator	2	5+
Mid-Term Wedge	2	5
Current Profit Maximizer	1	3
Total Years	5	13+

FIGURE 8.13 Financial Transformation Journey

that some companies never seem to get out of the FVA state. We predict these companies will flame out when the financial markets turn bearish.

There are three important uses of this chart. The first is to help you predict how long your journey may be from your current state to achieving your end state of more than 20% GAAP EBITDA. You simply identify what state you think you are in today and make a decision about whether you plan to run through the remaining states quickly (left column values) or if it will require more time (right-hand column values). For each year of your journey, your goal would be to complete the revenue mix and margin exercise shown in Figure 8.14. You should be able to explain why you think you are moving through states at a fast pace or a slow one.

Once this exercise has been completed for each year in your projected journey to 20% EBITDA, anyone in the company will be able to quickly see both the financial and the portfolio journey you need to pursue. You can then apply these ratios to your revenue projections to begin to compute actual dollar profits and losses along the way. This may be helpful in assessing the total capital required to get to the profit horizon event.

Revenue Mix and Margin Exercise
YEAR X

REVENUE STREAMS	CORE SUBSCRIPTION	PROJECT SERVICES	ANNUITY SERVICES	TRANSACTION SERVICES	
Type	Offer A Offer B	Service A Service B	Service A Service B	Service A	
Mix %					100%
COGS %					
GM %					
S&M %					
R&D %					
G&A %					
OI %					

X =   FVA = 1-5+ years   MTW = 3-5 years   CPM = 1-3 years

FIGURE 8.14 Revenue Mix and Margin Exercise

The second great use is to benchmark your current financial performance against our target states. If you look different, why is that? Are your costs lower in some areas and higher in others? Is your portfolio diversifying as the company changes states and approaches new targets? These financial models are by no means the only way to be a successful XaaS business, but they do seem to be characteristic of many we see.

Finally, if you are a traditional tech company, you can use this model to determine your point of entry into the XaaS market. As we have emphasized, we think these companies are smart to consider entering at scale in a CPM state. If managed correctly, they can use their huge scale to skip the FVA/FPI state and maybe even the MTW state. By forcing all their customers onto the XaaS offer, they can literally enter the market as a CPM and achieve GAAP profits in their first or second year.

XaaS Playbook Plays

Two plays that help a management team answer the question, "Can we make money with this XaaS offer?" are identified in this chapter:

Play: Identify Your Target Financial Metrics

Objective: Identify the metrics that will be used to determine if the company is on track to meet its business model objectives.

Benefits:

- Prioritizes critical metrics to track.
- Provides talk track for both employees and investors regarding how the company is defining success.

Players (who runs this play?): Core players: CFO, CEO, and board. Review team: board.

Play: Model Your XaaS Profitable Economic Engine

Objective: Identify the specific revenue streams the company intends to monetize. Identify the mix and margin expectations for each revenue stream. Determine the number of years in your journey to target GAAP profitability.

Benefits:

- Identifies the target financial model for the company.
- Identifies investment requirements.
- Set expectations on target margins for each revenue stream.

Players (who runs this play?): Core players: CEO, CFO, product development, services, marketing. Review team: CEO, CFO, board.

9 | The Case for Managed Services

This book is about conducting successful XaaS offers. For companies that have been selling technology as an asset, the pivot to selling technology as a service can be overwhelming. The many things to consider and worry about can make this seem like a bridge too far. But a first step that traditional technology companies can take on this journey to help them ease into the XaaS marketplace is to stand up a managed services capability.

In this chapter, we'll explore the special case of managed services (MS) as entrée into XaaS. For the past several years, we have been aggressively studying and benchmarking how enterprise tech companies of all sorts are incubating and growing MS businesses. So, let's discuss the pros and woes of how, why, and when to build your MS offer. Specifically, we will cover the following ground:

- The explosion of managed service revenues.
- Trends driving managed services.
- The many flavors of managed services.
- Why product companies fear managed services.
- Why companies should embrace managed service opportunities.
- Success tactics when incubating managed service capabilities.

By the end of this chapter, management teams should clearly understand why managed services is the fastest growing service line in the technology industry and why this opportunity shouldn't be ignored.

The Explosion of Managed Services

We benchmark the overall revenue mix of technology companies at a level of detail not available in the standard 10-K. One of our objectives with this data is to clearly understand how the economic engines of technology companies are changing over time. MS revenues have been present in the industry for years. In 2013, our data showed that 23% of the companies we benchmarked had some type of MS revenue stream. By the end of 2015, 46% of companies were reporting an MS revenue stream. That is a doubling of MS offers in just two years.

Not only are more companies jumping into MS, but MS is also starting to become meaningful revenue. The average revenue mix for companies that benchmark their managed services business with TSIA indicates that MS has blossomed to 12% of total company revenues, as seen in Figure 9.1.

More importantly, the average annual growth rate of these MS revenues exceeds 30%. This growth rate is far outpacing the average growth rate for product revenues we see in the industry today. In our last T&S 50 snapshot of 2015, product revenues, on average, were shrinking 8%! (See Figure 9.2.)

Finally, MS revenue streams are proving more and more profitable. The TSIA MS benchmark reports average MS gross margins greater than 40%. Some MS providers are generating gross margins just slightly south of 70%. In our annual survey on overall organizational structure, we ask technology companies to simply report the general profitability profile of every service line they have, the results of which are seen in Figure 9.3. For the past two years, MS has been reported as the second most profitable service activity, right after highly lucrative support services.

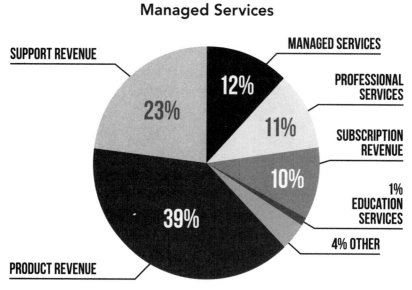

FIGURE 9.1 Revenue Mix for Companies that Benchmark MS

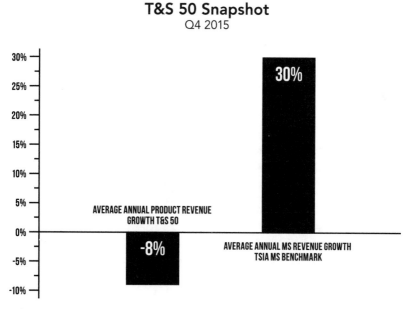

FIGURE 9.2 MS Revenue Annual Growth Rate

Which best describes the financial performance of the following service lines for the most recent fiscal year?

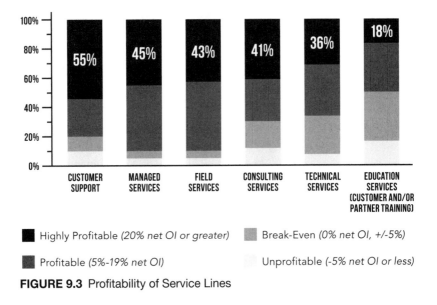

FIGURE 9.3 Profitability of Service Lines

So, MS is undoubtedly a rising star in the economic engine of technology companies. But why?

Trends Driving Managed Services

Multiple trends are driving the demand for managed services. Many of these trends were heavily discussed in our last two books, but let's do a quick review:

- **Reducing Operational Complexity.** Customers no longer want the headaches of running IT operations, especially if they don't view this as a core competency of the company.

- **On-Demand Capacity.** Customers don't want to pay for IT capacity they don't need. MS models are much more flexible and allow the customer to buy capacity as required.

- **OpEx versus CapEx.** Some customers (clearly not all) have a preference for spending operating dollars and not capital dollars when it comes to technology. CapEx leads to having big, lump-sum payments and then owning assets that must be depreciated over time. Migrating IT expenses to OpEx typically leads to smoother, more predictable expenses over time.

- **Value Beyond Technology.** Customers look for technology providers to apply unique insights to help maximize the business impact of technology. One common value proposition is MS offers that feature accelerated technology adoption versus do-it-yourself tech.

- **Economies of Scale.** Technology providers can create environments, tools, and processes that support multiple customers. These economies should allow providers to deliver technology environments more cost effectively than customers can create as a one-off.

- **Strategic versus Tactical.** *CIO* magazine published an article citing the growing demand for managed services. The magazine reported that CIOs are interested in leveraging outside vendors to manage day-to-day operations so internal IT staff can focus on strategic initiatives.[1]

Generically, TSIA sees these trends resulting in five common MS offering value propositions, listed below and shown in Figure 9.4.

- **Monitor.** Monitor technology availability and performance for the customer.

- **Operate.** Operate the technical environment on behalf of the customer.

- **Optimize.** Work with the customer to optimize technology costs, improve technology adoption, and maximize the business impact of the technology.

- **Transform.** Help the customer implement and integrate a new set of technology capabilities.

Common MS Offering Value Propositions

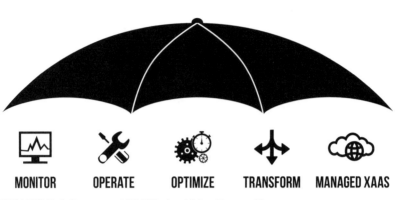

MONITOR   OPERATE   OPTIMIZE   TRANSFORM   MANAGED XAAS

FIGURE 9.4 Common MS Offering Value Propositions

- **Managed XaaS.** Technology may be on site, hosted, or a hybrid of the two. The solution is typically comprised of product (hardware and/or software), professional services, support, and operations elements bundled into a single per-unit, per-month price governed by a managed services agreement. Hardware and/or software is owned by the managed service provider.

Importantly, current and future generations of MS don't look anything like the low-margin outsourcing businesses of the past. Ideally, services are cloud-enabled, delivered from a remote network operations center. Delivery resources are typically shared across multiple clients. The product elements within the MS offer may be hosted and/or on premises; they may be single tenant or multi-tenant.

In September 2015, *Forbes* cited a study that more than half of IT managers expect to use multiple managed service providers (MSPs) within the next two years; a whopping 85% are at least somewhat likely to use MSPs.[2]

So, if you have a customer who is demanding one of the MS value propositions previously cited and you don't have an offer, you may lose that customer. How many customers can you afford to lose until you bring an MS offer to market that the market clearly wants?

The Many Flavors of Managed Services

Before you decide whether your company should pursue an MS business, it is important to segment the different types of MS businesses. TSIA segments MS offers based on the following five questions:

1. Is the offer standard across many customers or unique for each customer (as defined in Chapter 6 on portfolio power)?

2. Is the value proposition differentiated (again, referring to Chapter 6)?

3. Regardless, whether the technology is on site or not, can the services be delivered off site (virtually)?

4. What are the specific value propositions of the offer as defined by TSIA's five classic value propositions for MS offers?

5. Does the MS provider own the technology assets under management, or does the customer own the assets?

So, let's map two different example offers:

1. **Off-Site Monitoring.** The customer would like you to monitor technology that's been purchased from your company. You have unique capabilities to deliver this monitoring remotely.

2. **On-Site Operation.** The customer wants the technology to be present on their site, but they don't want to manage the environment. You need to provide some on-site services to manage their environment. Also, they do not want to own the technology.

Figure 9.5 maps these two offerings on our offering grid. The grid has been further segmented to show whether an offer is being delivered on site or off site. A solid line around the offer means the MSP owns the technology assets. A dotted line around the offer means the customer owns the technology assets.

Offering Grid A

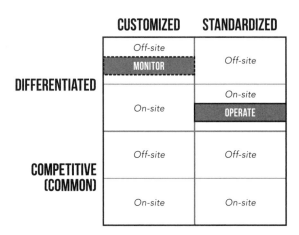

FIGURE 9.5 Offering Grid A

The question quickly becomes, "What are the high-growth and profitable MS offers?" This is exactly what we have been studying since 2013. There is no doubt that standard, off-site offers, where the customer owns the asset, have the greatest potential to drive the highest MS margins with the least financial risk to the provider (Figure 9.6).

Offering Grid B

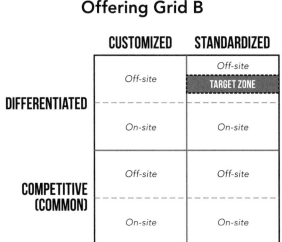

FIGURE 9.6 Offering Grid B

Breaking our benchmark data down into more detail, here are the highest-to-lowest margin MS offer types:

- Customer premised, customer owned, remotely monitored.
- Customer premised, customer owned, remotely operated.
- Hosted, customer owned, remotely monitored.
- Hosted, customer owned, remotely operated.
- Hosted, provider owned and operated.

Also, the data clearly shows that standard offers are more profitable than custom offers. On average, there is a nine-point profit improvement if an MS offer can be standardized across customers.

Unfortunately, we see that customers often start MS conversations with a host of custom requests. In fact, many of these offers are actually created "in the field" to meet the needs of specific deals. That is not the right way to approach your MS business. Instead, it reflects a common scenario where headquarters are hesitant about launching an MS business when their customers clearly want it. So, rather than lose the deal and the customer, sales makes one up. In some of these early deals, customers are often interested in the provider owning the assets.

Here's a better way: To accommodate early customer requests, successful MSPs are making three moves on the offer chessboard, listed here and seen in Figure 9.7.

- **First Move.** Work with strategic customers to define a differentiated MS offer. You can lean toward customers owning the assets, but you may need to be flexible. Perhaps you can arrange for a third party to carry the paper on the assets while you provide the managed service. Begin signing MS contracts.
- **Second Move.** Begin identifying the common building blocks of customer needs. Create a "standard" set of LEGO® building-block MS capabilities customers can string together into an offer that meets their needs.
- **Third Move.** Maximize every opportunity to leverage technology and off-site labor to deliver the offer.

Offering Grid C

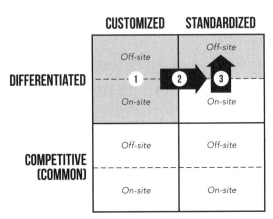

FIGURE 9.7 Offering Grid C

So far, we have talked about the compelling and special case of MS in the enterprise tech business circa 2016. We have helped define the drivers for MS offers. We have also helped define the different types of MS offers and how technology providers are successfully maturing their MS offers. Despite this help that we regularly offer to members, though, we still see many traditional product companies incredibly resistant to exploring MS conversations with eager customers. Why?

Why Product-Centric Companies Say No to Managed Services

George Humphrey vice president of research for the Managed Services practice at TSIA, refers to this dilemma as "the battle of the CFOs." In one corner, we have the customer CFO. In their role, they are keen to acquire some of the benefits listed earlier—reduced operational costs, predictable IT costs, and improved ROI from technology investments. In the other corner sits the technology provider CFO. Their role is to protect the financial business model. They are extremely reticent to sign off on any offers that may increase company risk, reduce cash flow, or impact the margin profile of the company. The customer is asking for managed services, but the CFO and other executives at your company are quick to raise the following concerns:

- **We don't own customer assets.** When negotiating MS deals, customers may not want to purchase the technology assets being managed. This means the provider has to carry the cost of these assets on their books. CFOs may be loath to reflect lower retained earnings on the balance sheet as a result of these added costs.

- **Delayed revenue recognition.** If the customer is not paying for the assets up front, that means the revenue for this technology will trickle in as part of a long-term service contract. Not ideal! We are a product company—we recognize product revenue, and we recognize it as soon as legally possible!

- **Service revenue intensive.** These MS deals are going to increase service revenues and decrease product revenues. Our financial model indicates how much revenue should be coming from products versus services. We will start looking like a services company to the street—which is not what we historically said we were.

- **Increased risk.** When we sell technology assets, the customer is ultimately responsible for achieving their target business results. With these MS contracts, we are taking on increased responsibilities. We are introducing new risks to the business. We may fail to meet contract SLAs and pay penalty clauses. The customer may be dissatisfied and cancel halfway through the contract. We might make an error in the customer environment and be sued.

- **Channel conflict.** Other executives beyond the CFO and CEO will start chiming in with their concerns. The executive who owns channel partners will be concerned that new MS offers conflict with partner offers. "We are stealing the bread from our partners' mouths. They will jump to selling the product of our competitors."

- **Complex sales cycle.** The sales executive may have concerns about the ability of sales reps to sell these complex MS offers. Also, by introducing an MS option, the customer selling cycle will most likely elongate—which is death to a sales force driven to close deals as quickly as possible and collect the cash.

- **Smells like outsourcing.** In the end, isn't MS really just another word for outsourcing? And isn't outsourcing one of the lowest-margin businesses in the technology industry?

The concerns and objections mount among executives, so there may be many reasons not to pursue this business. Yet, our point of view is that product companies should absolutely be pursuing MS opportunities when strategic customers begin knocking on the door for these services.

Just Say Yes

Despite the concerns listed here, we believe product companies should aggressively assess their opportunity to provide managed services for the following five reasons:

1. There is a compelling market opportunity for managed services.

2. Managed services is not IT outsourcing.

3. Managed services is an effective short-term defense against new XaaS competitors.

4. MS offers force the creation of new capabilities required to compete in the XaaS economy.

5. You could lose customer, after customer, after customer.

As cited previously in this book, market research firm Gartner signaled that worldwide IT spending was actually shrinking by 5.5% in 2015.[3] This opinion correlates with what we see in our T&S 50 data as we track the largest providers of technology solutions on the planet. Yet, the managed services market opportunity is exploding. Research firm MarketsandMarkets forecasts that the managed services market will grow from $107.17 billion in 2014 to $193.34 billion by 2019, at a compound annual growth rate of 12.5%.[4] For technology companies looking for growth, managed services becomes a compelling market opportunity.

Today's MS offers are not like yesterday's outsourcing offers. The traditional value proposition of IT outsourcing was simple: your mess for less. Outsourcers focused on cost reduction. As outsourcing became more competitive, margins for outsource providers eroded. But today's MS offers from product companies are anchored on unique capabilities designed to unlock the full potential of a technology solution. Benefits go beyond cost reduction into other areas, such as revenue growth and risk reduction. Also, MS offers can be much more targeted to specific technologies or problem sets. Product companies are not asking to take over the entire IT operation for a customer. We are seeing an explosion of product companies wrapping a managed XaaS offer around their core products. This offer is creating differentiation in the marketplace when contrasted with product companies that are only interested in selling a product to the customer and then leaving. With your MS offer, you create value far beyond commoditized technical features by reducing total operational complexity.

When it comes to financial concerns about asset risk and revenue recognition, many manufacturers successfully use third-party financing to give customers more of the OpEx price model they crave without all the negative baggage. It helps them:

1. Minimize the financial risk of carrying infrastructure costs on their books. This tends to affect valuation for traditional companies.

2. Get immediate revenue recognition on the product portion of the deal.

Be aware, though, that many financial auditing firms will tell you that you still have to recognize the revenue on the product over the duration of the service contract because the "value" of the product is directly linked to and inseparable from the value of the service. Service providers, VARs, and system integrators don't want the financial risk and burden of carrying all those assets on their books.

Cloud providers are somewhat exempt from all of this because, from day one, they embrace this business model. They know all revenue is recognized over the duration of the contract. They know there are inevitable costs of service that are asset and infrastructure based. Cloud investors also understand this. Manufacturer investors don't.

In the book *Zone to Win*,[5] our friend Geoffrey Moore discusses the importance of playing defense during significant market transformations. When entrenched market leaders are threatened by new offer types that disrupt the status quo, the recommendation is to respond with offers that slow competitive disruption. These "neutralization" offers don't have to go toe-to-toe against the new competitors. These defensive offers simply need to provide some new options to existing customers that may delay their choice to jump to the competitive offers. MS offers for entrenched product companies are a classic example of a neutralization offer. A large and strategic customer that previously purchased technology assets from you is now asking for a XaaS option. You meet them halfway with a special MS offer. The MS contract keeps the customer on your books and creates runway for you to develop a XaaS offer.

Finally, establishing MS offers is a forcing function for developing new organizational capabilities that will be required to compete in the XaaS economy. In our work at TSIA, we define and track "organizational capabilities." We define organizational capabilities as "the ability to perform actions that achieve desired results." We organize the capabilities into the nine categories shown in Figure 9.8.

In each of these categories, there are capabilities that organizations must master in order to scale and optimize their MS business.

Organizational Capabilities Categories

CATEGORY	EXAMPLE CAPABILITIES
Strategy and Planning	Annual business planning, aligning product and service strategies, stakeholder engagement and alignment.
Markets	Segmentation model, customer model, market requirements, competitive analysis.
Offers	Specific offer definition, offer development life cycle, offer management, bundling, SLA definitions, licensing and entitlement methods, pricing strategy.
Financial Model	Defining target revenue mix, margin profiles, investment profiles, and profit profiles for offer types.
Go to Market (GTM)	Defining alternate direct/indirect go-to-market models by offer type including application ecosystems.
Product	Development capabilities, technology capabilities, tools and applications required to deliver offers.
Operations	Automation platform, services delivery resource optimization, support channel optimization, workforce planning.
Sales and Marketing	Direct sales structure, automation platform, sales metrics, sales methodologies, marketing programs.
Partner Management	Partner selection, partner enablement, outsourcing management.

FIGURE 9.8 Organizational Capabilities Categories

As previously mentioned, taking on MS deals typically requires product companies to develop new organizational capabilities. As an example, sales and finance must collaborate on new pricing, revenue recognition, and compensation models. Delivering MS offers will require the services organization to build capabilities related to monitoring customer environments, driving adoption, and helping customers optimize costs. Overall, we have identified more than 100 capabilities required to master a managed services business but are relatively immature in most product companies. Figure 9.9 provides a sampling of these emerging capabilities.

Ideally, you would build out all the capabilities in our capabilities inventory before you take on your first MS customer.

Emerging Capabilities for Managed Services

SERVICE CAPABILITY	DESCRIPTION
In-Use Assistance Request	Customers can open service requests directly from within our products.
Business Value Mapping	We have developed and apply a business value-mapping framework to new service offering design in order to anticipate how we will help customers improve their business performance.
Automated License/ Feature Enablement	Our product has the ability to remotely turn on unused licenses and features without the manual involvement of a sales resource.
Consumption-Based Pricing Models	We have developed models for charging customers based on what they specifically consume.
Converging Service Resources	We successfully share billable and non-billable resources across existing service organizations.
Managed Service Sales Team Org Structure	We have implemented an effective organizational structure for selling managed service offerings.

FIGURE 9.9 Example Emerging Capabilities Required for MS

But more typically, by piloting new MS offers, product companies begin the journey of developing these new capabilities. All of these emerging capabilities will serve a product company well as customers pull them into the new XaaS economy.

Picking the Right Customers

Although we are encouraging product companies to aggressively pursue emerging MS opportunities, we do not believe all opportunities are created equally. One of the significant concerns executives have regarding the additional risk being assumed in MS deals can be summarized in one sentence: *"What if the customer doesn't do what they need to do to achieve the target outcomes of the MS contract?"*

This is a real concern and a healthy question to ask. The intuition is to solve this challenge contractually—to design contracts that hold customers accountable to deliver their end of the deal. When you look into the technology industry today, you'll find two common types of service contracts: (1) contracts crafted by technology providers that are centered on meeting service level agreements, and (2) contracts crafted by system integrators that cover large, complex technology implementations. Figure 9.10 captures these two contract examples.

Common Service Contract Types

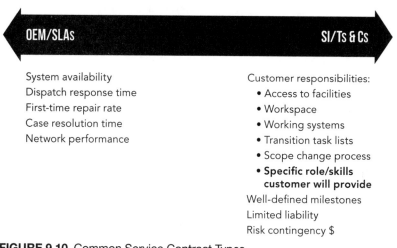

System availability
Dispatch response time
First-time repair rate
Case resolution time
Network performance

Customer responsibilities:
• Access to facilities
• Workspace
• Working systems
• Transition task lists
• Scope change process
• **Specific role/skills customer will provide**
Well-defined milestones
Limited liability
Risk contingency $

FIGURE 9.10 Common Service Contract Types

The purposes of these two contract types are different. SLA-based contracts are designed to meet customer expectations regarding technology availability. From the provider's perspective, these contracts minimize risk when technology goes down if the provider has been meeting all of their SLAs. Product companies are very familiar and comfortable with these types of contracts. SI contracts centered on detailed terms and conditions are designed to minimize risk if an implementation project fails. As shown in Figure 9.11, neither of these contract types really fit the bill for

Missing Outcome-Based Contracts

Prove technology failure is not our fault

Prove project failure is not our fault

FIGURE 9.11 Missing Outcome-Based Contracts

creating a contract that is designed to create an MS partnership with the customer to achieve targeted business outcomes.

When first exploring MS contracts that are designed to achieve specific business outcomes, we believe that attempting to craft a detailed contract that will drive customers to execute their side of the activities is not time well spent. *Successful managed service relationships are not achieved through contracts.* Initial MS success will be achieved by working with the right customers.

The recommended tactic when incubating MS is to identify the attributes required in a customer to make them a viable candidate for an MS offer. There are at least four attributes we believe a provider should test for before attempting an MS relationship with a customer:

1. **Do senior customer executives view you as a strategic provider?** If you spend your time with procurement or mid-level IT managers, it is not likely you will be able to influence the customer to execute the practices required to achieve a target outcome. Even worse, great progress and measurable results may not lead to increased customer spending.

2. **Does the customer have a history of listening to your recommendations?** If not, an MS relationship is high risk. Why will they start listening now?

3. **Has the customer demonstrated reasonable project management and IT governance capabilities?** If not, this customer will struggle to work with you to implement the technology and practices required to achieve targeted outcomes.

4. **Do you have the ability to benchmark the customer's current performance on targeted KPIs?** If the customer refuses to share data or does not have the ability to generate the data, this is a significant red flag. How can you improve performance KPIs if you do not know the current starting point?

This list is just a starting point. Technology providers should build on it to create a comprehensive set of customer attributes that should exist before engaging in an MS relationship. This approach will minimize the risk that a customer will not do what they need to do. It is worth mentioning that profiling your MS customers is an ongoing effort. Well-structured deals that look profitable when being assembled may take a turn for the worse during the life of the contract. Continually measuring MS performance is crucial.

For decades, customers have qualified suppliers to ensure a good fit. When it comes to taking on more responsibility in achieving customer outcomes, suppliers need to qualify customers. Ongoing, focused client management allows you to "fire" (not renew) non-profitable deals and to double down on customers that are profitable and growing. This new approach will not come naturally to many sales reps that historically viewed any customer with a budget as an eligible prospect. If you are simply selling a technology asset to a customer who then assumes responsibility for getting benefit from it, that tactic is fine. But if you are relying on customers to successfully adopt or attain specific business outcomes from your technology in order to achieve your revenue or margin goals, you must qualify their willingness and readiness to take the necessary actions. No contract, no matter how detailed, will replace the need for applying a solid customer profile tactic.

Incubating Managed Services: Key Success Tactics

When incubating an MS business, the first three questions that must be answered are the same as those for any other XaaS offer:

1. What is the offer portfolio and pricing model, and who are we selling it to?

2. What is the customer engagement model that we will use to sell and deliver this offer?

3. What are the financial keys that will allow us to make money with this offer?

The TSIA Managed Services discipline engages with product companies to help them establish or optimize their MS businesses. Through that work, we have identified a set of success tactics to consider as you explore MS opportunities with your customers:

- **Make finance your friend.** If your finance group is not on board with pursuing MS offers, there is a high probability that the MS business will quickly atrophy from a lack of approved contracts. Finance needs to believe in this business, and they need to understand the financial models of MS.

- **Understand the net-new capabilities that will be required to successfully deliver an MS offer.** MS offers do require you to be intimately involved in IT operational practices. Common customer handshakes that must be mastered include applications management, capacity management, information security management, and release management. Mastering these processes will most likely require new organizational capabilities for your company.

- **Understand the new sales skills that will be required to land MS offers.** Our benchmark data is clear on this point. The existing product sales force will struggle with this offer. Yet, we know from our data that the most common approach is to attempt to sell new MS offers through the existing sales force. Our recommendation is to incubate a dedicated sales capability that specializes in selling MS offers. In TSIA benchmark data, we see that companies relying on their existing sales force to sell MS are seeing annual MS growth rates of 5%. Companies that invest in a dedicated MS sales force are seeing annual MS revenues grow an average of 39%. Also, dedicated MS sales reps secure deals that are almost 20% more profitable than the deals being sold by generalist sales reps.

- **Establish key performance indicators and measure them regularly.** One of the surprising facts we discovered is how many product companies have established MS offers with no clear definition of the KPIs that should be used to understand the health of an MS offer. If they did have KPIs, they often had no idea what "good" should look like for that KPI. This is not untrodden ground. The technology industry understands what metrics to measure related to MS. In addition, we have specific benchmarks on what pacesetting companies achieve on these metrics. Figure 9.12 provides a sampling of the KPIs we recommend MS organizations track.

Top 10 Metrics MSPs Should Be Tracking

METRIC	HOW TO CALCULATE
Total Recurring Revenue Growth Rate	Total current year recurring MS revenue minus previous year total recurring MS revenue. Divide the difference by the previous year total recurring MS revenue. Convert to percentage.
Top-Line (Cap Net-New) Recurring Revenue Growth Rate	Most current full year new revenue minus previous year new revenue. Divide the difference by the previous year net-new revenue. Convert to percentage.
Total Base Revenue Growth	Most current full year revenue from existing customers (excluding revenue from new customers) minus previous year base revenue. Divide the difference by the previous year base revenue. Convert to percentage.
Total Bookings Revenue Growth (a.k.a. total contract value growth)	Total value of existing contracts minus the total value of previous year contracts. Divide the difference by the previous year total contract value. Convert to percentage.
Total Customer Growth Rate	Most current full year number of customers under contract minus previous year number of customers under contract. Divide the difference by the previous year number of customers under contract. Convert to percentage.
Gross Margin	Subtract all direct costs from the total managed services revenue. Divide that number by the total managed services revenue. Convert to percentage.
Net Profit (Net OI)	Subtract the total direct and indirect costs from the managed services revenue. Divide that number by the total managed services revenue. Convert to percentage.
Revenue Renewal Rate	Total current year MS revenue minus previous year total contract value. Divide that number by the previous year total contract value. Convert to percentage.
Contract Renewal Rate	Number of contracts up for renewal minus the number of customers that do not renew their contracts. Divide that number by the number of contracts. Convert to percentage.
Client Satisfaction Rate	Simple 1:5 scale provides enough insight into client-by-client performance. Customer success/client management team should engage in ongoing review of simple scoring of client satisfaction during regular contract performance reviews.

FIGURE 9.12 Top 10 Metrics MSPs Should Be Tracking

- **Pilot, pilot, pilot.** As previously mentioned, it is very important to identify the right customers for your MS offers. Not all customers are good candidates for this type of relationship. Once you start identifying customers, the initial MS engagements should be approached as pilots designed to help you mature the offer. It is unlikely your first MS offer will spring from the heads of your offer designers fully formed. Early customers should understand you are partnering with them to help define the best offer possible for both sides.

- **Invest in automation early.** The most profitable MS organizations we benchmark have implemented commercial, off-the-shelf tools and platforms to help automate aspects of their MS operations. Key tools can be seen in Figure 9.13 on the next page.

- **Don't ignore the channel.** There is no doubt that when a product company decides to work with customers directly as a provider of managed services, channel partners get nervous. However, our point of view is that MS offers actually unlock an entirely new class of service opportunities for your partners as well. We will discuss this more in Chapter 10.

Summary Comments

Product companies, historically, have resisted building service capabilities that are not directly related to installing and supporting their own products. However, we are at an interesting juncture in the history of the technology industry. We sit at an inflection point where old business models collapse and new business models emerge. Managed services represents a unique opportunity for product companies to start navigating through this inflection point. There is clearly a market appetite for these services. There is solid evidence product companies can be very successful with these services. If you are not currently investigating MS offers, we strongly recommend you revisit that decision.

Components of a Managed Services Delivery Platform

TOOL	PURPOSE
Configuration Management Database (CMDB)	This is really the heart of any managed services operation. A CMDB pulls data from all other service management tools to enable the operations team to have full, in-depth insight into a client's complete operations environment.
Event Monitoring and Notification	These systems monitor remote systems to detect specific error conditions or alarms and use rules to take an action depending on the error situation detected, such as creating an incident or sending a notification email.
Proactive Monitoring for Applications	These platforms monitor software deployments to track usage statistics, as well as detecting any error conditions, and use a rule system to notify IT or support to take the appropriate action.
Proactive Monitoring for Infrastructure	These platforms monitor device-level performance such as hardware outages, memory utilization, hard-drive failures, port failures, etc. Devices include, but are not limited to, servers, switches, routers, access points, session border controllers, hard drives, power systems, etc.
Proactive Monitoring for Network	These platforms monitor statistics related to enterprise networks, capturing usage data, as well as helping to pinpoint outages or network slowdowns when users experience connectivity problems.
Event Correlation	These tools analyze and identify incidents that have a high likelihood of being related. Automated correlation dramatically aids in faster restoral time or even prevention of application failure.
Service Desk	Service desk is responsible for the governance of incident and problem management. This is where events not resolved through automation result in tickets to be worked by the operations and engineering staff.
Orchestration	An orchestration application facilitates the integration of multiple tools required to operate an information technology environment. This may include connecting device management, application monitoring, infrastructure monitoring, and correlation tools, as an example.
Release Management	Release management is the process of managing software releases from development stage to software release, as well as tracking the delivery/upgrade of software versions at customer sites.
Capacity Management	Capacity management software ensures that IT capacity meets current and future business requirements in a cost-effective manner, triggering automated warnings if volumes are nearing maximum capacity for a hardware component, software program, network, or other technology.
Reporting/Analytics Platforms	Reporting/analytic platforms are analytic-based reporting platforms used to do sophisticated trend reports and create reporting portals such as a services dashboard.

FIGURE 9.13 Components of a Managed Services Delivery Platform

Playbook Summary

Two plays are identified in this chapter:

Play: Saying "YES" to MS

Objective: Determine whether the company should explore MS offers.

Benefits:

- Itemizes the industry trends driving the explosion of MS revenues.
- Itemizes key success tactics the company will follow to minimize risk when incubating MS.

Players (who runs this play?): Core players: CEO, CFO, head of marketing, head of services, head of product development.

Play: MS Opportunity Map

Objective: Identify potential opportunities the company has for MS offers.

Benefits:

- Creates a common taxonomy for the types of MS offers the company could pursue.
- Creates an understanding of what types of MS offers are the most profitable.

Players (who runs this play?): Core players: product development, product marketing, services marketing. Review team: CEO, CFO, sales and services leadership.

10 | Changes in the Channel

One of the best, most effective plays that traditional tech companies have learned to run is the creation, care, and feeding of a huge network of channel partners.

Companies like Cisco, HP, and Oracle have vast global reseller channels that generate the majority of their total revenue—sometimes more than 80% of it. In some segments like SMB, the channel might account for 100% of the revenue. So naturally, these OEMs spend lots of cycles on trying to keep the channel big, healthy, and happy.

But let's look one level deeper into most channel partner networks. From the OEM's perspective, the channel performs two critical roles:

- It puts more salespeople into the market than the company does directly. They can reach the nooks and crannies that the OEM can't.

- It delivers product-attached services that the company does not want to perform directly.

The channel looks something like Figure 10.1.

Traditional Partner Bucket Brigade

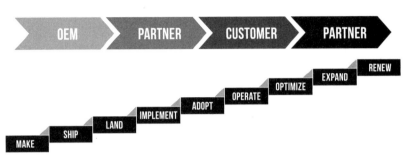

FIGURE 10.1 The Bucket Brigade

You can see these roles reflected in the revenue streams of channel companies like system integrators or VARs. The vast majority of their revenues come from the margins they make by reselling the OEM's products and from the professional services they deliver to implement them. Take those two revenue streams away and most of the world's channel companies would collapse.

Imagine what would happen if a traditional tech company that got most of its revenue through the channel stood up a new XaaS offer that the end customer could subscribe to directly in the cloud and that didn't require much in the way of implementation services.

This scenario is already happening all over the industry. And, as you might expect, it can represent a fundamental challenge to the longstanding agreements between most OEMs and their partners. Obviously, there is a range of cloud-based offers, some of which still do require complex customizations, integrations, and implementations. But if you look at what AWS is achieving on a direct basis with minimal third-party requirements, you get a glimpse of the problem.

The fact is that OEMs and resellers alike are about to face one of the most disruptive eras in the long history of their partnership. Who does what? How does money get made by either party?

Who owns the customer? All these questions and more must be reexamined quickly and effectively.

Let's examine some of the specific challenges we face.

The "VA" in VAR

There aren't many channel partners out there today who don't feel they are adding value to the OEM's solution, but let's push back on that assumption a little bit. Sure, being able to successfully conduct a sales cycle creates value. It is valuable to the customer who learns how technology can benefit them. It is also valuable to the OEM because they didn't have to pay the salary, commissions, and benefits of the salespeople. And, yes, implementation services like planning, installation, customization, integration, and training also add value. They allow the customer to master the complexity of the solution faster and more effectively than they could have on their own.

But our question is this: When the sales and implementation phases are all completed, what's really different about the solution the customer inherits from a particular partner? If the customer had bought exactly the same OEM components from a different channel partner, how would the eventual solution be different? If they bought a Cisco-based network from partner A versus partner B, what lasting value differences would they be able to point to? Most likely, not many. As we mentioned, just how much of the total revenue of most channel companies comes from something other than product resales and product-attached implementation services? In many cases, probably not much.

What happens if the customer could subscribe directly for a new XaaS offer? Or what if the partners are all reselling the same OEM XaaS offer and then simply signing the customer up for it on the OEM's partner portal? How will the partner add value? And if the need for complex, on-site implementation services is dramatically reduced, then what?

We think the first challenge we have to overcome is redefining what partner-added value truly means in the age of the cloud and XaaS. And, by the way, we know from our experience with channel companies that they are smart enough to already be asking these questions of their OEMs and, in most cases, they are not satisfied with the answers.

The OpEx Pricing Problem

The next problem is the subscription nature of most XaaS offers. Most cloud and managed service offers are priced either on a pay-for-consumption or monthly subscription basis. They are funded out of the customer's OpEx budgets, not their CapEx budgets. That means the revenue and the cash come to the reseller and the OEM over time, not up front.

In these cases, it's really not a problem for the OEM. After all, it probably doesn't cost them much to have one more incremental customer on their core XaaS platform. And it was the partner who paid the sales costs on the deal. So, the OEM can wait for the money to come in.

However, for the channel partner, it's a bigger problem. It was their sales team who got the deal. They had to pay the salaries of that team during the sales cycle. Salespeople live and die based on commission. They are often affectionately referred to as "coin operated." They live for that big check sitting out there if they close the deal. But if the customer isn't paying much up front to subscribe to the XaaS offer, who is supposed to pay the sales costs? Who writes that big check to the salespeople? Is it the reseller who takes that risk? The OEM? If neither wants to take that on, will salespeople be happy getting paid a little bit each month as the customer eventually consumes the service and pays their monthly bills?

The LAER Problem

In several chapters of the book, we have discussed the new customer engagement models associated with profitable XaaS. LAER (land, adopt, expand, renew) is all about process-driven engagement activities involving many different players at both the provider(s) and the customer. Land selling teams hand the customer to implementation teams, who then hand them to customer success teams, who will sometimes bring in expansion sales specialists. Sometimes they will hand the customer back to the land sales team if the upsell opportunity is large enough. In LAER, the process owns the customer, not the salesperson on the deal. Importantly, many of these organizations like customer success and expand selling are net-new investments. They are costly to build and operate. They can also be complex, requiring new skills and systems. Not all resellers will have the appetite to build them.

Furthermore, many of these activities are data initiated. By that, we mean that the customer's actual usage data, combined with the provider's consumption analytics and success science models, are triggering specific sales and service interventions. That means someone needs to collect that data and pay to build the analytics and models, and then needs to monitor the customer every day to make sure the right interventions are happening at the right time. Without direct access to the customer's usage data, the LAER model becomes significantly less effective. What's more, some of the LAER engagement actually occurs through the product itself.

For these reasons, we think that the OEM will be best positioned to perform some of the important engagement activities required in profitable XaaS. Although there may be some large partners who have the resources and desire to do it for themselves, we think the majority of partners will not want or be able to.

This is an entirely different thought about managing customer engagement than the traditional indirect customer model. Let's face it: most channel partners consciously tried to hide the identity of their customers from the OEM. They were worried that the OEM would begin to deal directly with them, especially if they were a larger company. Now we are proposing that both the partner and the OEM may be active in every account, every time! That is going to be quite a sea change for all three parties. The customer isn't used to that model, and it's an historically unnatural act for both the OEM and the partner. Nonetheless, it is likely to occur, and everyone needs to start deciding who does what.

The Skills Problem

This is a challenge shared by the OEM, so there will be lots of empathy on both sides. Most of the skill sets in play in most channel companies are product focused. That means they employ salespeople who can talk about the product, sales engineers who can demo the product, professional services teams who can install the product, and technical support teams who can troubleshoot the product. That's great, and those needs are not going away overnight in a XaaS world.

As we discussed in Chapter 7, new skills are needed. We need experts in vertical markets, business process consultants, solutions engineers, and outcome engineers. The people who have these skills are unicorns: They are hard to find and hard to keep. They have the unique ability to think like a businessperson but also be a product expert. They can interface with senior business buyers, not just IT and procurement staff. Sourcing, hiring, developing, and retaining this precious talent is going to be a defining characteristic of successful XaaS partners. It is closely related to redefining the "VA" in VAR. Not all channel partners will have the wherewithal to add these resources. Yet, not having the talent needed to put "VA" in your VAR story could prove fatal.

The Data Access Problem

As we mentioned, many of the engagement activities in the LAER life cycle are data driven. Absent the data, LAER becomes a costly, almost unwieldy, model. You have people running every play on every customer instead of being only at the right places at the right times.

So, where is this precious XaaS data sitting? In the OEM's data center. Yes, some larger partners have their own XaaS offers and platforms. The data for those applications are sitting in the partner's data center. However, the OEM XaaS parts of the solution are collecting and storing the data at the OEM.

If we are going to be data driven in our customer engagement model and the data is holed-up on the OEM's servers, how are the channel partners going to get access to it? Well, it turns out that is only half the problem. The other half is getting the customer's permission to access it. Even if the OEM and their partners can work out a technical solution for sharing the data in some form, the customer may not be comfortable having their usage data being shoveled all over the world. So, there are multiple challenges to contend with in this thread. We need to decide what data is relevant, whether an individual partner has secure capabilities to access it, whether the partner has the ability to act on the data if they can get to it, and whether the end customer is going to sign up for the whole scheme in the first place.

We think there is a better way to approach the dilemma.

The Software Problem

Many channel partners are woefully understaffed with software developers. As we are going to assert later in this chapter, the value-add of lots of partners is going to be in new kinds of applications and services. In both cases, most of that value needs to be delivered via software.

In a traditional channel relationship, the OEM did most of the software development. They shouldered the big R&D spend and gave products to the partners to resell. Yes, the partners could customize it if the customer paid them to, but with the exception of some of the largest partners, customers did not expect the partners to come to the table with much software of their own.

That is about to change. With software costs and development times coming down, app exchanges and marketplaces speeding time-to-market, and IoT spawning unlimited new application possibilities, software is becoming the game. But even if a channel partner isn't into building applications, software is still critical. New kinds of project and annuity services are being delivered remotely via software more and more every day. We think successful channel partners are going to need more skills and capability to build software.

The Capital Problem

These last several challenges culminate in the issue of capital investment. Who is going to fund the expense line of swallowing the fish? If there are all these required new capabilities, are individual partners really going to be willing or able to fund the required investments? This is particularly difficult when the returns for these investments are perceived to be in the distant future when enough subscription customers have been added. Even then, the replenishment of capital occurs slowly as monthly revenues recur and the model becomes profitable.

The reality is this: Not all partners are going to be able to fund all the capabilities that they want to have (and the OEM wants them to have, too).

Once again, we think some unnatural acts are going to occur. The "aha" thought is that not all these capabilities need to be built individually by every partner. Many of them can be built once—by the OEM—and then provided to all the partners. This is the most efficient possible use of capital and, fortunately, it puts the responsibility mostly on the one player who can afford it, the OEM.

A second tricky capital question is: Who carries the paper on an asset that is being "rented" as part of a XaaS deal? Does the OEM do that? Or maybe that is the channel partner's problem. Or maybe one of them needs to find a third-party financing entity that will take it on. It's yet one more hot-potato issue as we pivot toward more XaaS deals.

The Legacy Customer Problem

Too, we cannot forget that channel partners have an existing installed base of customers. The vast majority of these customers have purchased technology as an asset. When do these customers get migrated to new XaaS offers? How can a channel partner add more value to these legacy customers who are not ready to migrate to new XaaS offers? After all, these existing customers are the ones paying the bills today. As we stressed in Chapter 5, we think there is a case to be made for an aggressive posture on moving legacy customers onto XaaS platforms. However, we know it's tricky and it can be unnerving to move customers before they are really willing.

Let's turn away from challenges and starting heading toward solutions. Before we do that, though, let's summarize the important questions we need to answer:

- What strategic, value-creation activities do partners need to engage in?
- What are the new financial models for partner companies?
- How do salespeople get compensated when a partner resells OEM XaaS offers?
- How do direct and indirect LAER teams interact?
- How will the requirement for new partner skills be met?
- How do we overcome the security concerns of customers?
- How does the channel avoid the need to make huge capital investments for XaaS offers?
- How does the channel put its customers on a successful XaaS migration path?

We certainly don't have exhaustive and proven answers on all of these questions, but we do believe that a few big ideas can make them all seem more doable.

Selling Customer Business Outcomes Creates Significant New Opportunities

B4B[1] was an entire book with a single message: What customers want from their tech suppliers is changing . . . rapidly. They don't want shiny objects called "features"; they want business outcomes. The beauty of XaaS is that it exponentially increases the ability to give them what they want. The time to value is faster, the cost to implement is less, the operation of the solution can largely be done by the provider, and the potential to innovate the customer's business model is at an all-time high. To top it all off, most of the risk in the relationship shifts from the customer to the provider. After all, if the customer is not getting the return, they can stop. Sometimes, they can stop at the end of the contract. With other offers, they can stop immediately. From many customers' perspectives, XaaS blows the doors off technology as an asset. The deal is simple: Give me business outcomes or get outta here.

However, many issues surround this new landscape of customer business outcomes:

- Delivering outcomes usually takes an ecosystem of providers, not just one.
- The keys to achieving outcomes from XaaS usually vary industry to industry.
- Outcomes are often vague and need to be specified so that the provider and the customer have common expectations.
- Often, customers don't really understand how XaaS solutions can revolutionize some or all of their business.
- The biggest impediment to achieving outcomes is usually adoption.
- The biggest impediment to adoption is frequently suboptimal business processes within the customer.
- The conditions for delivering successful customer business outcomes begin in presales. Sales needs to have discussions they aren't used to having.

- Providers need to qualify customers just as much as the customer qualifies the supplier.
- OEMs and channel partners need to work in concert to deliver the business outcome to the customer.
- The provider will play new roles traditionally performed by in-house IT or that went neglected by the customer altogether.

Here is the key point: Buried in all these challenges is the answer to the new definition of the "VA" in VAR for XaaS. Successful XaaS channel partners of the future:

- Will be educators, business model experts, and solution architects . . . painting business outcome visions that electrify CEOs and CFOs alike.
- Will work seamlessly with OEMs and other value-adding partners inside the partner network and with companies adjacent to their offer but important to the overall outcome. They will have "certified" multivendor solutions.
- Will offer vertical market solutions. As software eats the tech stack, more configurability and easier customization allow vertical nuances to create value far more frequently than in the past. Every layer in the stack is now "smart." That means hospitals will use the same XaaS offer in a different way than a bank or a manufacturer. XaaS partners need to understand and amplify those vertical market opportunities.
- Will play a unique and differentiated role in achieving the customer's outcome. They will fill a gap in the ecosystem: This could be through software or through services. However, they represent a point of differentiation. They do some specific thing that is different from or better than other partners in the ecosystem. That is why the increasingly vertical go-to-market nature of XaaS is so exciting. There are so many gaps in vertical solutions that partners can fill! It doesn't mean the only way to add value is through vertical solutions, but it is ripe

with opportunity, especially in emerging areas like IoT. If you can find horizontal value-add areas, by all means fill the gap.

- Will have sales teams able to tie the key features of the solution to the financial outcomes of the customer. The outcome chain methodology we cover in Chapter 7 does this.

- Will have a customer success offer. Whether they deliver it directly or they leverage the OEM's customer success function, someone is on the job for every customer.

- Will have a business process consultative capability. They monetize that capability as part of the presales, implementation, and adoption phases of the relationship.

- Will have annuity offers to help the customer operate and optimize the solution. They will offer managed, adoption, or information services that optimize outcomes and reduce operating costs. They will also offer unique software or consulting that differentiates them from every other partner in the OEM's network. This is core to the profitable partner financial model for XaaS—a defense against the killer Cs.

In short, the pivot to business outcomes opens the door to all kinds of new value-adding opportunities. Tasks that used to be performed by the customer (or that didn't get done at all) can now be performed by providers. This is your chance to replace classic product-attached services with new, much higher value-adding operate and optimize services. The tech industry is maturing—no more bright, shiny objects. Successful channel partners will have a clear and specific set of roles in the customer's outcome chain.

Just look at all the new service opportunities we identified in Chapters 3 and 4.

There are a dozen new "optimize services" lines that can be added to the seven traditional product services lines. Though some are project-based services, most are annuity services, which we know can be delivered at very high gross margins if done correctly. Figures 10.2.1 through 10.2.4 document the evolution of the technology services portfolio.

Overall Revenue Opportunity
TECHNOLOGY INDUSTRY

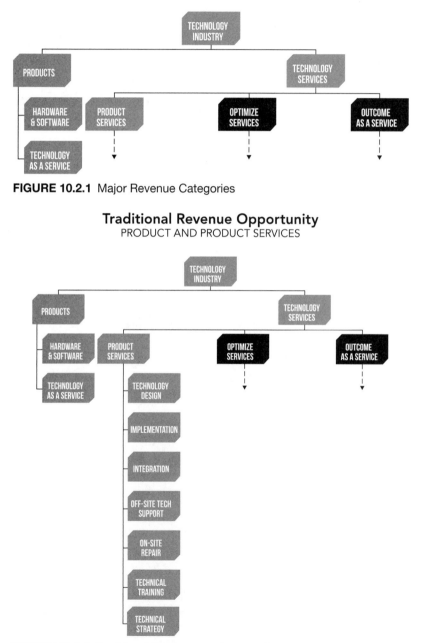

FIGURE 10.2.1 Major Revenue Categories

Traditional Revenue Opportunity
PRODUCT AND PRODUCT SERVICES

FIGURE 10.2.2 Traditional Product and Product Service Revenue Categories

Emerging Revenue Opportunity
OPERATE AND OPTIMIZE SERVICES

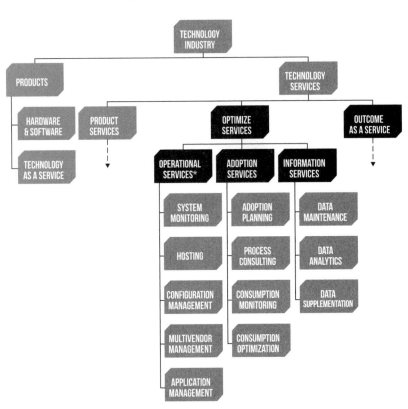

Also known as managed services.

FIGURE 10.2.3 New Operate and Optimize Service Revenue Categories

One problematic hurdle is the coordination problem when multiple OEMs and/or partners are required to deliver a business outcome to the customer. Often the field teams don't play nice in the sandbox. Having each provider trying to be the leader of the combined team is a recipe for disaster. The sales and technical teams need to be thoughtful and to plan carefully. They need to keep in mind that getting the deal is more important than leading the sales cycle. Three good rules of thumb: One is that the provider who is the highest in the stack, i.e., closest to the application level, is probably most important to the customer and, therefore, may be best suited

Emerging Revenue Opportunity
OUTCOME SERVICES

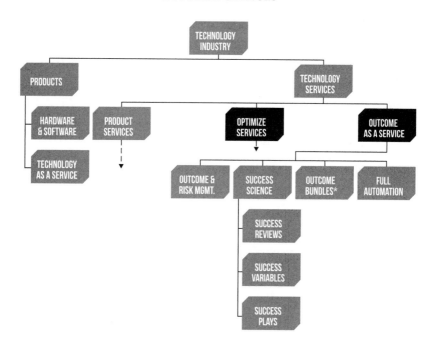

Also known as managed services.

FIGURE 10.2.4 New Outcome Service Revenue Categories

to lead the deal. Second is that vertical trumps horizontal. Sales and technical resources with deep vertical expertise and who can converse with the business executives at the customer should be doing most of the talking. Business users don't care about all the technical complexities. They are paying for someone else to do that. They want to talk about how the business value will be realized. Finally, we think that the OEMs should be orchestrating the first and most important "certified multivendor solutions," including coordinating sales activities. Then, like taking the training wheels off of a bike, the partners will master sales coordination between multiple players.

We believe that the pivot to customer business outcomes will create many new chances to unlock value for the customer. We think channel partners can play a large and profitable role in delivering the outcomes either through their proprietary software, their vertical or business process expertise, or through their optimize services portfolio.

Leveraging the OEM's XaaS Platform

As we mentioned, we don't think it makes sense for certain investments to be replicated at partner after partner. Instead it makes sense for the OEM to make the investment once and then let the partners access the asset.

Remember our illustration in Chapter 4 and shown here in Figure 10.3?

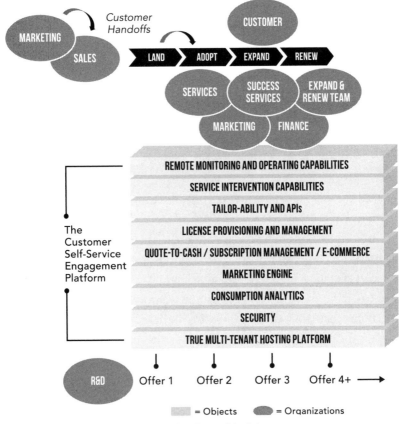

FIGURE 10.3 XaaS Self-Service Business Model

We call it the XaaS customer engagement technology platform. Again, the concept here is that the OEM builds a sophisticated technology platform that has three main attributes:

- The product offers attach to the platform. They can be provisioned, used, and managed from it.

- The customers interact directly with the platform. They place orders, use products, get marketing and training information, and they can even pay bills. It becomes a significant part of the overall customer experience. The platform is part of the OEM's brand as well. It is a big part of their differentiation.

- Internal delivery functions such as services success and finance also leverage the platform. It feeds the internal systems with information about what to do for a particular customer and when to do it. It is the same for marketing and expand selling. Marketing can use the platform to deliver customized messages to buyers and users through the products that are attached to it. Expand selling can reach buyers to chat and transact.

Just to be clear, this platform is not a single piece of software. It is a stack of many objects, most of which will be purchased from third parties. However, there is a need to knit them all together, build the application layers, connect the offers, and integrate to the internal systems of the sales, marketing, and service organizations. That will likely be done in-house. But here is the point: This isn't cheap. It absolutely does not make sense for every channel partner to attempt to build their own platform. This is why we believe channel partners should be heavily lobbying OEMs to establish these platform capabilities. So, if you are an OEM, brace yourself for this tsunami of partner requests!

What does make sense is that the individual channel partners can get the "keys" to access and integrate to the OEM's platform. That means the partner can rely on the platform to undertake many of the post-land activities. They can simply be a user of the platform to enable and inform both their service delivery offers as well as their expand and renew sales motions. This approach also solves the data access problem. The partner doesn't need to house or see the actual customer usage data: That data remains on the OEM's platform. But the platform uses advanced analytics and models to pass actionable interaction triggers or customer health scores to the partner.

Even more powerful is the idea that the platform can become the actual operating platform for the "operate" and "optimize" services of the partner. Imagine offering a managed service to the end customer that the partner sells and operates, but they are using the OEM's managed service platform as their service management system. Through the platform, they get fully processed indicators of the customer's system performance and adoption. They can manage the technology or intervene with end users. They can add new customers and upgrade existing ones. They may even be able to use the platform to price and bill for their offers. The partner might use it under the OEM's brand or perhaps the OEM allows the partner to co-brand the platform. Wouldn't that be nice! Well, it's happening today. There are many variations, but one version might look like Figure 10.4.

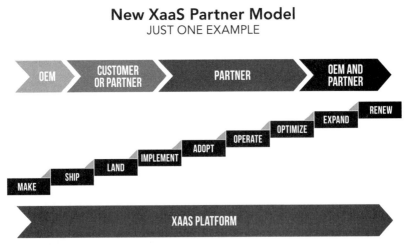

New XaaS Partner Model
JUST ONE EXAMPLE

FIGURE 10.4 New XaaS Partner Model Example

Larger partners who resell many OEM solutions may be building some form of customer-facing platform of their own. In that model, their platform will be integrating to many OEM platforms. The OEM platforms can still provide the same value, but they are simply passing information back and forth to the partner's platform. The partners' customers and staff only experience the partner platform, but it is fueled by information coming from the OEM. In this case, it is in the OEM's best interest to offer the most robust integration possible. That's because the better they work with the partner's platform, the more of their XaaS offers the partner will sell.

These approaches also act as an accelerator to closing the software skills gap for partners. If the OEM builds the platform, SaaS applications, and services with the channel in mind, partners will be able to tailor rather than build from scratch. OEMs will let partners stand up creative applications and services but do so far faster, less expensively, and with lower maintenance costs.

The New Financial Models for Partners

Essentially, many channel partners face the same exact fish model problem as the OEM. They, too, must keep the traditional, asset sale-plus-service business as robust as they can during their transition to a subscription business model. That is going to provide some financial air cover for the investments they need to make and cushion the short-term impact on revenue of switching customers to subscription pricing models like managed services or SaaS. There is no sense in waiting to get started. Traditional asset-based sales revenues are dropping across the industry. Next year isn't going to be better for those revenue streams; it's likely to be worse. Now is the time to begin the journey of swallowing the fish.

If channel partners are going to be using the same financial approach to modeling the transition as the OEMs are, we can borrow some content from Chapter 8.

Most partners have the same five revenue streams as OEMs:

- Asset revenues (reselling technology as an asset)
- Technology subscription revenues (reselling technology as a subscription)
- Annuity services revenues
- Project services revenues
- Transaction revenues

And, like all businesses, each revenue stream has its normal costs:

- COGS (cost of goods sold) and gross margin (revenue minus COGS)
- S&M (sales and marketing)
- R&D (research and development)
- G&A (general and administrative)

So we suggest that channel partners need to complete the financial model exercise in Chapter 8 for each year of their transition. They need to allocate revenue across the five revenue categories each year in a way that reflects three important concepts:

- The decline of traditional asset revenue
- The rise of subscription revenue
- The replacement, and eventual growth, of traditional project and annuity revenue streams with new offers

We are not going to repeat all of Chapter 8, but if you are a channel partner, we suggest you read it and do the exercise. Also, our data tells us that a majority of channel partners have a majority of their revenue coming from the first data stream (reselling technology as an asset). This industry transition to XaaS will be just as disruptive to the economic engines of partners as it will be to the OEMs. We expect some large OEMs may be able to leverage their extraordinary cash piles to provide business financing to qualified, key partners as they migrate to the new model.

One part of the financial model we do want to touch on specifically is related to commissions (or points, margin, or discounts) that are extended to the partner for signing up the customer. This is a very interesting topic, and one that is new to most companies. So, let's get a few concepts on the table. Thus far, we see the following trends emerging:

- Salespeople get commissioned on committed customer revenue (the part of the contract the customer can't cancel).

- Most companies don't want their salespeople living on residual income from previous years' sales; thus, they are limiting the commissions to first-year committed revenue.

An interesting analog to the commission problem of a XaaS offer is from the insurance industry. According to *The Wall Street Journal*, insurers pay their independent agents anywhere from 15% to 20% of the first-year premium (for auto insurance) to more than 50% (for life insurance).[2] Many OEMs may hate the idea of paying 20% to 50% of their first-year revenue in commissions to the partner. Most partners are going to hate paying all of it to the sales team.

But, here is why you do it with a smile: In insurance, those high sales commissions on first-year revenue can work out to be less than 1% on the total lifetime spend of the customer. It's basically to be viewed as just another financing, P&L, or cash flow challenge in the XaaS world. In TSIA's view, we agree: You don't want the salesperson making money on the renewal in years 2, 3, and 4. You want them making money on the land and expand phases. And, who pays the up-front commissions? It's simple: Where does the customer pay? Do they sign up and pay with the partner? Or do they sign up and pay with the OEM? Whoever they commit to, that's who subsidizes the sales effort. That's what insurance companies do every day, and they have a lot more experience at optimizing this model than we do.

Vertical, Vertical, Vertical

Everyone needs a niche. In traditional tech, the OEM's niche was often defined by a layer in the stack or a toolbox for managing it. As a result, most OEMs and their channel partners sold basically the same solutions from industry to industry.

We think, more than ever before, that niches are going to be important. That's where differentiation will occur and how optimal margins will be realized. But what kind of niches will be sought by customers? If you believe that the influence of the business buyer and their obsession with business outcomes will continue to increase, we suggest there are (at least) three great places to play:

- Business process experts
- Managed service experts
- Vertical experts

Let's take a look at each one.

Business buyers are responsible for adeptly executing processes within their organization. Most people agree that weak business processes is one of the primary causes of poor technology adoption and low value realization. For many years, IT departments were in charge of buying technology, and their mandates to vendors were often to ascribe to their company's current systems and processes. They developed RFPs that were based on how they thought things should work. They spent millions to customize software and incorporate legacy systems into new solutions.

Today's business buyers seem to be increasingly open to a new way of thinking. They often see XaaS companies as consultative partners. They expect the provider to tell them what best practices look like. They want to ascribe to what is proven to work in the industry, not to their old processes and systems. That opens the door for thousands of partners to specialize in business process optimization services.

Another characteristic of business buyers is that they don't want to spend time administering or optimizing technology. They want someone else to manage it for them. Even IT departments whose budgets are being pinched and who want to deploy their talent to advancing new corporate capabilities rather than maintaining existing ones are now open to more managed services from their providers. This is another great new subscription revenue stream for partners. Please read Chapter 9 for more details.

Finally, we think that the industry—both suppliers and customers—is realizing that there is a lot more value to vertical solutions than horizontal ones. We mentioned this earlier in the chapter as part of delivering customer business outcomes, but we really want to stress the huge opportunity that vertical "everything" represents.

The math in the new niche opportunities created by "going vertical" is staggering. If you figure that 50% of the tech stack—starting at the network and security level and moving up through data management, analytics, collaboration, and applications levels—has hundreds of vertical optimization opportunities per industry, and there are hundreds of significant micro-verticals, then the number of opportunities to specialize and add unique value is immense.

All of these vertical value-adds require two basic ingredients: some experts and some customers willing to work with you. Only the partner can pick their spot. They need to identify good vertical markets that fit their vision. Hopefully, they already have some of both assets in the targeted industry(s). But their vertical value needs to be built on a real-world knowledge of that industry. They can develop software that fills a gap, provide business process services on critical tasks, provide benchmarks or analytics, and create a solution architecture—just for a single vertical or micro-vertical!

And the Internet of Things is going to light vertical opportunities on fire! We can't stress how many new opportunities are likely to be created for vertical value-add over the next decade. Some partners are going to make a killing by being the 800-pound gorilla in their niche. Security will go vertical; collaboration will, too. So will high-performance networks and analytics. Don't forget the hundreds of software applications and web service opportunities.

Evolving these new offers—especially service offers—must be done with care. Traditionally, services were synonymous with people. We think that is an antiquated notion. We think services should be a combination of people and software with a trending toward software. We encourage partners to pursue a line of thinking that we laid out in the book *Complexity Avalanche*.[3] In it we suggested that services be thought of as going through three "ages" (Figure 10.5).

In this progression, you are applying your best and brightest people to service engagements in the early stages. Their mission is to uncover the keys to success and the toughest challenges along the way. Then, you tell them that you are going to fund the development of tools to scale the value-creating motions; automate the repetitive, low-value ones; and build applications to shrink the challenges. Eventually, you will build those tools into the actual products you are delivering to the customer. The product itself then has the "option" of performing the tasks for itself. You can choose to make that an embedded but differentiating part of your solution or you can monetize it separately. But in any case, you should think about services development in this way. Once you have worked the smart people out of the delivery model, you move their focus to the next new service opportunity even higher up the value chain and repeat the cycle. Obviously, this is one reason partners need better software development capability.

The Three Ages of Services

FIGURE 10.5 The Three Ages of Services

We think tens of thousands of channel partners need to augment their traditional value-add of filling a local market "integrator" niche with a vertical market "expert" niche at the national or international level. But remember, you are going to need to partner with other partners who offer complementary vertical offers or skills to deliver full business outcomes to customers. It truly takes an ecosystem.

Picking the Right Customers, Migrating the Existing Customers

In traditional tech, any customer with budget was a good customer. In XaaS, that's not necessarily true. After all, traditional tech was a pay-up-front world. If the customer was willing to part with the money, the OEM or the partner made money. Pretty simple. Of course, we all wanted the customer to succeed and buy more, but we were willing to gamble on the outcome because the risk was on the customer's shoulder. But in XaaS, the customer might pay little or nothing up front. They might be locked in for multiple years but maybe not. The up-front costs to sell, implement, and train might have been absorbed by the provider in order to get the subscription. And, whatever commitments were made might have been for a pilot where the provider is smothering the customer with expensive love in the hope that the pilot will explode into an enterprise relationship.

The bottom line is that in XaaS, the risk is with the provider. The profits in the deal may be in year 2—or in years 3 or 4. Those profits may depend not only on renewal but also on expansion. As we said in Chapter 7, new customer engagement models are needed. That goes for channel partners, too. LAER is for them to execute just as much as for the OEMs. Please refer to that chapter for more details.

But, here is the main point: If the customer is not ready to do what they need to do to succeed with your XaaS offer, then you should not take the deal. Yes, that's right, walk away. If they are not ready to engage with you to adapt their business processes, train their end users, utilize your expertise, run the customer success playbook that you gave them—if they don't view you or your offer as a true partner to listen to—then focus your finite resources on a customer who will. This is a tough message for the sales force to hear. This is an issue for frontline sales management. It is up to them to spot these deals and not spend many cycles on them. They are uniquely positioned in that they are close enough to the deal to spot the trouble signs. They are mature enough to understand the problem. They need to be supported by executive management when they make the call. Believe me, we know of deals where tens of millions in losses have been incurred by providers over this issue.

This is also the principle that will guide you through the customer migration process. First, focus on migrating customers that are ready, willing, and able to engage in these new models. For customers that are resistant or unable, keep them on the legacy models. At some point, though, they will need to move. You will need a road map of incentives to make them move, along with disincentives if they stay. At some point, you may need to turn the fire all the way up and force them onto your XaaS offer. In the interim, understand that they will be a diminishing revenue stream. Once again, this is a tough message for your sales reps to internalize.

Leveraging the Scale Advantage of Traditional Tech

One of the premises of this book is that there has been an unfair playing field that, so far, has given the advantage to "born in the cloud" start-ups over traditional tech companies. In other words, so far, the ability to be innovative and disruptive has trumped the competitive advantages of scale enjoyed by traditional tech OEMs and partners. However, we think that's a swing of the pendulum that can be driven back in the other direction.

As we mentioned previously, many pure-play XaaS companies are largely rooted in doing business in their home country. Most US SaaS companies get the vast majority of their revenue from the

US market. This is the same for start-up enterprise XaaS companies in Germany and China. In addition, most pure-play XaaS companies espouse the "best of breed" value prop. They argue—right or wrong—that customers should pick from a menu of highly focused providers and knit them together to form complete solutions.

That's great except for one thing: Some customers don't buy into that strategy. Maybe they are global companies that want a consistent experience across all their locations worldwide. Maybe they prefer a deeply integrated solution from a company with a broad portfolio of core offers, not just one. Or they want one data partner that can operate globally and yet meet local country requirements. In any case, this is another way for partners to add value. If you have that scale, have an international sales and services capability, or represent a broad portfolio of XaaS offers that you have already built the software to knit together, then maybe you can be the only qualified provider in the eyes of that customer. Scale is still an advantage, even in the XaaS world. We think the pendulum is about to swing that way again. Just look at the investment focus of AWS and Salesforce. It's about broadening the portfolio and their geographical footprint. That is what happens when innovations begin to mature and need to become "industrial strength."

Traditional IT Sales and Services Don't Go Away, They Just Trend Down

These new capabilities are not for every channel partner and certainly are not required on every deal. There is still value to be created by simply reselling products and delivering traditional systems integration, implementation, and support services. That is still a huge market today. Lots of money is being paid out by end customers for those services.

However, it's not a trend that is likely to increase. IT budgets are plateauing or shrinking, and as much as half of technology decisions are being made by business users. Many XaaS offers are simply easier for them to try and require less of a service wrapper. There are many, many signs that channel monetization activities around traditional IT are not going to be a source of growth unless you can take share from a competitor. It's going to be a tough road if that is your only growth strategy.

While IT may be trending down, though, things like IoT are trending up. So, if you know how to connect PCs, why can't you connect IoT devices? If you can plan and manage an on-premise IT implementation, why can't you manage an off-premise SaaS rollout? Fortunately there are many opportunities to repurpose and redirect existing resources into higher-growth areas. Yes, there are new things to learn and maybe even new OEMs or ISVs to partner with. But, as we have repeatedly pointed out, selling business outcomes to business buyers is where the real growth is going to be. Partners need to get on that train somehow.

The bottom line, as we said in *B4B*, is that these are AND strategies we are advocating, not OR ones. We think you will want to engage in your traditional monetization activities AND invest in these new capabilities. Go ahead and grab as much of the trillion dollars or more that customers spend on traditional products and services as you can. Hybrid computing is here for a long while. But, if you want your company to grow, if you want strategic customers instead of price shoppers, if you want to continue to innovate and attract great people . . . if you want those things, you will need to act.

So, Imagine . . .

Just like the smoke is starting to clear on profitable XaaS business models, we think the next-generation partner business model is beginning to take shape. We think the model has these characteristics:

- 70% to 80% of revenue is recurring.
- Recurring revenue comes from a balanced mix of technology subscription and value-added annuity services.

- Software and services dominate the portfolio.

- Value-added offers are built on top of the OEM's platform.

- The partner works with other partners in the ecosystem to deliver outcomes to the customer. They can also combine offers from multiple XaaS and traditional OEMs and act as a new style of SI.

- Their value-add is rooted in vertical industry, business process, or managed services expertise. Best-practice capture and conveyance are essential processes.

- Ongoing data analytics are central to the value proposition and are focused on "ongoing value over time" that fuels subscription services, not just project services.

- The partner doesn't care how the end customer originally subscribed to the OEM's core XaaS offer (direct or indirect). The partner can still add value and monetize that customer over time via services or software even if the OEM sold them originally. Customers are no longer "mine" or "theirs." They are all "ours."

- They offer their own form of LAER (see Chapter 7) working in concert with the OEM's customer success teams.

Playing Your Position

Think about the team roles of a quarterback and a wide receiver in America's National Football League. They each have their unique role to run in a winning play. They need different skills and carry the ball at different times, but they are both running one play. They feed off each other. They respect each other's contribution, and they count on each other's execution.

That's how we think about the next generation of channel plays. Much rides on the OEMs. They have to call the play and deliver the ball. Then, the channel partner needs to run with it, finding their own spots and breaking through the holes that lead to the score. If either party fails, there is no score. But, it starts with the OEM. What plays are in their playbook? What route do they want the partner to run? Can they deliver the ball?

Honestly, we think that many OEMs are late to the table with their XaaS channel playbook. Many resellers we know are unhappy with the answers to the hard questions they are asking. They talk to customers every day. They know what's happening out there. But they are dependent on their OEMs to explain how they will run the play and, more importantly, how they will make money. We hope this chapter helps frame some answers.

XaaS Playbook Plays

FOR OEMs:

Play: Model Your Profitable XaaS Partner Economic Engine Model

Objective: Use Chapter 5 to identify the specific XaaS revenue streams that you believe your partners should monetize. Identify the mix and margin expectations for each revenue stream. Model the number of years in their journey to target GAAP profitability for key partner segments.

Benefits:

- Identifies the target financial model for the partner types.
- Identifies investment requirements.
- Sets expectations on target margins for each revenue stream.

Players (who runs this play?): Partner strategy and enablement team, finance. Review team: CEO, CFO, CIO, and board.

Play: Sketch Out Your Partner Platform Strategy

Objective: Draw a picture of your XaaS operating platform and how partners will access, add value, and monetize it. Determine what services you want to enable and whether they will be OEM branded or white-labeled to the partners. Determine how LAER will be performed for customers brought onto the platform by the partner. Determine how the platform will integrate with the platforms built by your larger partners.

Benefits:

- Identifies the core requirements of the platform for your channel business.
- Identifies investment requirements.
- Provides specifications to CIO/CTO.

Players (who runs this play?): Partner strategy and enablement team. Review team: CEO, CFO, and CIO.

Play: Identify Key Vertical Opportunities

Objective: List those vertical market opportunities of greatest value. Identify existing partners who can fill the gaps in selling and delivering complete business outcomes in those markets. Note where you have holes and target new partners that can fill them. Begin to define go-to-market strategies that detail the financial, LAER, and coordination challenges that lie ahead to deliver the ecosystem outcomes at scale.

Benefits:

- Identifies the key vertical opportunities.
- Tells you what partners to focus on and what new ones to add.
- Lays out the to-do list of challenges that must be overcome.

Players (who runs this play?): Partner strategy and enablement team. Review team: CEO, CFO, and CIO.

FOR PARTNERS:

Plays: **We suggest partners run the Plays in Chapters 3, 6, 7, 8, or any other chapters that resonate with you.**

Endnotes

Chapter 1

1. Gladwell, Malcolm. 2002. *The Tipping Point: How Little Things Can Make a Big Difference.* New York: Back Bay Books.

2. Wood, J.B., Todd Hewlin, and Thomas Lah. 2013. *B4B: How Technology and Big Data Are Reinventing the Customer-Supplier Relationship.* San Diego, CA: Point B, Inc.

3. For a complete listing of companies in both indexes, visit http://www.tsia.com/financial-sets.html.

4. "Why a Subscription Model Could Be the Future for All Businesses," http://www.techradar.com/us/news/world-of-tech/man agement/why-a-subscription-model-could-be-the-future-for-all-businesses-1249302; "Wall Street Loves Workday, but Doesn't Understand Subscription Businesses," http://allthingsd.com/20121128/wall-street-loves-workday-but-doesnt-understand-subscription-businesses.

5. http://seekingalpha.com/news/2575935-wedbush-down-grades-autodesk-worried-about-business-model-transition?app=1&uprof=25.

6. http://marketrealist.com/2015/04/will-oracles-transition-cloud-impact-margins.

7. https://redmondmag.com/articles/2014/11/01/windows-cow.aspx.

8. http://www.marketwatch.com/story/sap-profit-down-23-after-cloud-move-2015-04-21.

9. http://seekingalpha.com/instablog/749739-vuru/3518265-adobes-adbe-strategic-shift-will-lead-to-growth-in-the-long-term.

10. http://www.reuters.com/article/2015/01/24/us-sap-cloud-profitability-idUSKBN0KX0FY20150124.

11. http://www.forbes.com/sites/connieguglielmo/2013/10/30/you-wont-have-michael-dell-to-kick-around-anymore.

12. http://www.reuters.com/article/2012/11/01/us-jdasoftware-offer-idUSBRE8A00N820121101.

13. http://www.reuters.com/article/2013/05/06/us-bmcsoftware-offer-idUSBRE9450F520130506.

14. http://www.theregister.co.uk/2015/10/16/dell_bought_emc_is_this_the_end_salvation.

15. http://www.ciodive.com/news/informatica-now-private-announces-new-leadership-team/412011.

16. http://fortune.com/2014/10/08/hp-split-meg-whitman.

17. http://marketrealist.com/2014/12/symantec-split-two-companies.

Chapter 2

1. http://www.mcafee.com/uk/products/security-as-a-service/saas-free-trials.aspx.

2. http://www.appfolio.com/benefits/pricing?_bk=appfolio%20property%20manager&_bm=e&_bc={creative}&_bt={creative}.

3. https://www.veeva.com/services/.

4. https://blog.kissmetrics.com/saasy-pricing-strategies/.

Chapter 3

1. There is a great article analyzing Amazon's elongated "unprofitability": http://ben-evans.com/benedictevans/2014/9/4/why-amazon-has-no-profits-and-why-it-works.

2. http://www.morningstar.com/InvGlossary/economic_moat.aspx.

3. Burton, Jonathan. August 2, 2012. "Follow the Buffett Strategy." *The Wall Street Journal.*

4. For those of you too young to remember this commercial: https://www.youtube.com/watch?v=TgDxWNV4wWY.

5. "Gartner Says Worldwide IT Spending to Decline 5.5 Percent in 2015," June 2015. http://www.gartner.com/newsroom/id/3084817.

6. Wood, J.B. 2009. *Complexity Avalanche: Overcoming the Threat to Technology Adoption*. San Diego, CA: Point B, Inc.

7. https://www.zendesk.com/benchmark-your-support/.

8. http://logisticsviewpoints.com/2011/08/22/sap-performance-benchmarking-in-supply-chain-management/.

9. https://aws.amazon.com/premiumsupport/trustedadvisor/.

10. http://www.jda.com/thought-leadership/retail-self-assessment/.

11. www.granular.ag.

12. www.travelclick.com.

Chapter 4

1. Wood, J.B., Todd Hewlin, and Thomas Lah. 2013. *B4B: How Technology and Big Data Are Reinventing the Customer-Supplier Relationship*. San Diego, CA: Point B, Inc.

2. http://organizationalphysics.com/2012/01/09/the-5-classic-mistakes-in-organizational-structure-or-how-to-design-your-organization-the-right-way/.

3. https://www.pac-online.com/sap-services-simplifies-customer-engagements-%E2%80%9Cone-service%E2%80%9D.

4. Moore, Jeffrey A. 2015. *Zone to Win: Organizing to Compete in an Age of Disruption*. New York: Diversion Books.

5. To watch the full presentation, visit: https://www.youtube.com/watch?v=0WOLc3a8lHg.

6. Wood, J.B., Todd Hewlin, and Thomas Lah. 2013. *B4B: How Technology and Big Data Are Reinventing the Customer-Supplier Relationship*. San Diego, CA: Point B, Inc.

Chapter 5

1. For more details on this analysis, review TSIA's quarterly T&S 50 webcast presentation. https://www.tsia.com/events/webinars/on-demand-webinars.html.

2. Wood, J.B., Todd Hewlin, and Thomas Lah. 2013. *B4B: How Technology and Big Data Are Reinventing the Customer-Supplier Relationship.* San Diego, CA: Point B, Inc.

3. http://www.wsj.com/articles/when-it-comes-to-tech-services-cloud-can-be-a-nebulous-term-1454375944.

4. http://www.adobe.com/aboutadobe/pressroom/pressreleases/201110/100311AdobeCreativeCloud.html.

5. http://ww2.cfo.com/revenue-recognition-accounting-tax/2015/07/intuit-manages-big-accounting-change.

6. http://www.sec.gov/Archives/edgar/data/769397/000076939714000018/adsk-0131201410xk.htm.

7. http://www.autodesk.com/products/perpetual-licenses/perpetual-licenses-faq.

8. Moore, Geoffrey A. 2015. *Zone to Win: Organizing to Compete in an Age of Disruption.* New York: Diversion Books.

9. Christensen, Clayton M. 2013. *The Innovator's Dilemma: When New Technologies Cause Great Firms to Fail.* Boston, MA: Harvard Business Review Press.

10. Herbold, Robert J. 2007. *Seduced by Success: How the Best Companies Survive the 9 Traps of Winning.* New York: McGraw-Hill.

11. http://fortune.com/2014/06/18/for-adobe-cloud-traction-leads-to-record-high-stock-price.

12. https://wedesignstudios.com/why-adobes-subscription-only-plan-sucks.

13. http://www.fool.com/investing/general/2016/01/28/why-servicenow-inc-stock-sank-today.aspx.

14. http://q4live.s1.clientfiles.s3-website-us-east-1.amazonaws.com/454432842/files/doc_presentations/2014/Salesforce%20Analyst%20Day%202014.pdf.

Chapter 6

1. Wood, J.B., Todd Hewlin, and Thomas Lah. 2011. *Consumption Economics: The New Rules of Tech.* San Diego, CA: Point B, Inc.

2. www.tableau.com.

3. www.liveperson.com/solutions/marketing.

4. http://www.workday.com/applications/human_capital_manage
   ment.php.

5. For more information on Tim Matanovich work, visit: http://
   www.valueandpricing.com.

Chapter 7

1. http://www.chaotic-flow.com.

2. TSIA 2015 Consumption Analytics Survey.

3. Lah, Thomas. December 3, 2014. "Defining the Customer Engagement Life Cycle." TSIA.

4. http://www.forentrepreneurs.com/2014-saas-survey-1/.

5. Wood, J.B., Todd Hewlin, and Thomas Lah. 2013. *B4B: How Technology and Big Data Are Reinventing the Customer-Supplier Relationship*. San
   Diego, CA: Point B, Inc.

Chapter 8

1. TSIA T&S Cloud 20, Q4 2015 snapshot.

2. 10-Q, posted November 20, 2015.

3. According to Wikipedia. https://en.wikipedia.org/wiki/DocuSign.

4. Ibid.

5. According to Wikipedia. https://en.wikipedia.org/wiki/LinkedIn.

6. Sharf, Samantha. July 20, 2015. "Why the 10% Drop in Software
   Sales Is the Most Important Number in IBM's Q2 Earnings Report.
   http://www.forbes.com/sites/samanthasharf/2015/07/20/why-
   the-10-drop-in-software-sales-is-the-most-important-number-in-
   ibms-q2-earnings-report.

7. www.veeva.com/services.

8. Shankland, Stephen. May 6, 2013. "Adobe Kills Creative Suite,
   Goes Subscription-Only." CNET. http://www.cnet.com/news/
   adobe-kills-creative-suite-goes-subscription-only.

9. McAllister, Neil. April 23, 2015. "Amazon Lifts Lid on AWS
   Money Factory, Says It's a $5 BEEEELLION Biz. *The Register*.

http://www.theregister.co.uk/2015/04/23/amazon_q1_2015_
earnings_cloud.

Chapter 9

1. "Why Businesses Are Turning to Managed IT Services," *CIO,* June
   2015, http://www.cio.com/article/2930498/it-strategy/why-busi-
   nesses-are-turning-to-managed-it-services.html.

2. "Your IT Wingman: The Agile Managed Services Provider,"
   Forbes-Tech, September 2015, http://www.forbes.com/sites/
   centurylink/2015/09/25/your-it-wingman-the-agile-man
   aged-services-provider/#2715e4857a0b408bd03b34da.

3. "Gartner Says Worldwide IT Spending to Decline 5.5 Percent in
   2015," http://www.gartner.com/newsroom/id/3084817.

4. "Managed Services Market Worth $193.34 Billion by 2019,"
   http://www.marketsandmarkets.com/PressReleases/man
   aged-services.asp.

5. Moore, Geoffrey A. 2015. *Zone to Win: Organizing to Compete in an
   Age of Disruption.* New York: Diversion Books.

Chapter 10

1. Wood, J.B., Todd Hewlin, and Thomas Lah. 2013. *B4B: How Technology and Big Data Are Reinventing the Customer-Supplier Relationship.* San Diego, CA: Point B, Inc.

2. http://www.wsj.com/articles/SB10001424052702304177104577
   305930202770336.

3. Wood, J.B. 2009. *Complexity Avalanche: Overcoming the Threat to Technology Adoption.* San Diego, CA: Point B, Inc.

Index